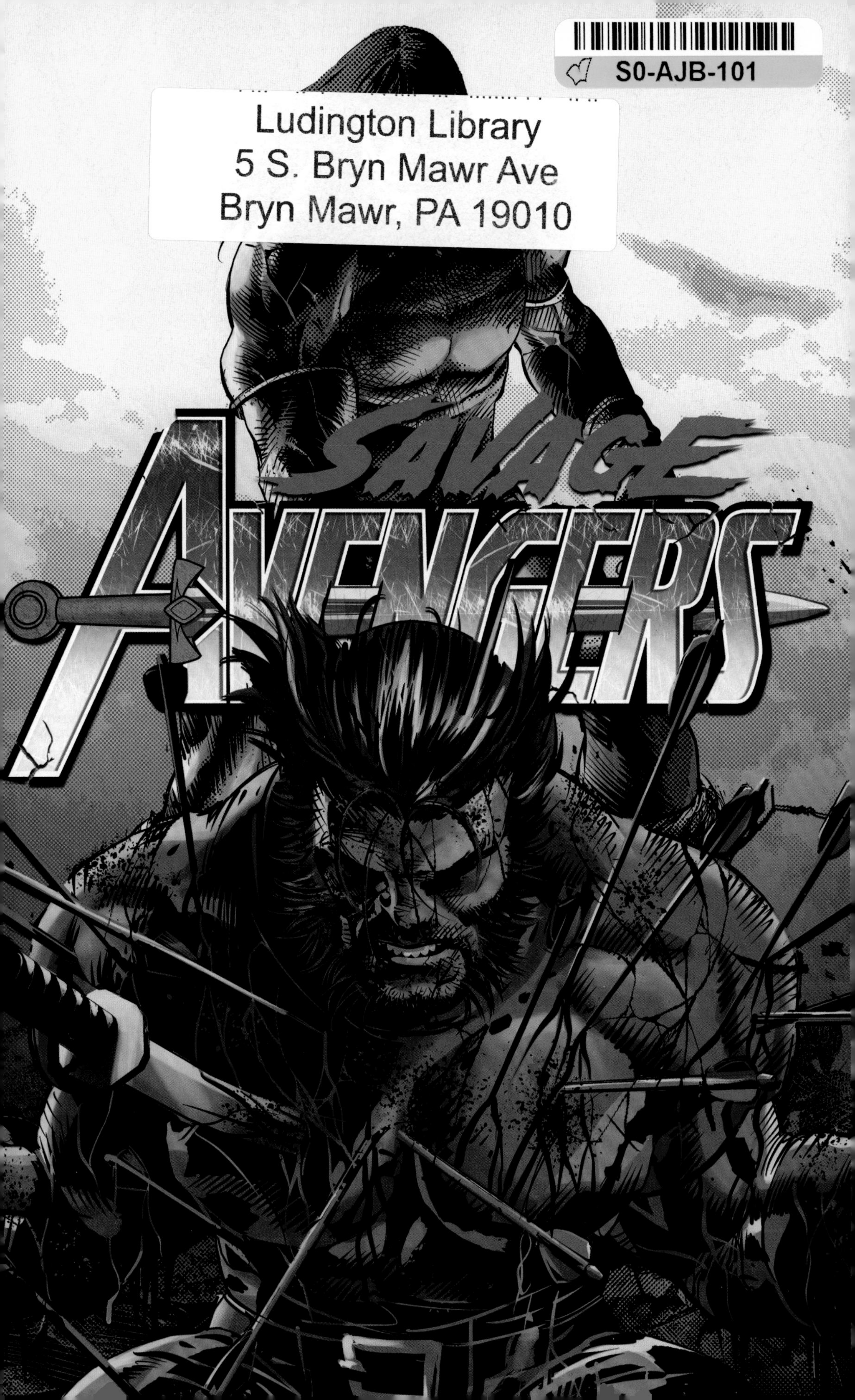
SAVAGE
AVENGERS

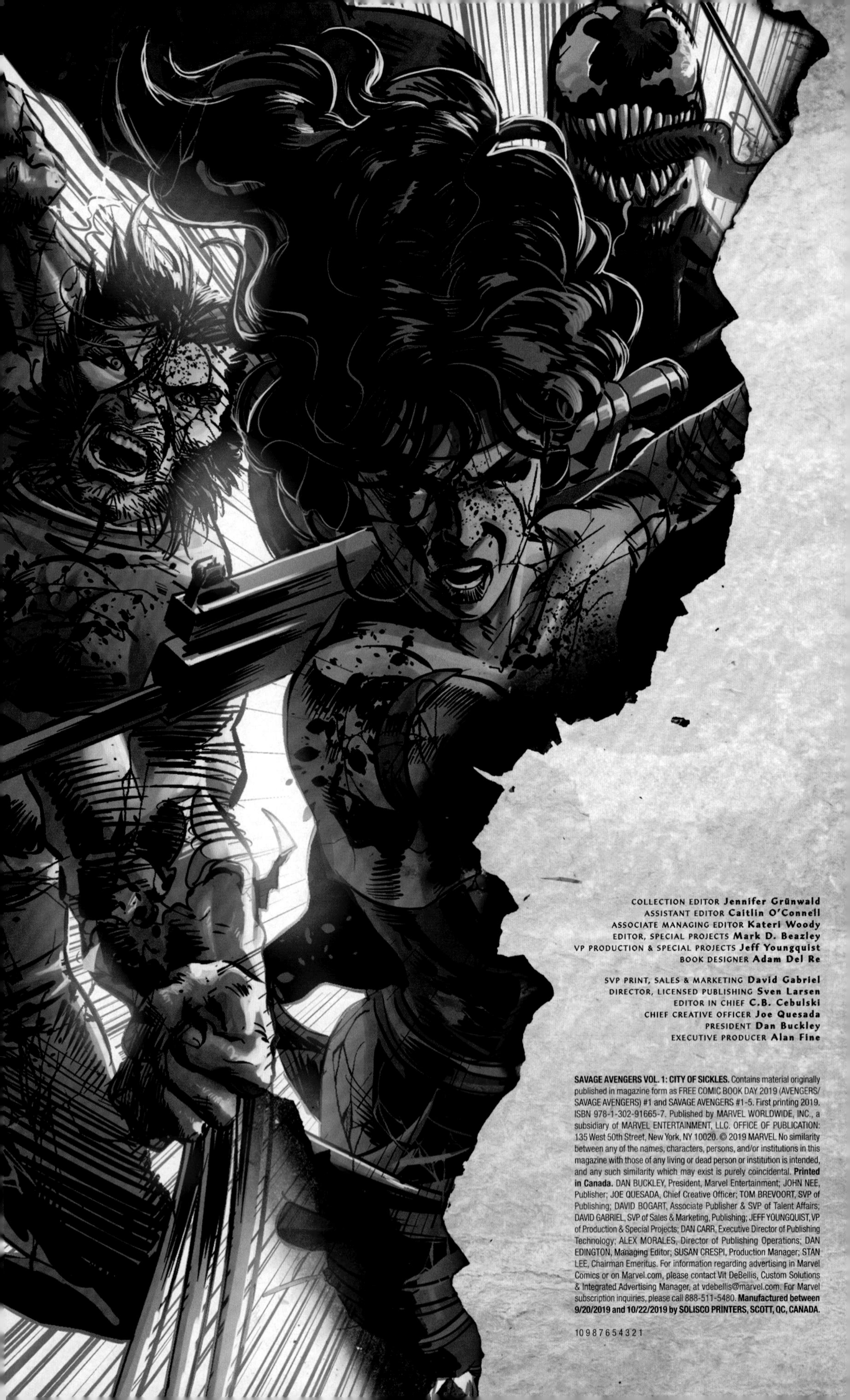

COLLECTION EDITOR **Jennifer Grünwald**
ASSISTANT EDITOR **Caitlin O'Connell**
ASSOCIATE MANAGING EDITOR **Kateri Woody**
EDITOR, SPECIAL PROJECTS **Mark D. Beazley**
VP PRODUCTION & SPECIAL PROJECTS **Jeff Youngquist**
BOOK DESIGNER **Adam Del Re**

SVP PRINT, SALES & MARKETING **David Gabriel**
DIRECTOR, LICENSED PUBLISHING **Sven Larsen**
EDITOR IN CHIEF **C.B. Cebulski**
CHIEF CREATIVE OFFICER **Joe Quesada**
PRESIDENT **Dan Buckley**
EXECUTIVE PRODUCER **Alan Fine**

SAVAGE AVENGERS VOL. 1: CITY OF SICKLES. Contains material originally published in magazine form as FREE COMIC BOOK DAY 2019 (AVENGERS/SAVAGE AVENGERS) #1 and SAVAGE AVENGERS #1-5. First printing 2019. ISBN 978-1-302-91665-7. Published by MARVEL WORLDWIDE, INC., a subsidiary of MARVEL ENTERTAINMENT, LLC. OFFICE OF PUBLICATION: 135 West 50th Street, New York, NY 10020. **Printed in Canada.** DAN BUCKLEY, President, Marvel Entertainment; JOHN NEE, Publisher; JOE QUESADA, Chief Creative Officer; TOM BREVOORT, SVP of Publishing; DAVID BOGART, Associate Publisher & SVP of Talent Affairs; DAVID GABRIEL, SVP of Sales & Marketing, Publishing; JEFF YOUNGQUIST, VP of Production & Special Projects; DAN CARR, Executive Director of Publishing Technology; ALEX MORALES, Director of Publishing Operations; DAN EDINGTON, Managing Editor; SUSAN CRESPI, Production Manager; STAN LEE, Chairman Emeritus. For information regarding advertising in Marvel Comics or on Marvel.com, please contact Vit DeBellis, Custom Solutions & Integrated Advertising Manager, at vdebellis@marvel.com. For Marvel subscription inquiries, please call 888-511-5480. **Manufactured between 9/20/2019 and 10/22/2019 by SOLISCO PRINTERS, SCOTT, QC, CANADA.**

10 9 8 7 6 5 4 3 2 1

CONAN THE BARBARIAN joined a band of Avengers on a dire mission to restore light to the universe. Their victory came at a cost for the Cimmerian. In the final battle, he was cast away by their enemy—but instead of landing back in the Hyborian Age, he found himself on present-day Earth...in the Savage Land.

SAVAGE AVENGERS
CITY OF SICKLES

Gerry Duggan
WRITER

Mike Deodato Jr.
ARTIST

Frank Martin
COLOR ARTIST

VC's Travis Lanham
LETTERER

David Finch & Frank D'Armata
COVER ART

Shannon Andrews Ballesteros
ASSISTANT EDITOR

Alanna Smith
ASSOCIATE EDITOR

Tom Brevoort
EDITOR

FOR CONAN PROPERTIES INTERNATIONAL

Mike Jacobsen
COORDINATOR

Frederik Malmberg
PRESIDENT

Jay Zetterberg
EXECUTIVE VICE PRESIDENT

Steve Booth
CHIEF OPERATING OFFICER

AVENGERS created by STAN LEE & JACK KIRBY

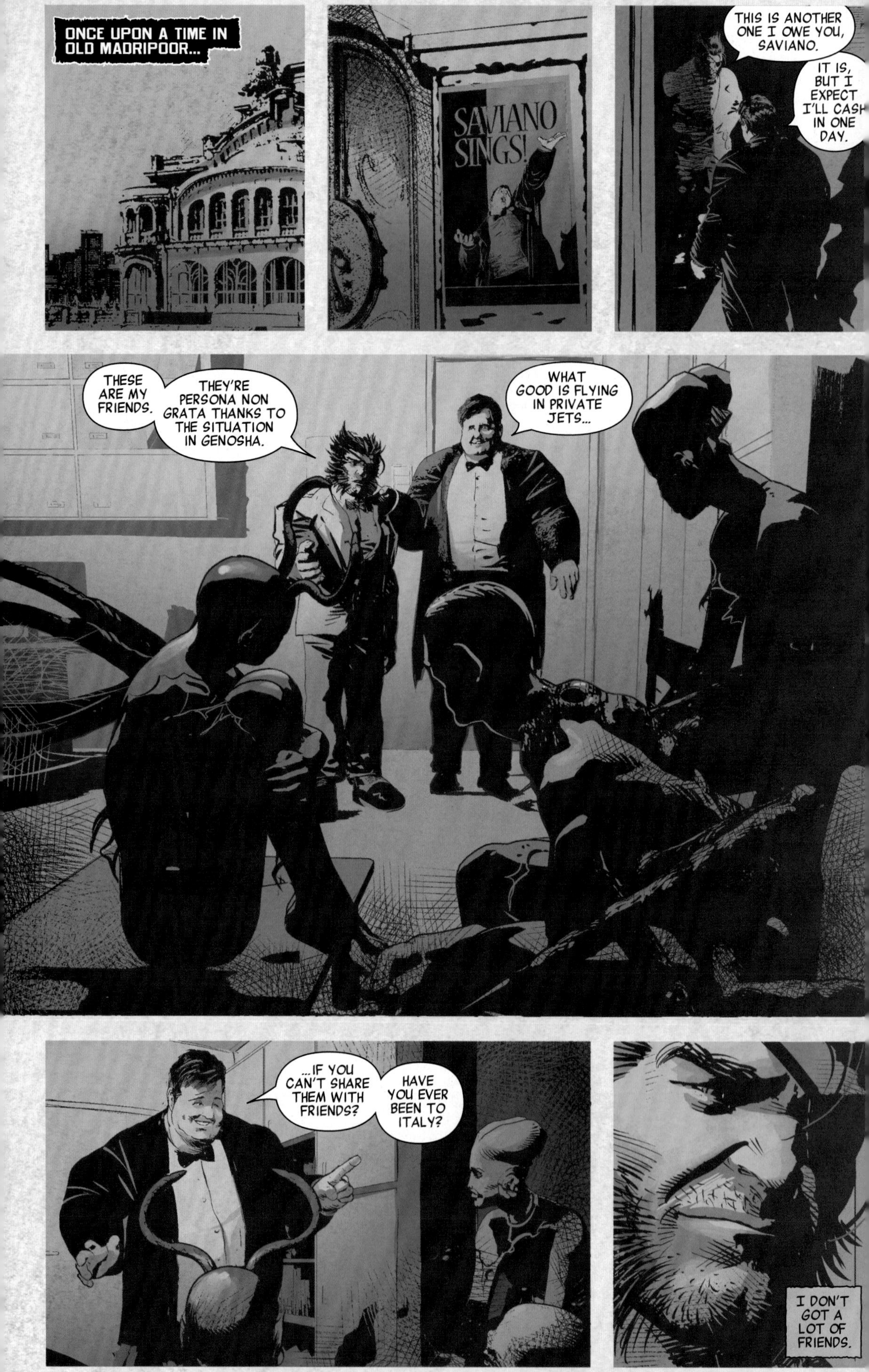
ONCE UPON A TIME IN OLD MADRIPOOR...
SAVIANO SINGS!
THIS IS ANOTHER ONE I OWE YOU, SAVIANO.
IT IS, BUT I EXPECT I'LL CASH IN ONE DAY.
THESE ARE MY FRIENDS.
THEY'RE PERSONA NON GRATA THANKS TO THE SITUATION IN GENOSHA.
WHAT GOOD IS FLYING IN PRIVATE JETS...
...IF YOU CAN'T SHARE THEM WITH FRIENDS?
HAVE YOU EVER BEEN TO ITALY?
I DON'T GOT A LOT OF FRIENDS.

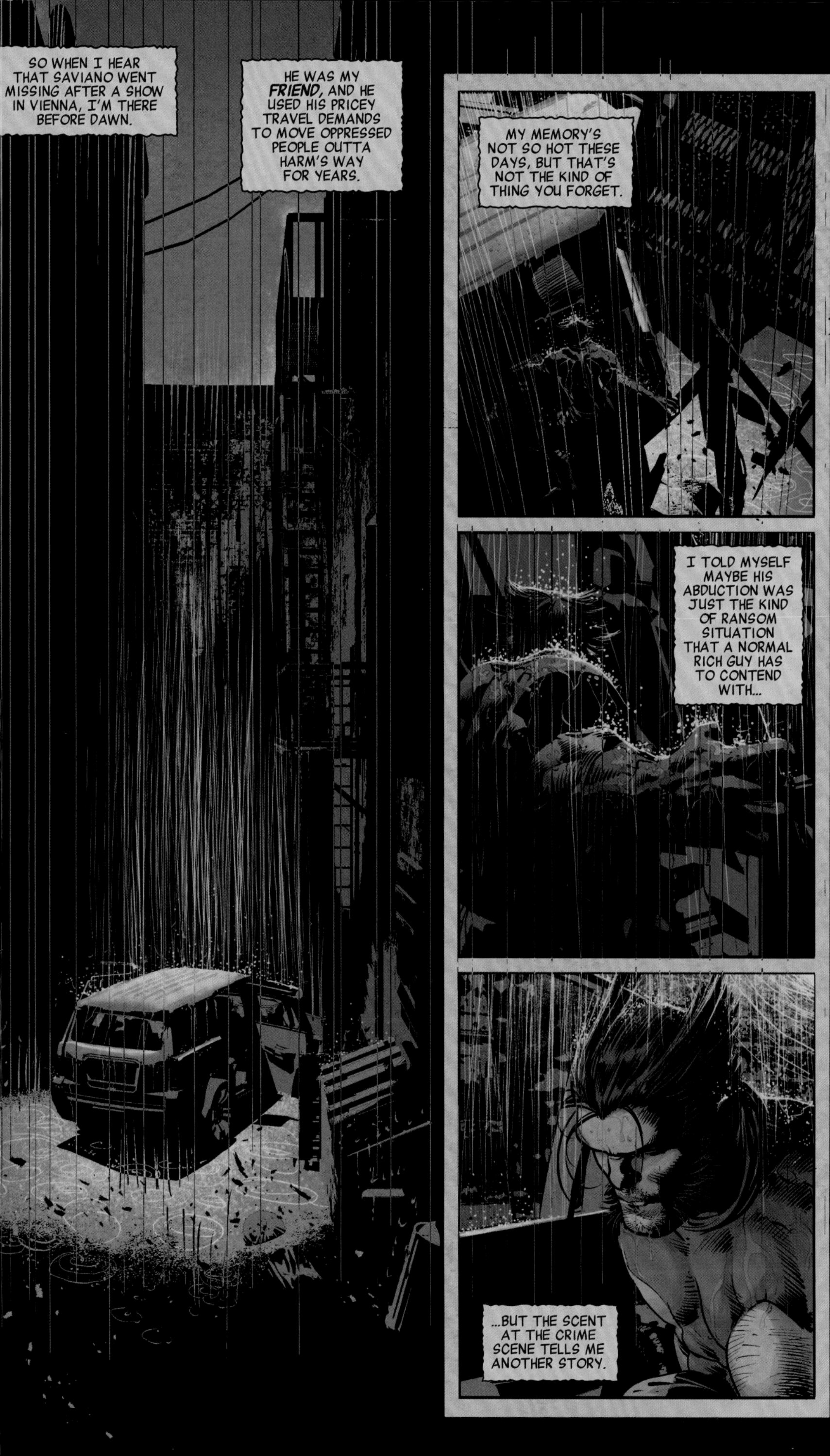
SO WHEN I HEAR THAT SAVIANO WENT MISSING AFTER A SHOW IN VIENNA, I'M THERE BEFORE DAWN.
HE WAS MY FRIEND, AND HE USED HIS PRICEY TRAVEL DEMANDS TO MOVE OPPRESSED PEOPLE OUTTA HARM'S WAY FOR YEARS.
MY MEMORY'S NOT SO HOT THESE DAYS, BUT THAT'S NOT THE KIND OF THING YOU FORGET.
I TOLD MYSELF MAYBE HIS ABDUCTION WAS JUST THE KIND OF RANSOM SITUATION THAT A NORMAL RICH GUY HAS TO CONTEND WITH...
...BUT THE SCENT AT THE CRIME SCENE TELLS ME ANOTHER STORY.

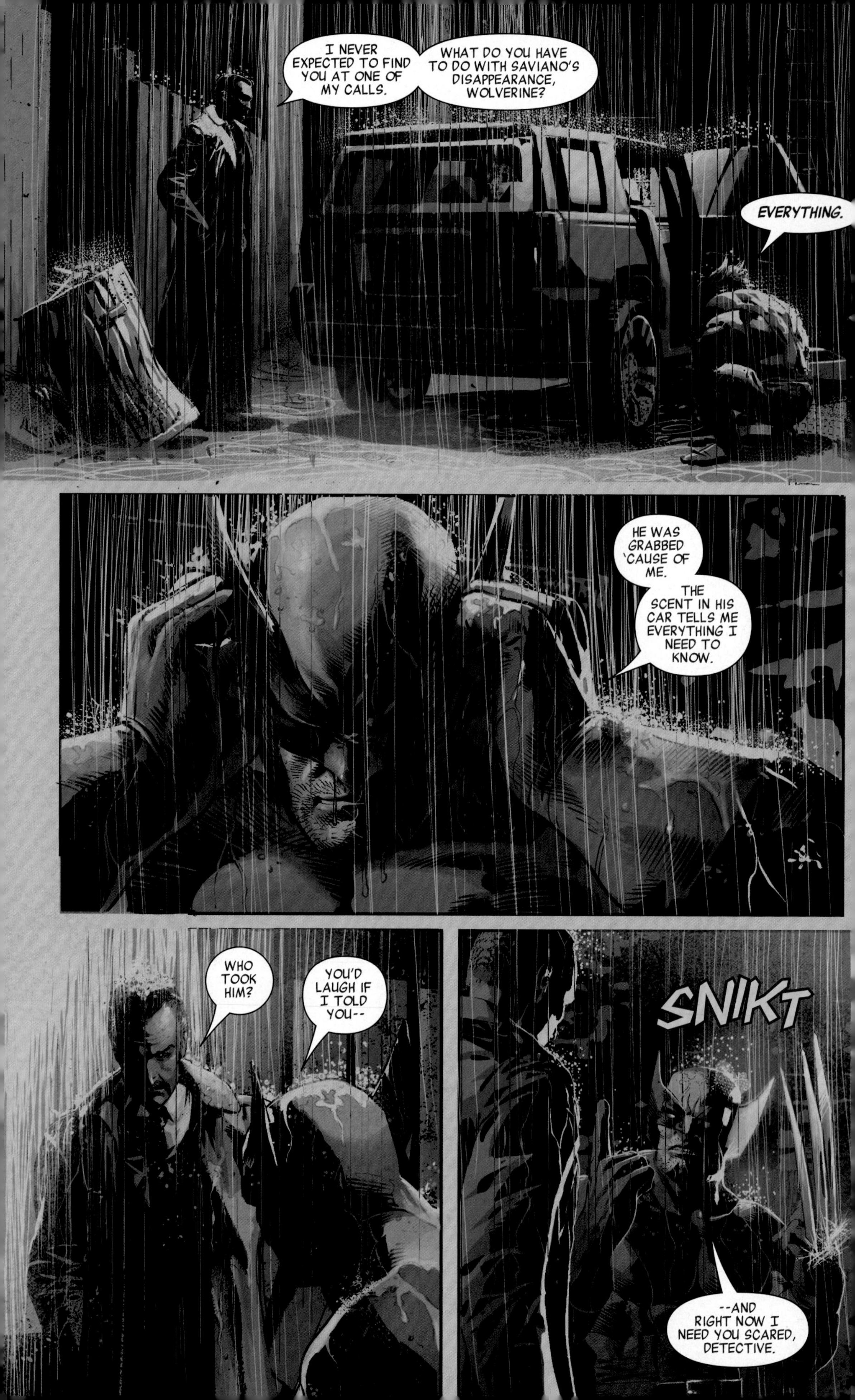
I NEVER EXPECTED TO FIND YOU AT ONE OF MY CALLS.
WHAT DO YOU HAVE TO DO WITH SAVIANO'S DISAPPEARANCE, WOLVERINE?
EVERYTHING.
HE WAS GRABBED 'CAUSE OF ME.
THE SCENT IN HIS CAR TELLS ME EVERYTHING I NEED TO KNOW.
WHO TOOK HIM?
YOU'D LAUGH IF I TOLD YOU--
SNIKT
--AND RIGHT NOW I NEED YOU SCARED, DETECTIVE.

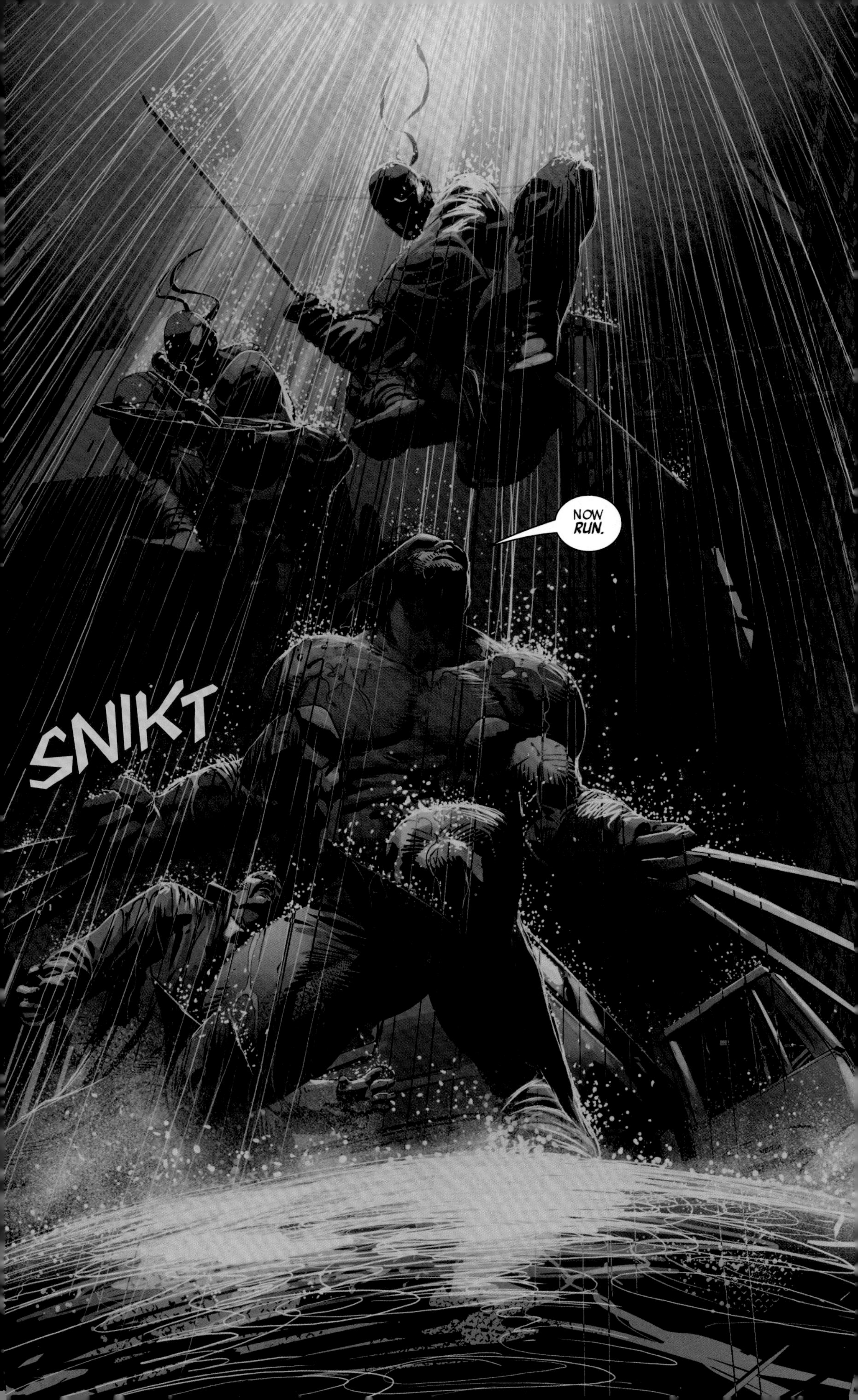
NOW RUN.
SNIKT

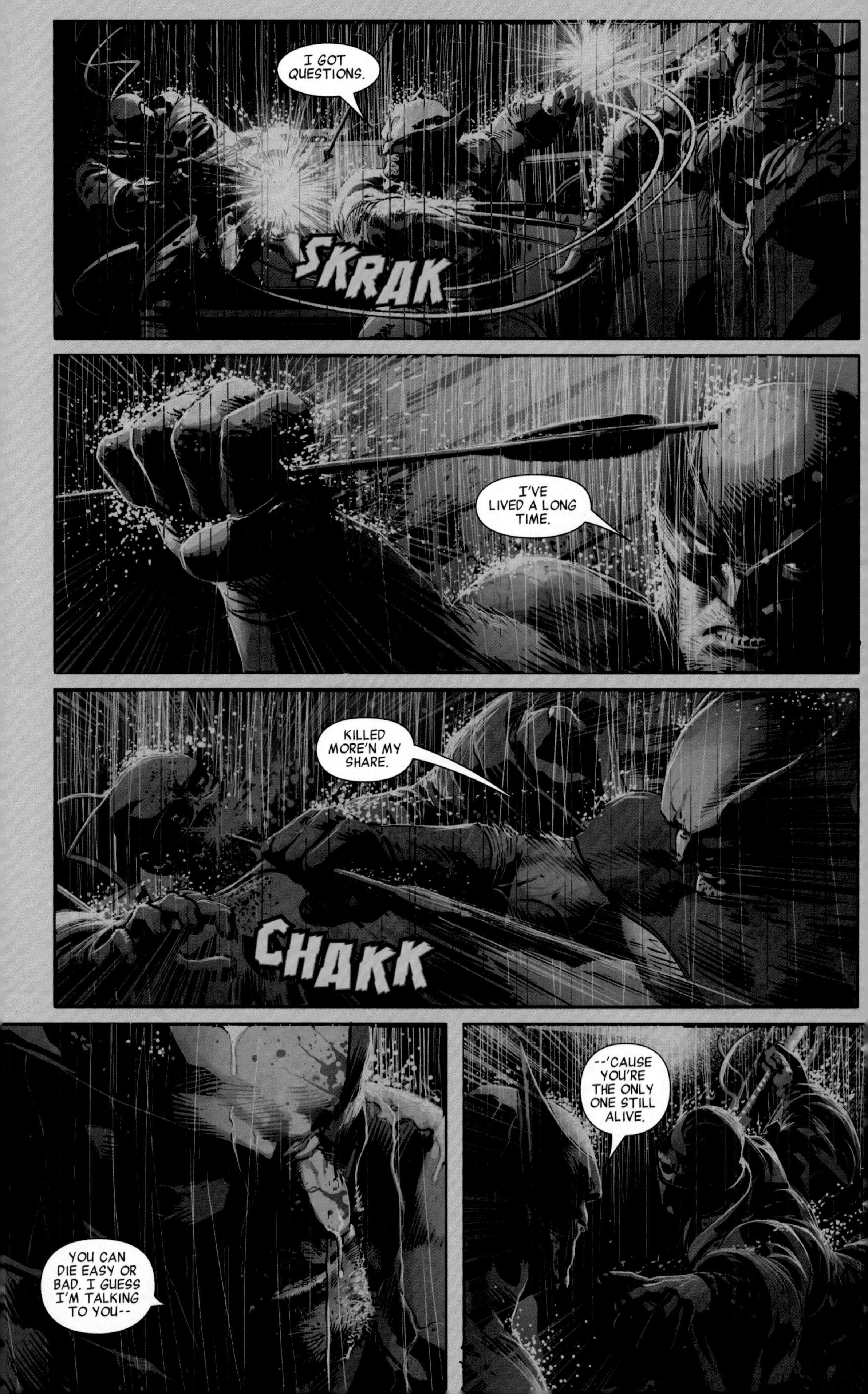
I GOT QUESTIONS.
SKRAK
I'VE LIVED A LONG TIME.
KILLED MORE'N MY SHARE.
CHAKK
YOU CAN DIE EASY OR BAD. I GUESS I'M TALKING TO YOU--
--'CAUSE YOU'RE THE ONLY ONE STILL ALIVE.

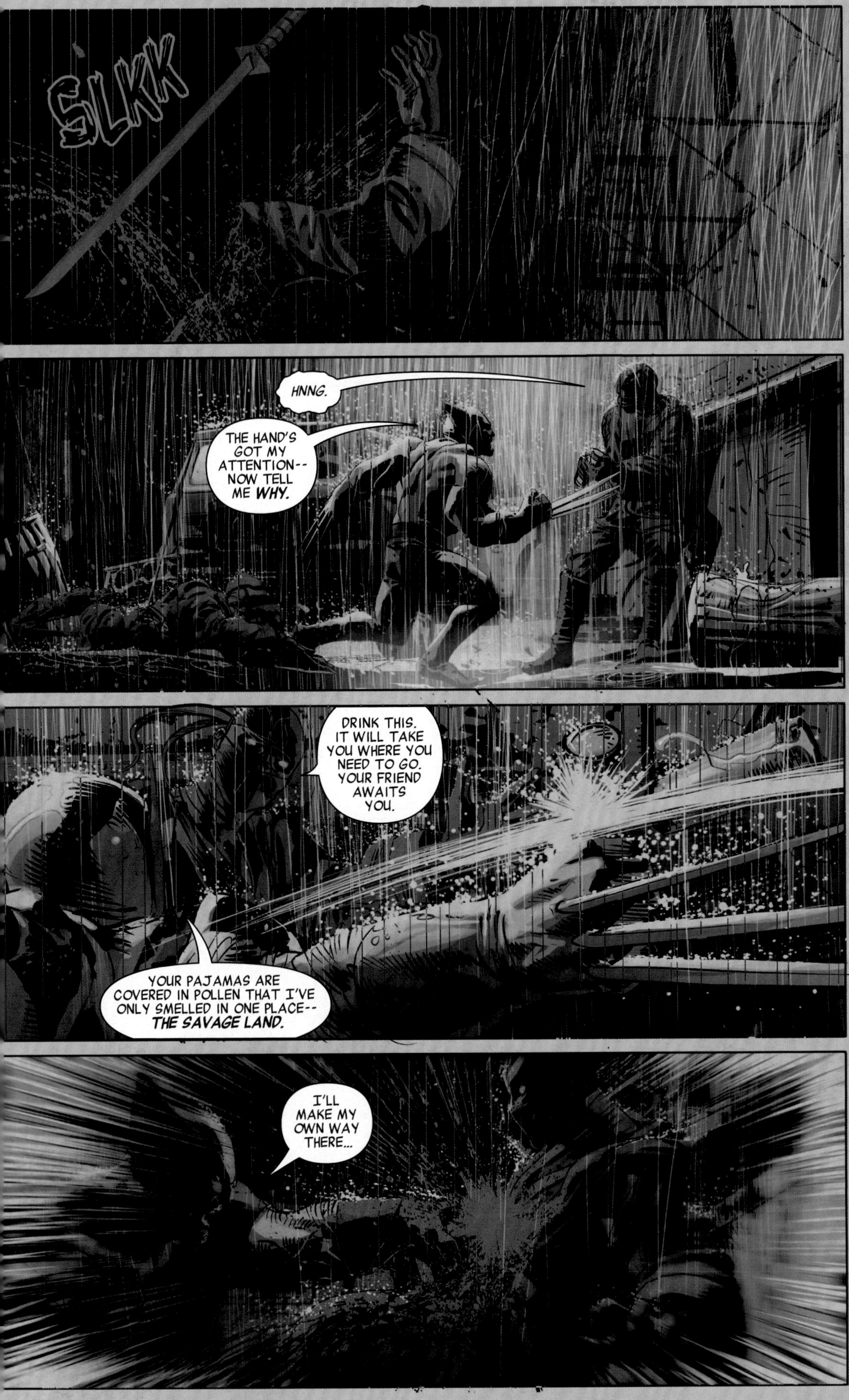
SLKK
HNNG.
THE HAND'S GOT MY ATTENTION-- NOW TELL ME **WHY.**
DRINK THIS. IT WILL TAKE YOU WHERE YOU NEED TO GO. YOUR FRIEND AWAITS YOU.
YOUR PAJAMAS ARE COVERED IN POLLEN THAT I'VE ONLY SMELLED IN ONE PLACE-- ***THE SAVAGE LAND.***
I'LL MAKE MY OWN WAY THERE...

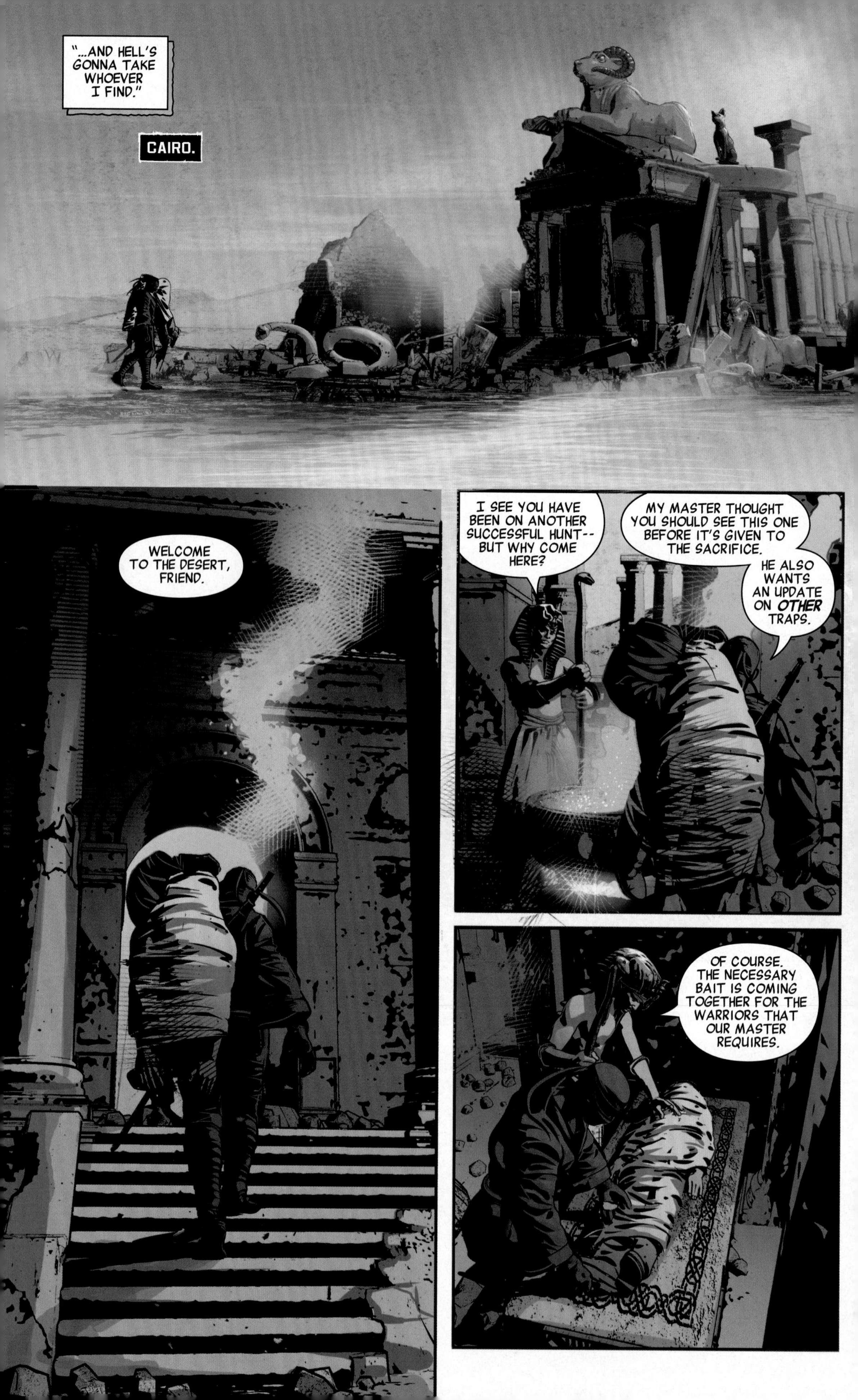
"...AND HELL'S GONNA TAKE WHOEVER I FIND."
CAIRO.
WELCOME TO THE DESERT, FRIEND.
I SEE YOU HAVE BEEN ON ANOTHER SUCCESSFUL HUNT-- BUT WHY COME HERE?
MY MASTER THOUGHT YOU SHOULD SEE THIS ONE BEFORE IT'S GIVEN TO THE SACRIFICE.
HE ALSO WANTS AN UPDATE ON OTHER TRAPS.
OF COURSE. THE NECESSARY BAIT IS COMING TOGETHER FOR THE WARRIORS THAT OUR MASTER REQUIRES.

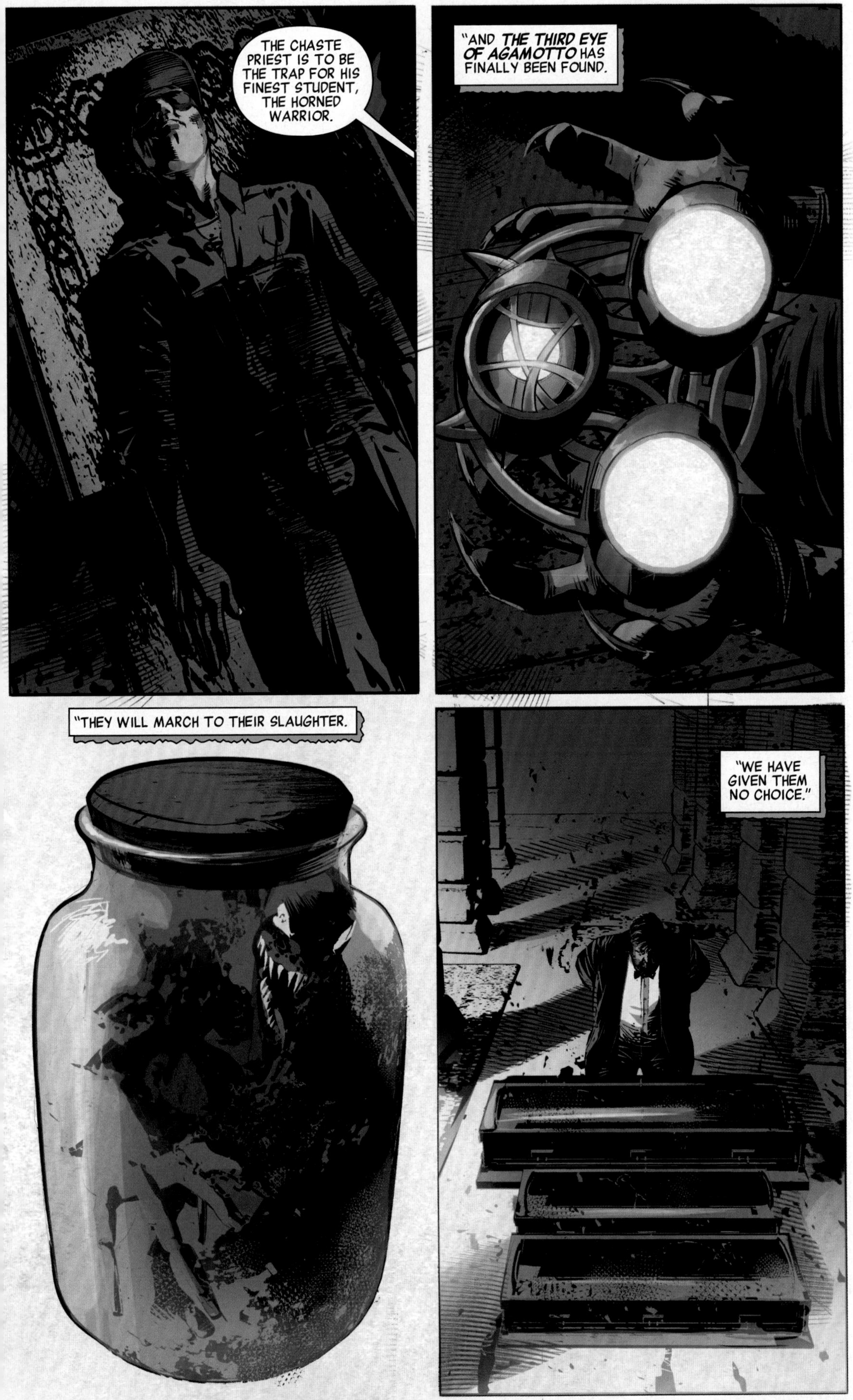
THE CHASTE PRIEST IS TO BE THE TRAP FOR HIS FINEST STUDENT, THE HORNED WARRIOR.
"AND THE THIRD EYE OF AGAMOTTO HAS FINALLY BEEN FOUND.
"THEY WILL MARCH TO THEIR SLAUGHTER.
"WE HAVE GIVEN THEM NO CHOICE."

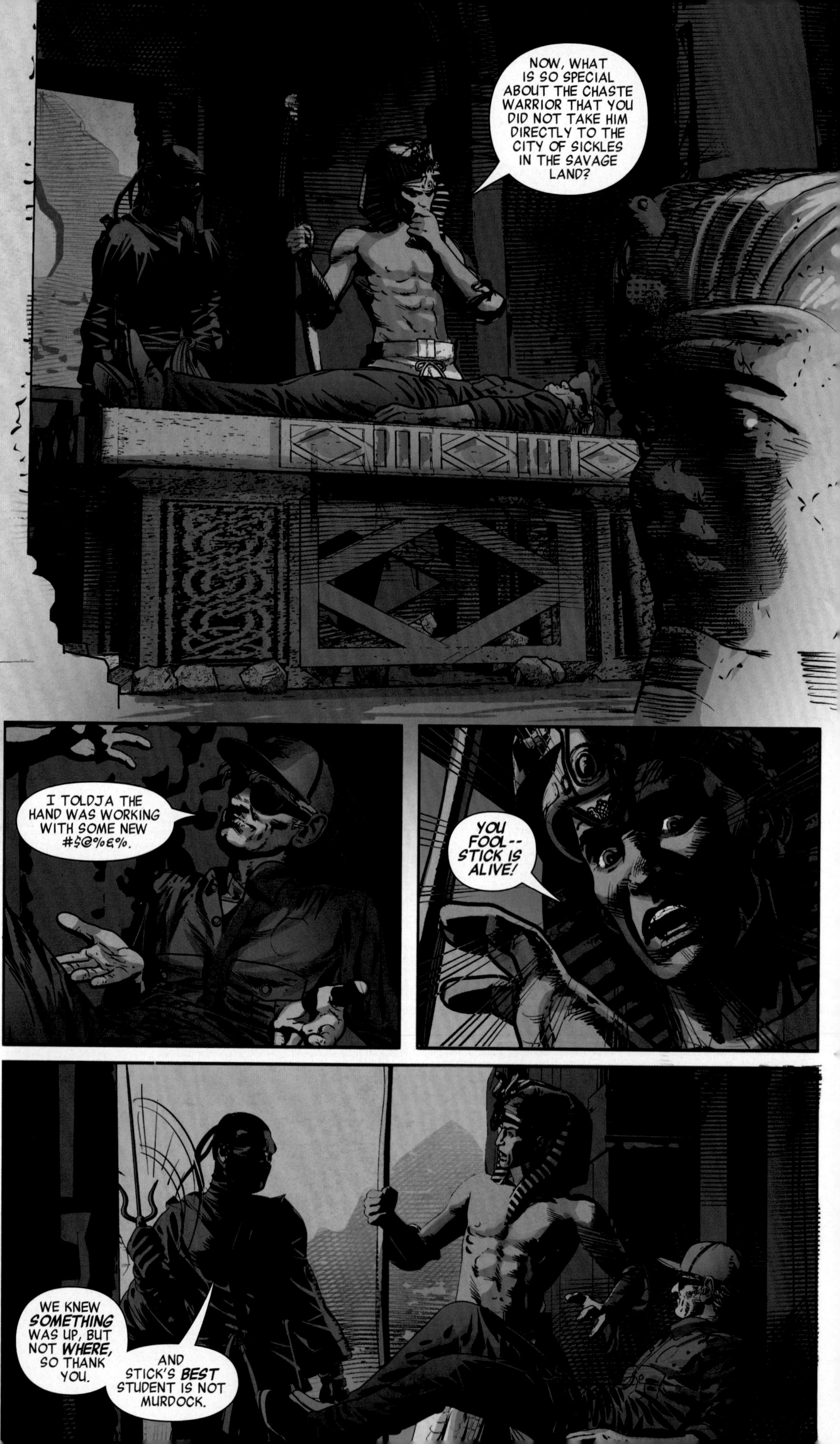
NOW, WHAT IS SO SPECIAL ABOUT THE CHASTE WARRIOR THAT YOU DID NOT TAKE HIM DIRECTLY TO THE CITY OF SICKLES IN THE SAVAGE LAND?
I TOLDJA THE HAND WAS WORKING WITH SOME NEW #$@%&%.
YOU FOOL-- STICK IS ALIVE!
WE KNEW SOMETHING WAS UP, BUT NOT WHERE, SO THANK YOU.
AND STICK'S BEST STUDENT IS NOT MURDOCK.

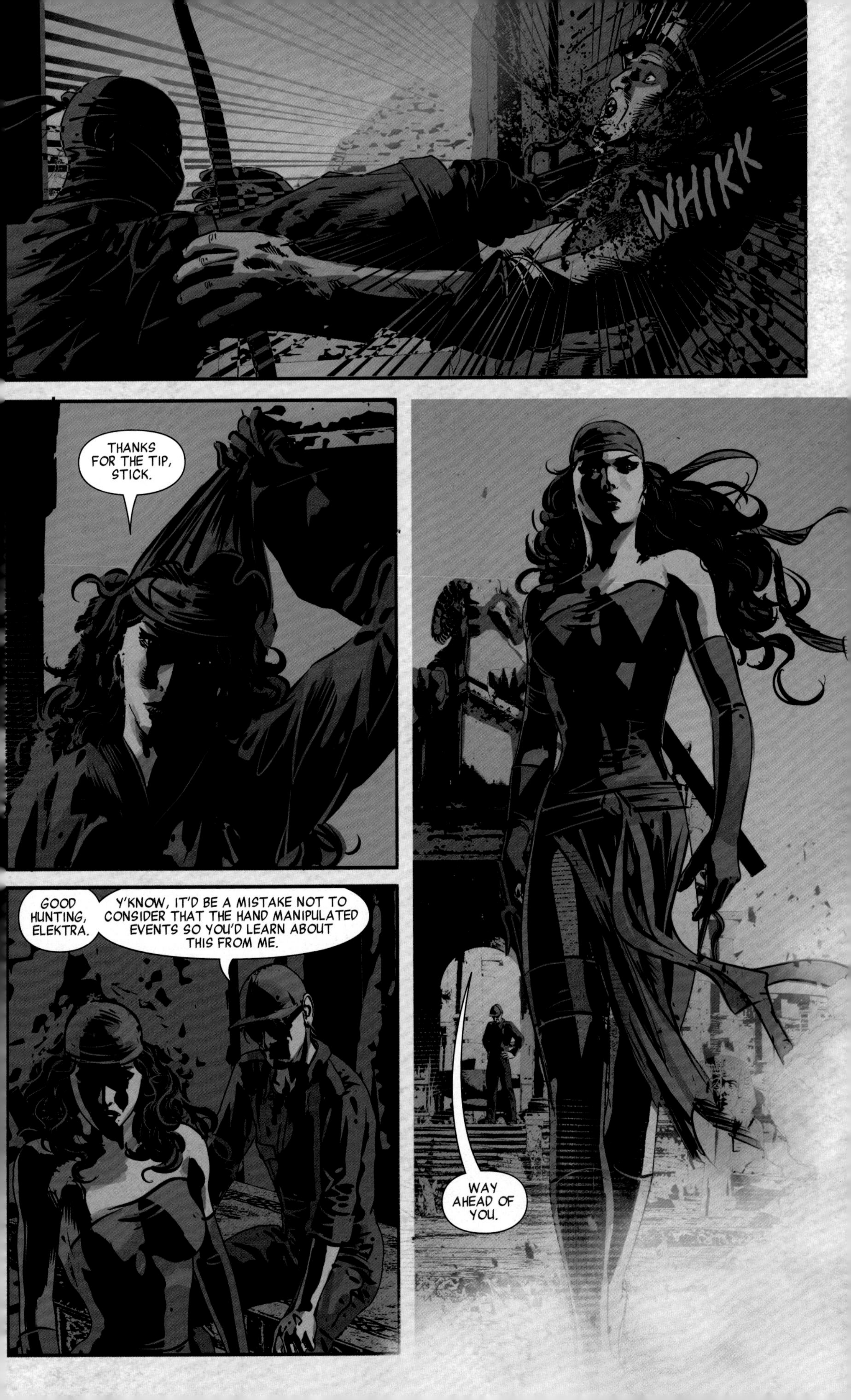
WHIKK
THANKS FOR THE TIP, STICK.
GOOD HUNTING, ELEKTRA.
Y'KNOW, IT'D BE A MISTAKE NOT TO CONSIDER THAT THE HAND MANIPULATED EVENTS SO YOU'D LEARN ABOUT THIS FROM ME.
WAY AHEAD OF YOU.

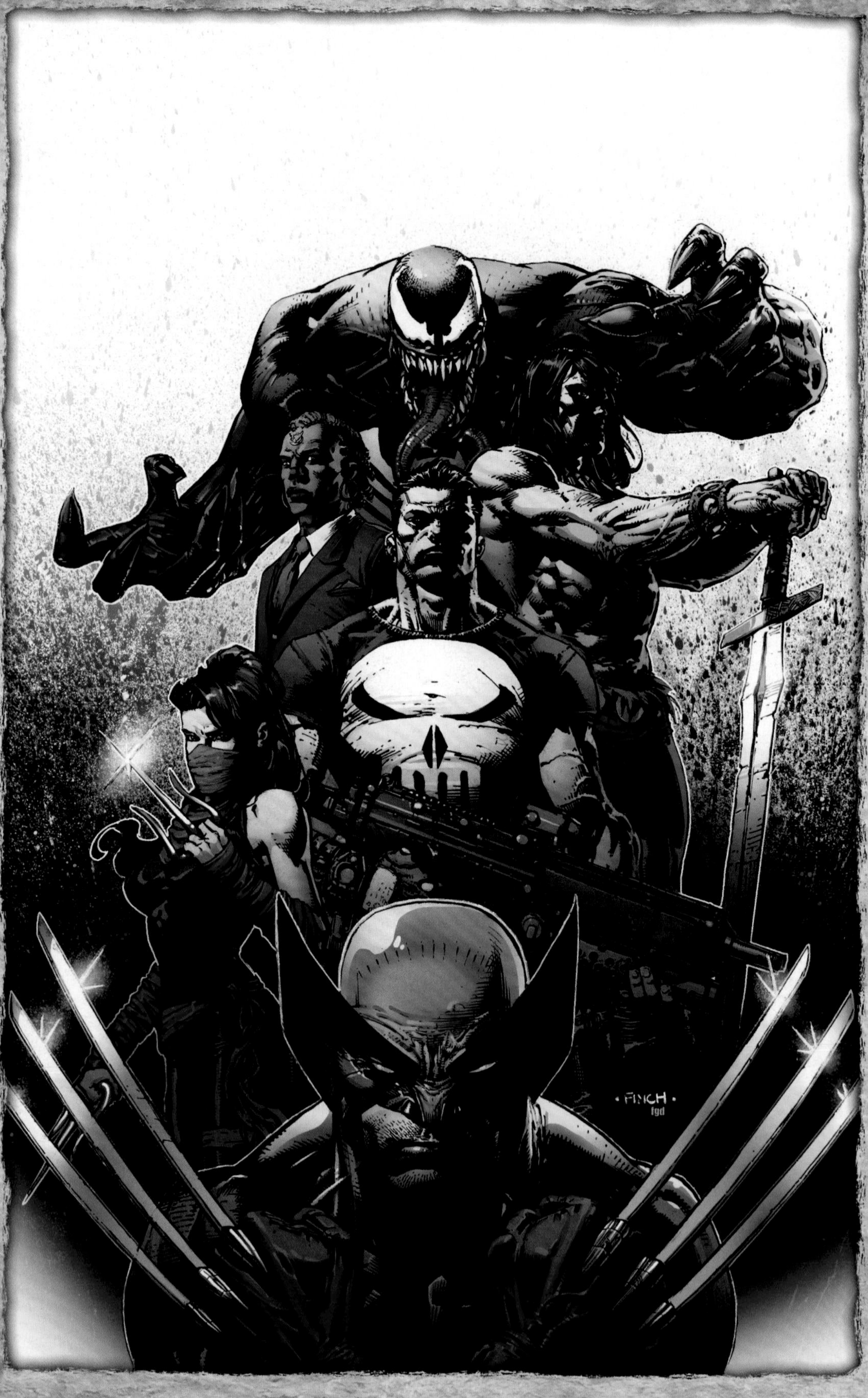
FINCH
fgd

1: ONCE UPON A TIME IN THE CITY OF SICKLES

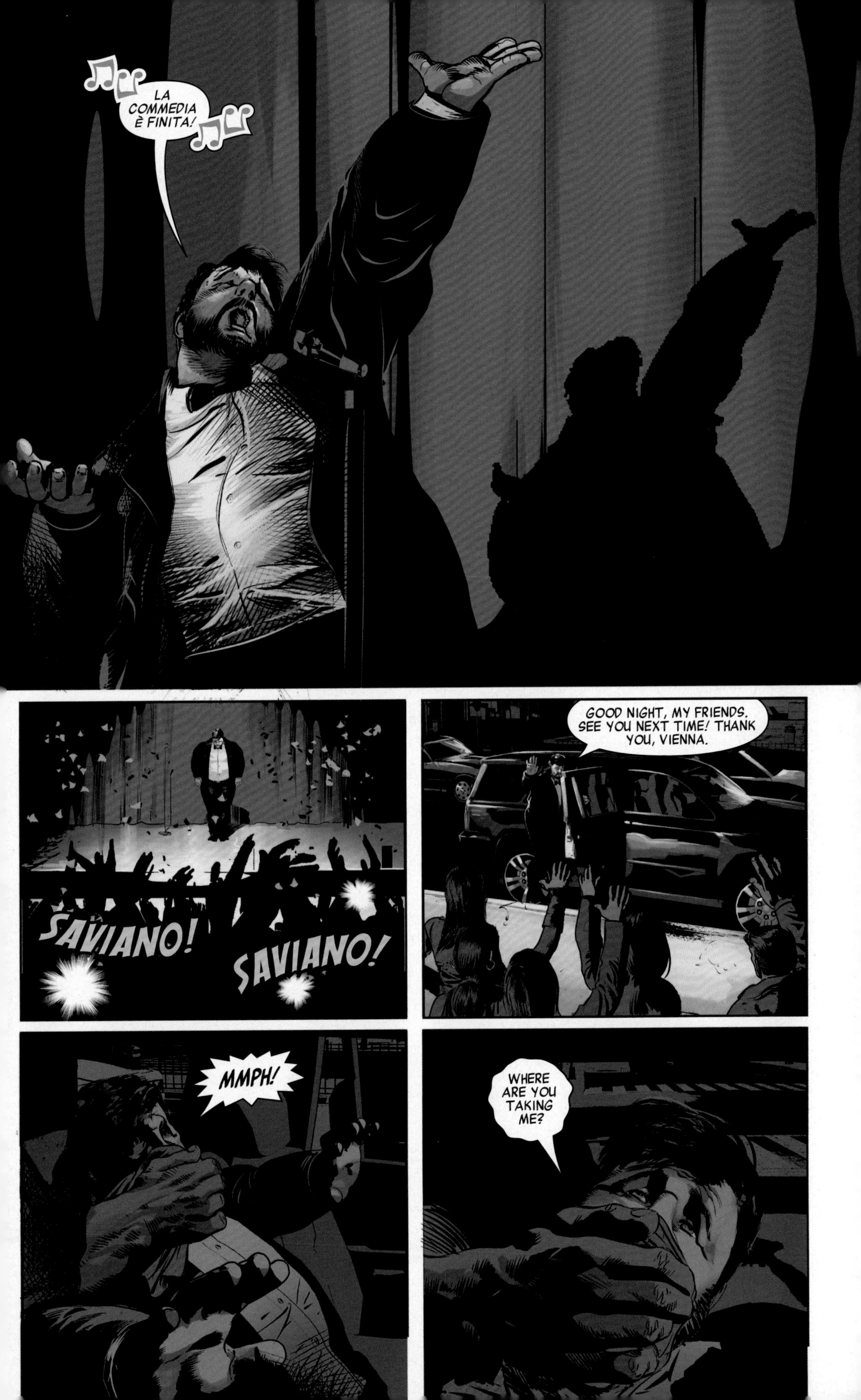
LA COMMEDIA È FINITA!
SAVIANO!
SAVIANO!
GOOD NIGHT, MY FRIENDS. SEE YOU NEXT TIME! THANK YOU, VIENNA.
MMPH!
WHERE ARE YOU TAKING ME?

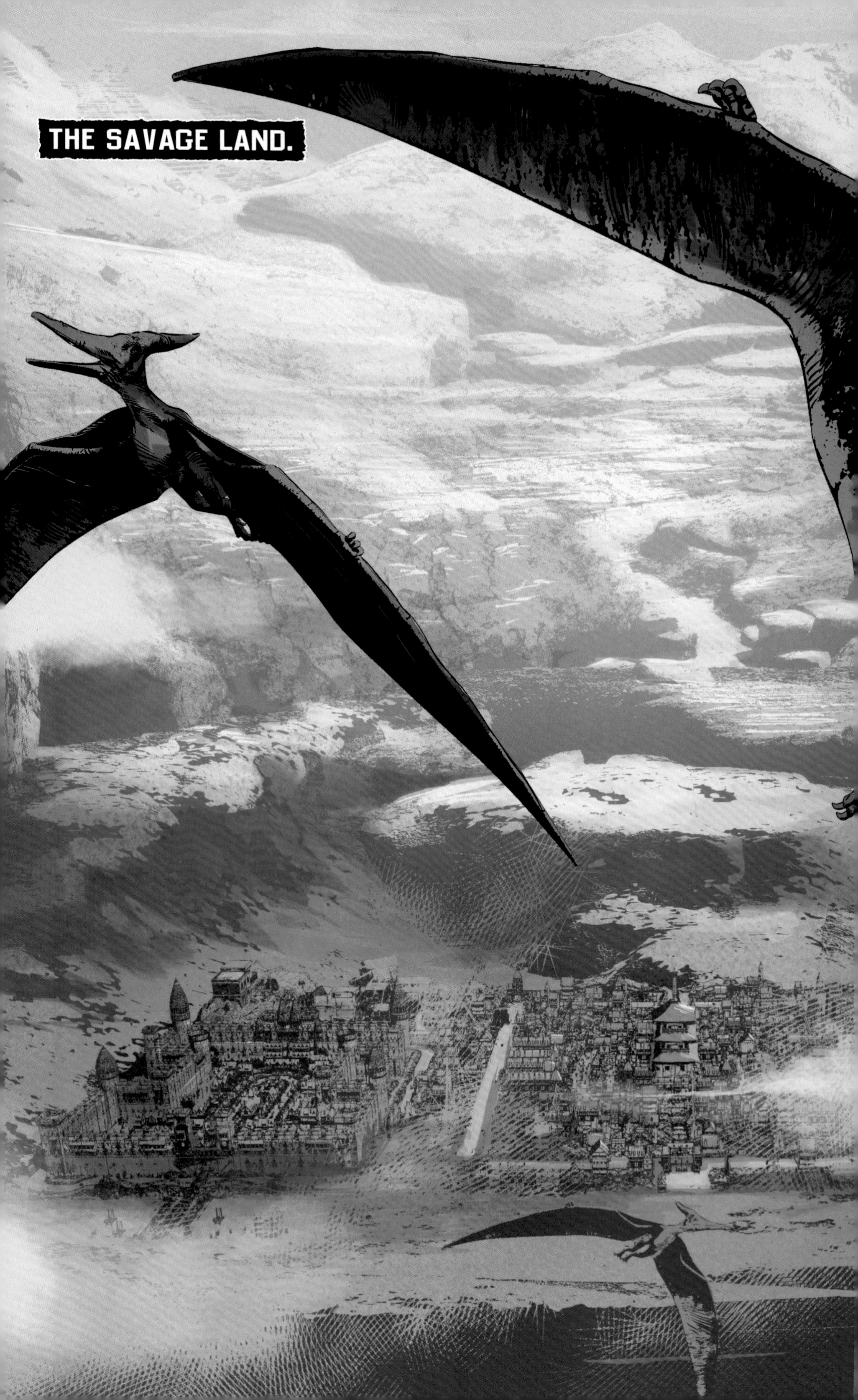
THE SAVAGE LAND.

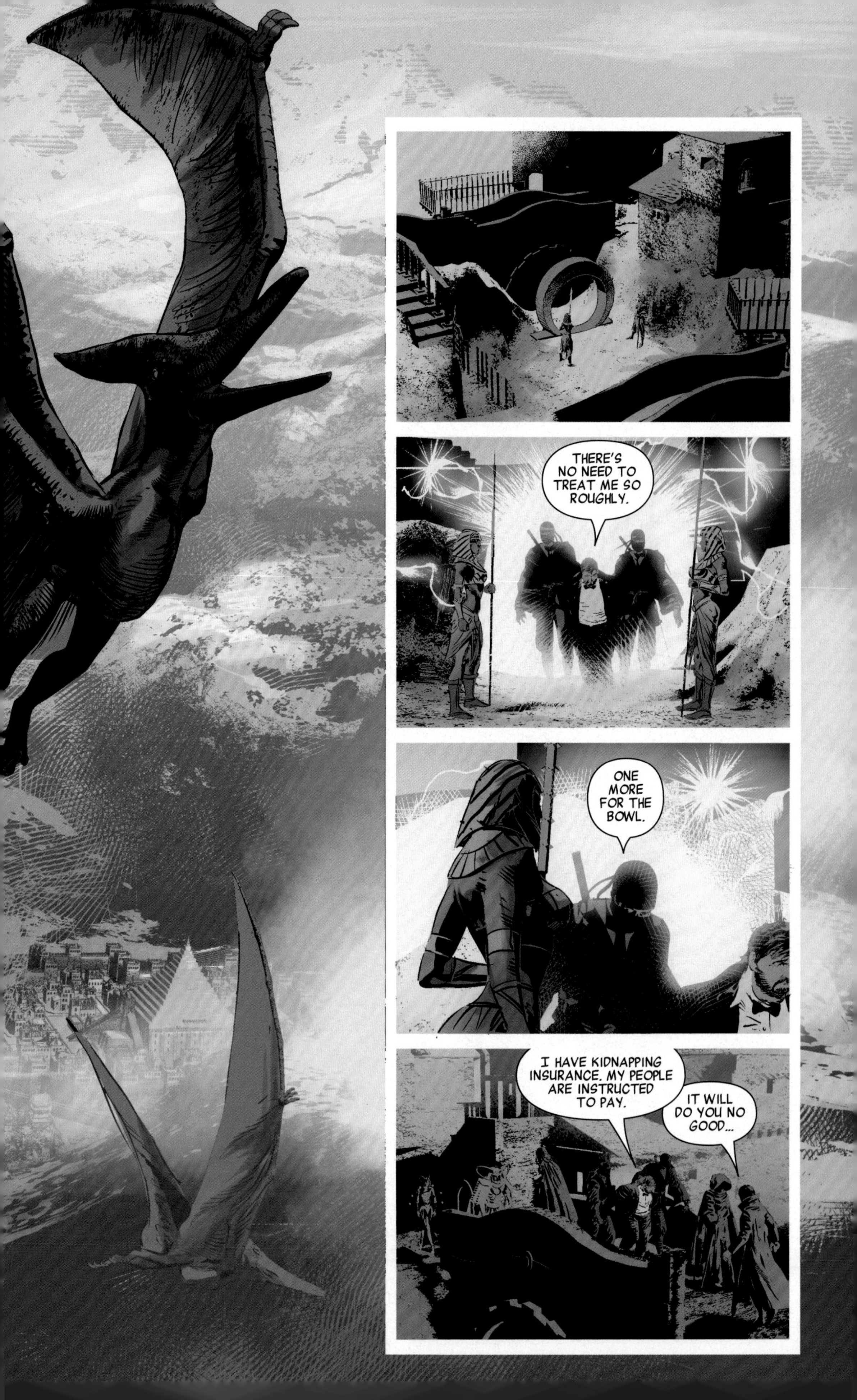
THERE'S NO NEED TO TREAT ME SO ROUGHLY.
ONE MORE FOR THE BOWL.
I HAVE KIDNAPPING INSURANCE. MY PEOPLE ARE INSTRUCTED TO PAY.
IT WILL DO YOU NO GOOD...

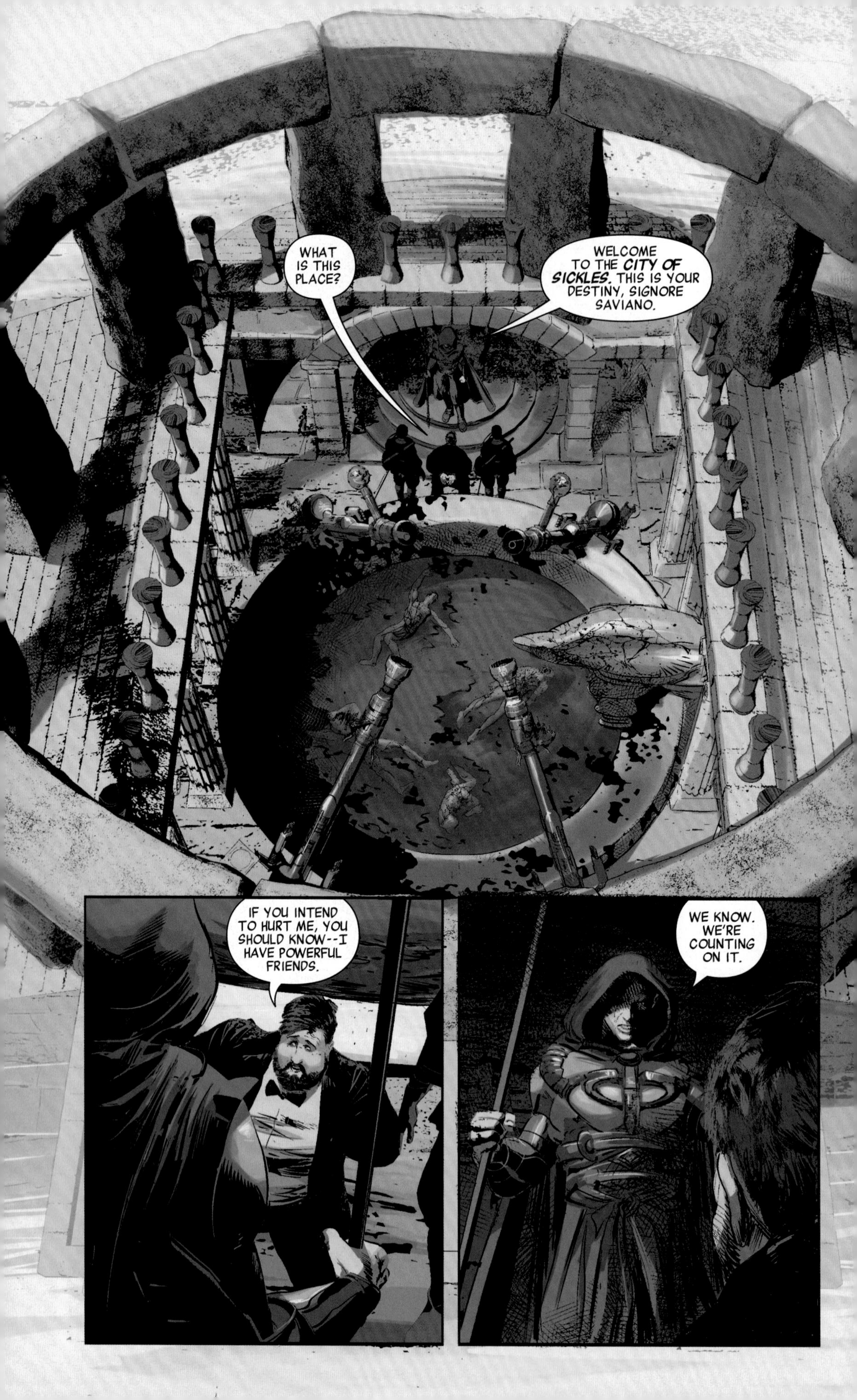
WHAT IS THIS PLACE?
WELCOME TO THE CITY OF SICKLES. THIS IS YOUR DESTINY, SIGNORE SAVIANO.
IF YOU INTEND TO HURT ME, YOU SHOULD KNOW--I HAVE POWERFUL FRIENDS.
WE KNOW. WE'RE COUNTING ON IT.

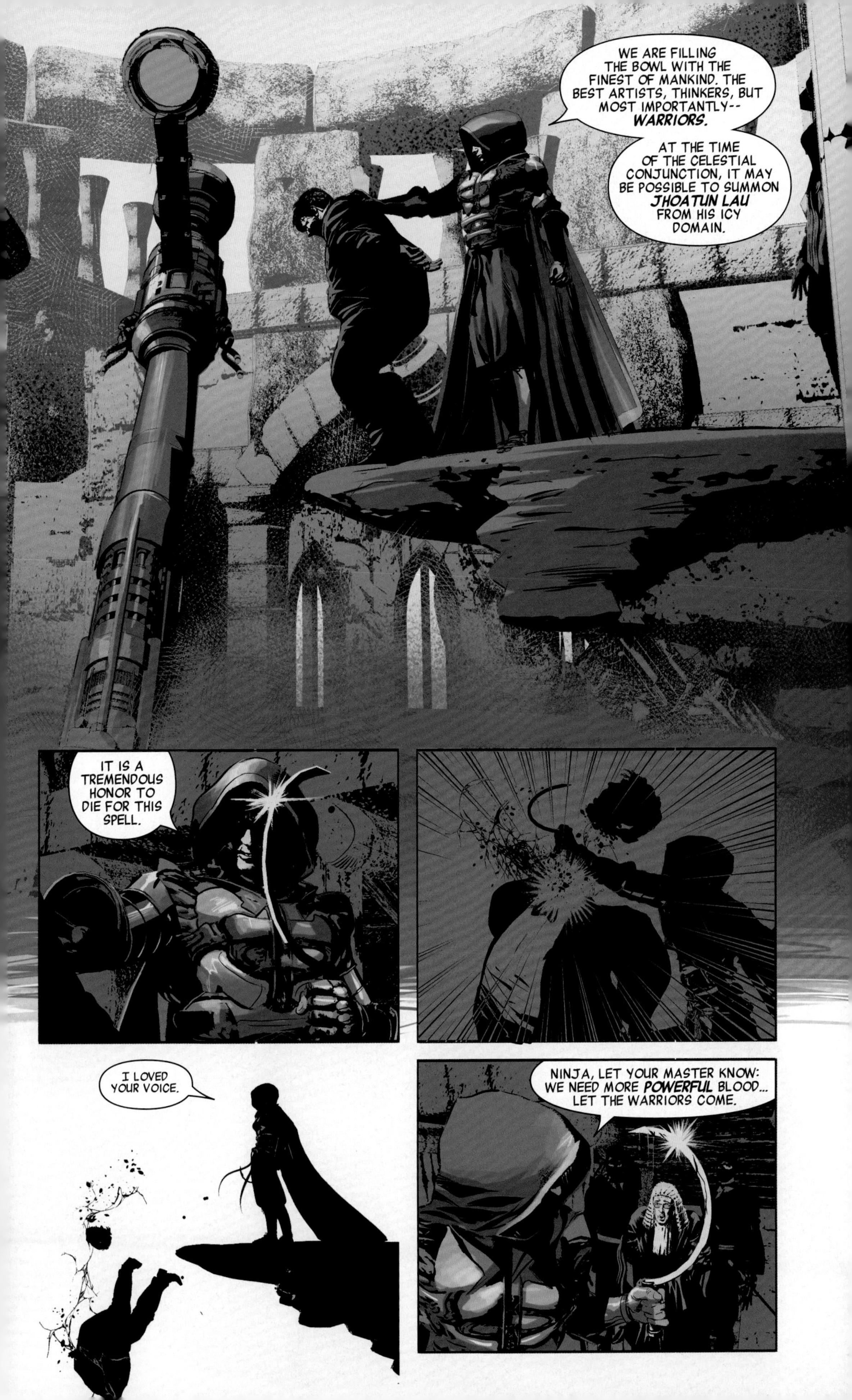
WE ARE FILLING THE BOWL WITH THE FINEST OF MANKIND. THE BEST ARTISTS, THINKERS, BUT MOST IMPORTANTLY-- WARRIORS.
AT THE TIME OF THE CELESTIAL CONJUNCTION, IT MAY BE POSSIBLE TO SUMMON JHOATUN LAU FROM HIS ICY DOMAIN.
IT IS A TREMENDOUS HONOR TO DIE FOR THIS SPELL.
I LOVED YOUR VOICE.
NINJA, LET YOUR MASTER KNOW: WE NEED MORE POWERFUL BLOOD... LET THE WARRIORS COME.

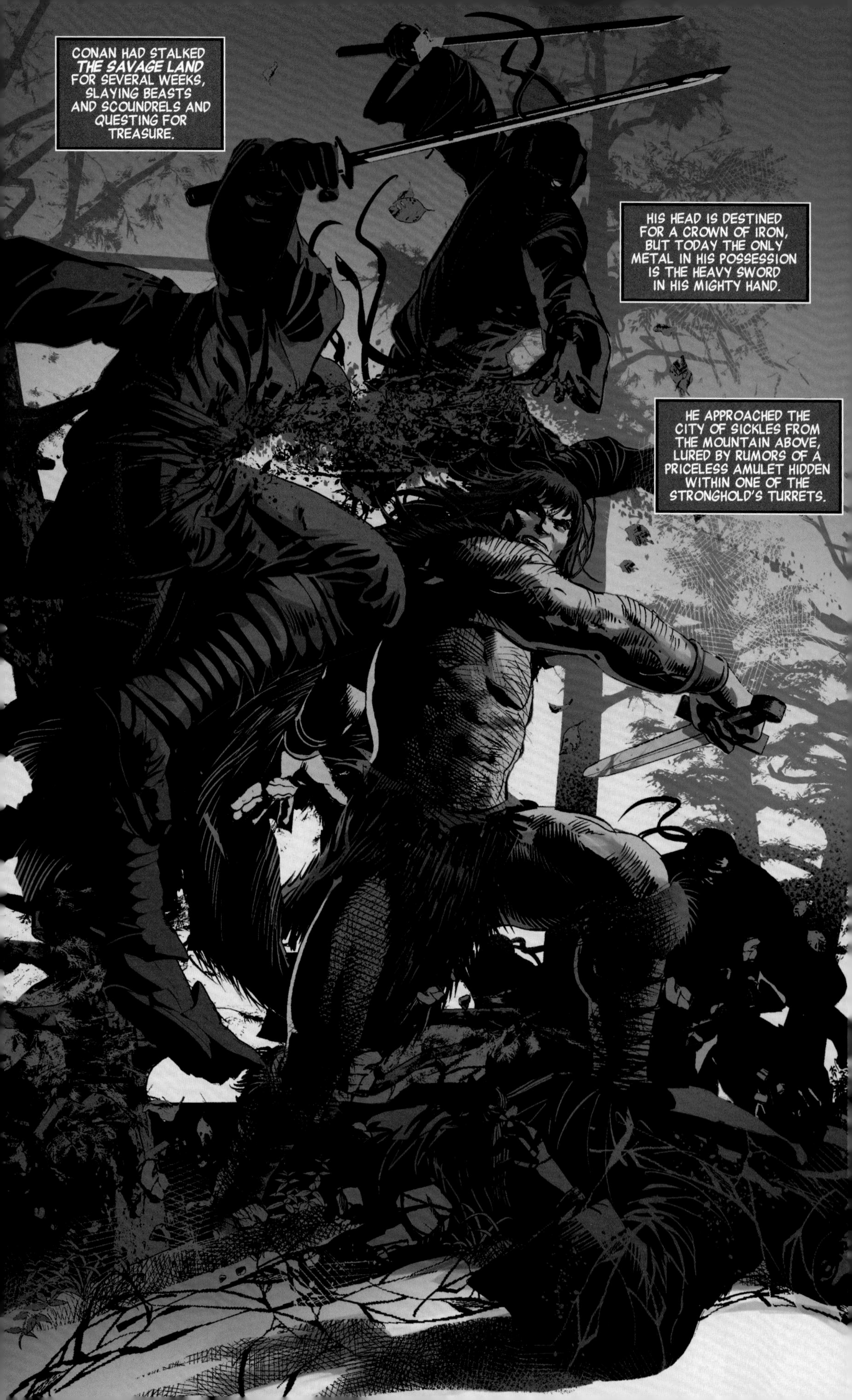
CONAN HAD STALKED THE SAVAGE LAND FOR SEVERAL WEEKS, SLAYING BEASTS AND SCOUNDRELS AND QUESTING FOR TREASURE.
HIS HEAD IS DESTINED FOR A CROWN OF IRON, BUT TODAY THE ONLY METAL IN HIS POSSESSION IS THE HEAVY SWORD IN HIS MIGHTY HAND.
HE APPROACHED THE CITY OF SICKLES FROM THE MOUNTAIN ABOVE, LURED BY RUMORS OF A PRICELESS AMULET HIDDEN WITHIN ONE OF THE STRONGHOLD'S TURRETS.

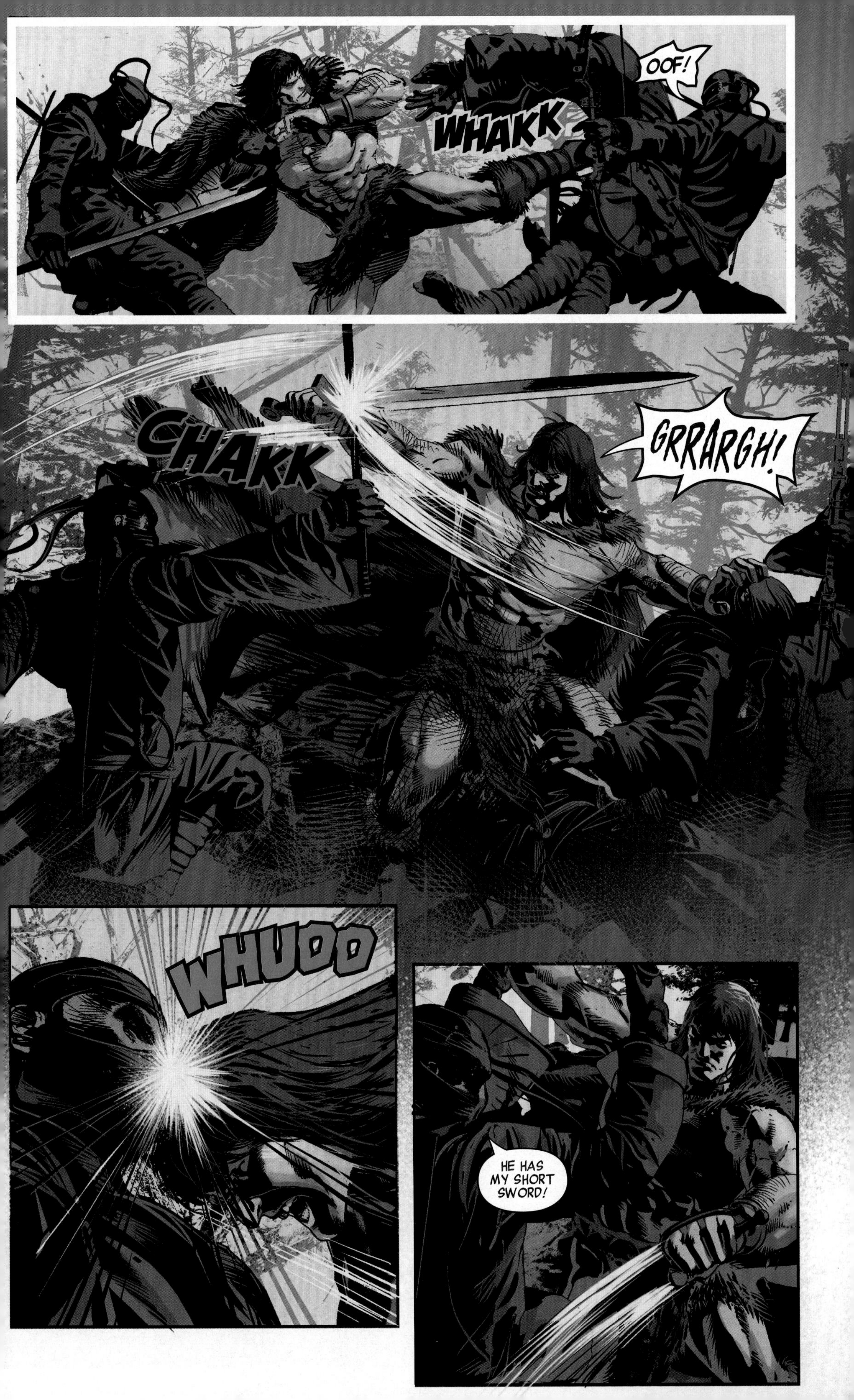
WHAKK
OOF!
CHAKK
GRRARGH!
WHUDD
HE HAS MY SHORT SWORD!

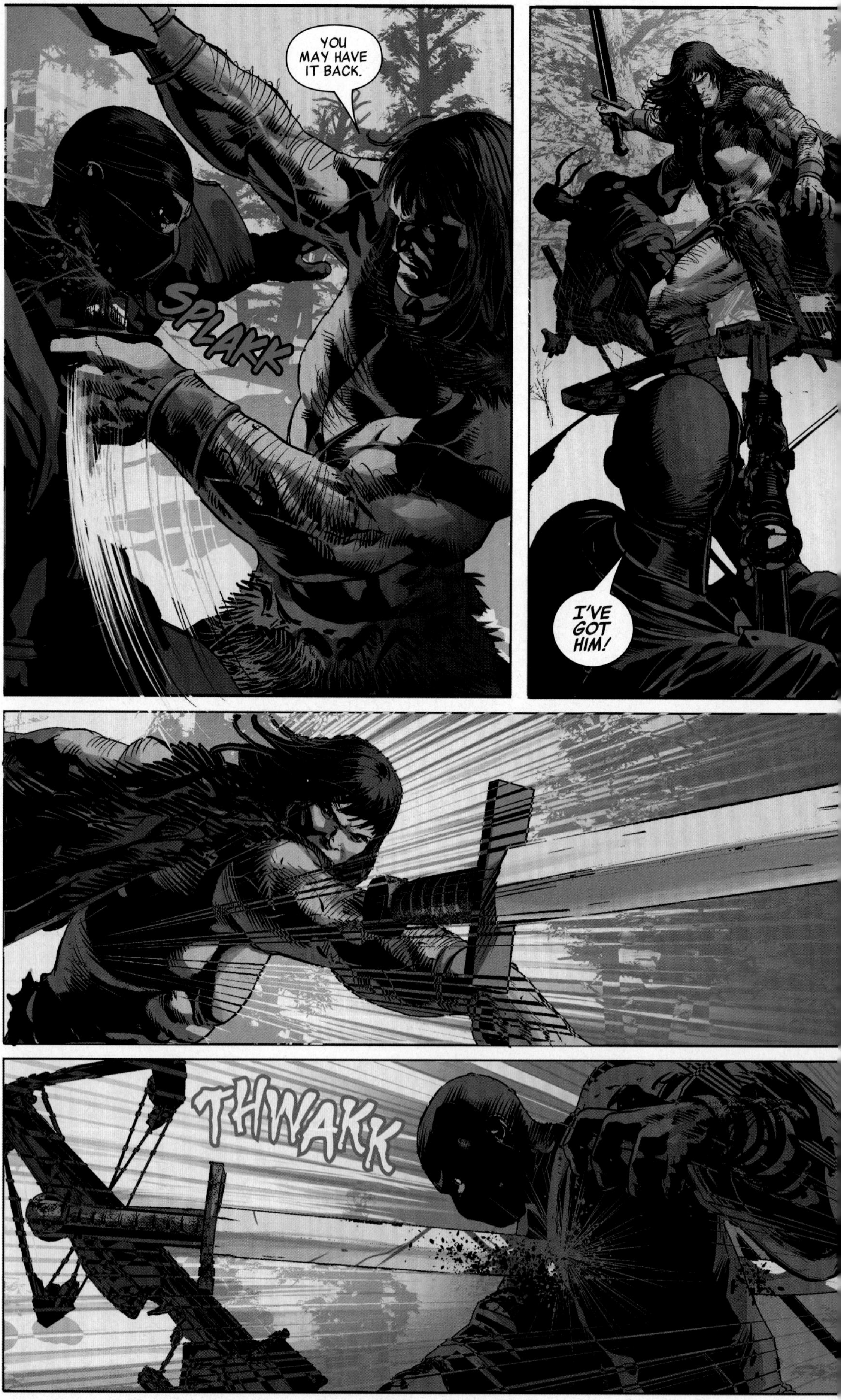
YOU MAY HAVE IT BACK.
SPLAKK
I'VE GOT HIM!
THWAKK

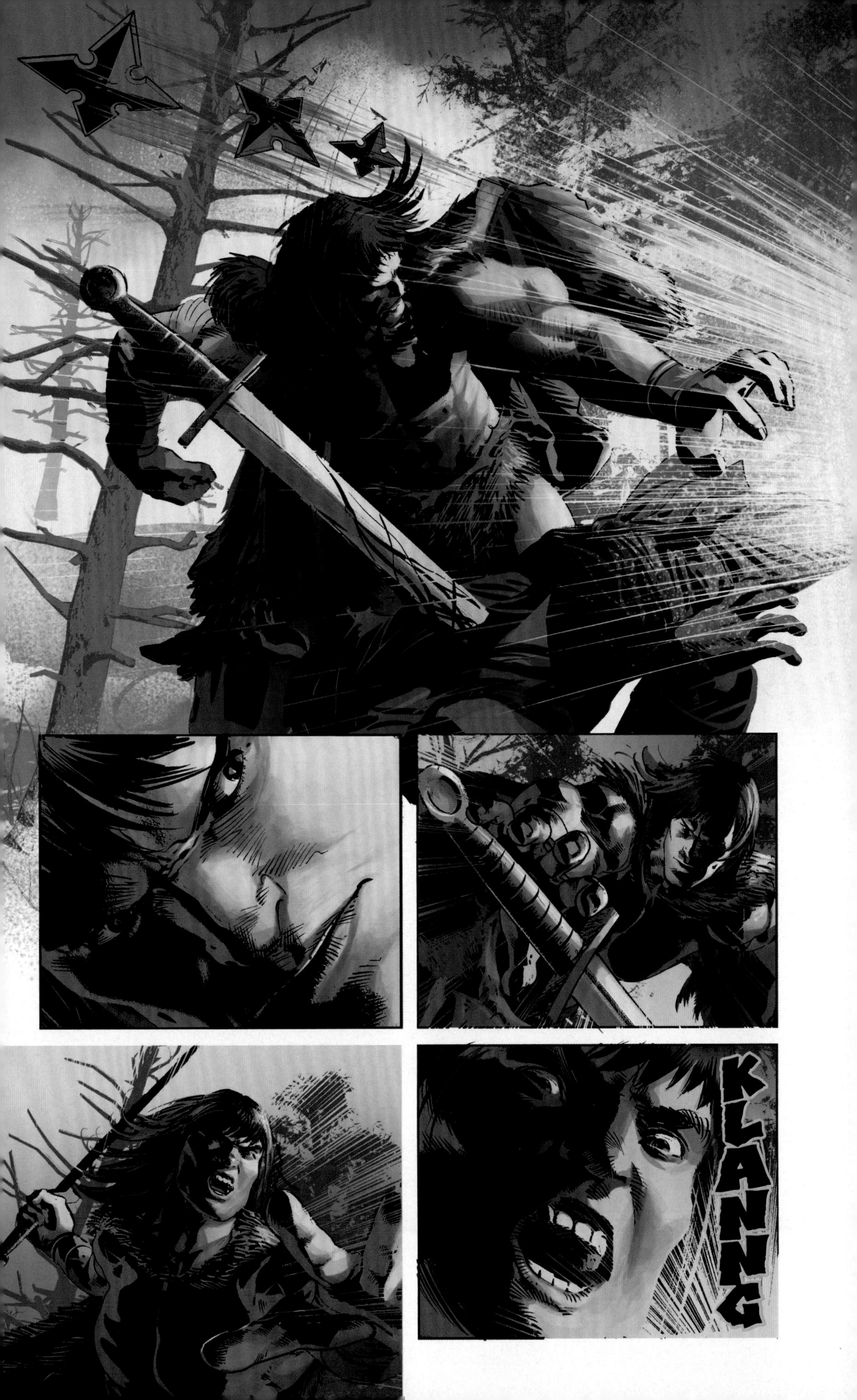
KLANG

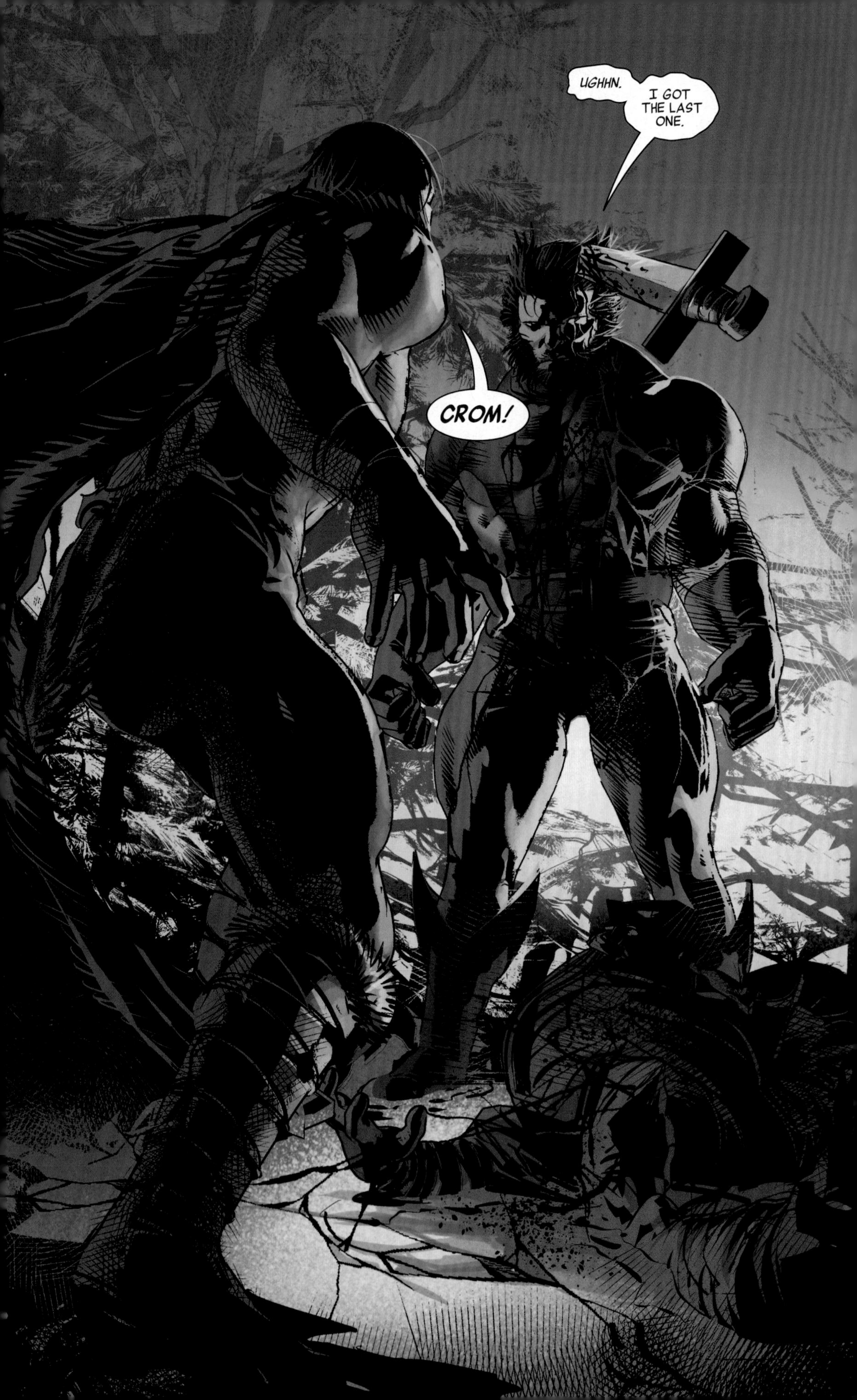
UGHHN.
I GOT THE LAST ONE.
CROM!

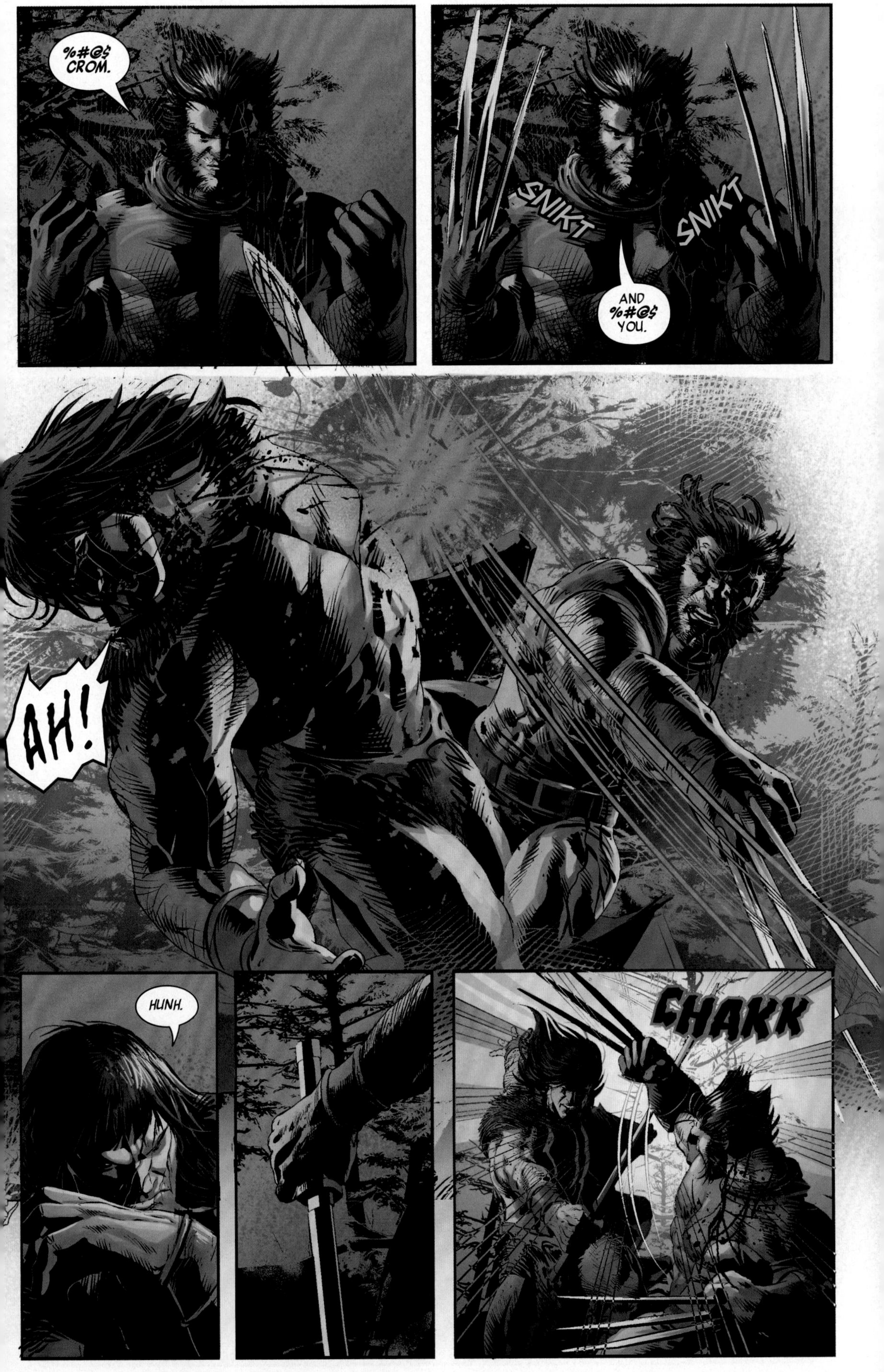
%#@$ CROM.
SNIKT
SNIKT
AND %#@$ YOU.
AH!
HUNH.
CHAKK

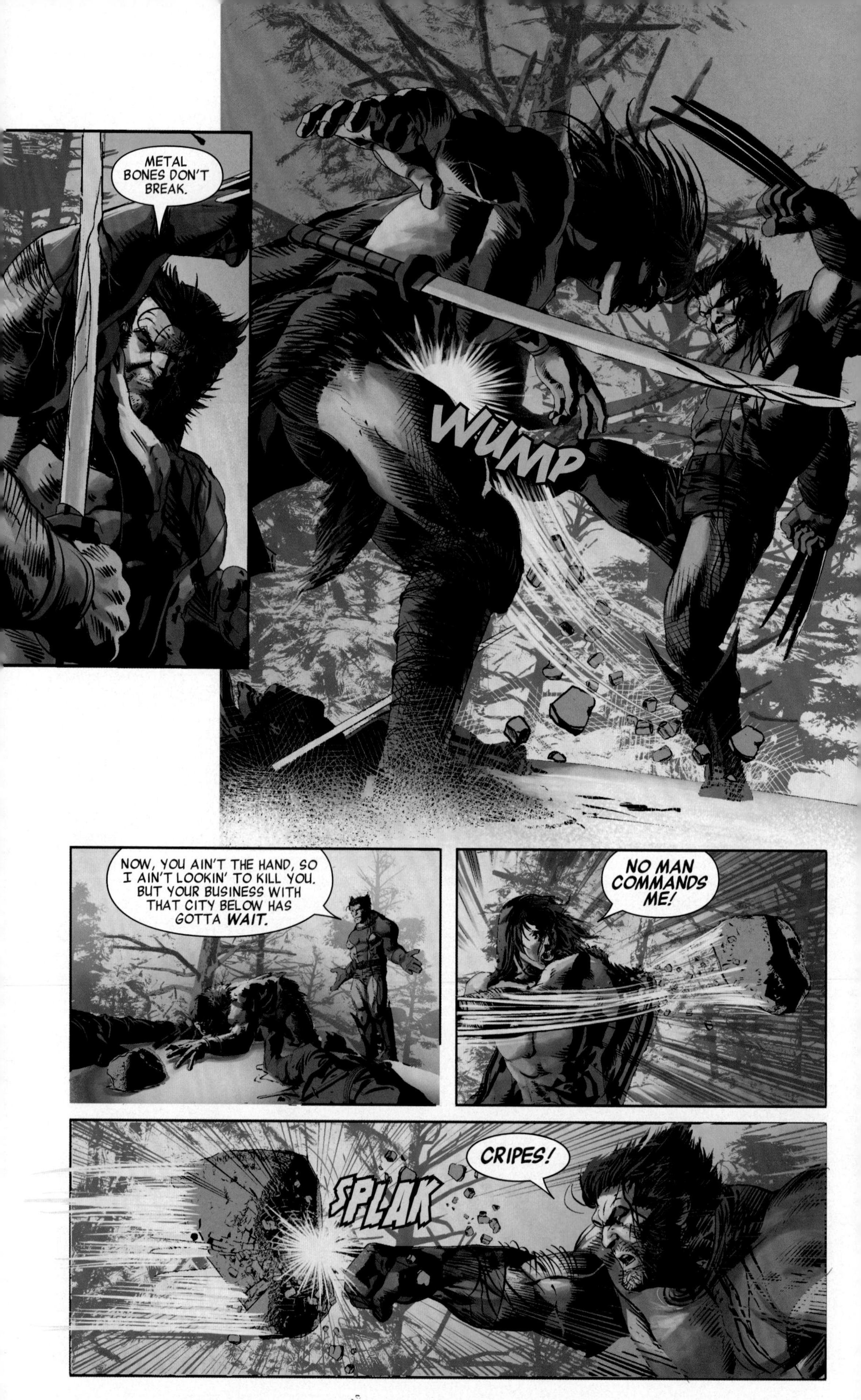
METAL BONES DON'T BREAK.
WUMP
NOW, YOU AIN'T THE HAND, SO I AIN'T LOOKIN' TO KILL YOU. BUT YOUR BUSINESS WITH THAT CITY BELOW HAS GOTTA WAIT.
NO MAN COMMANDS ME!
CRIPES!
SPLAK

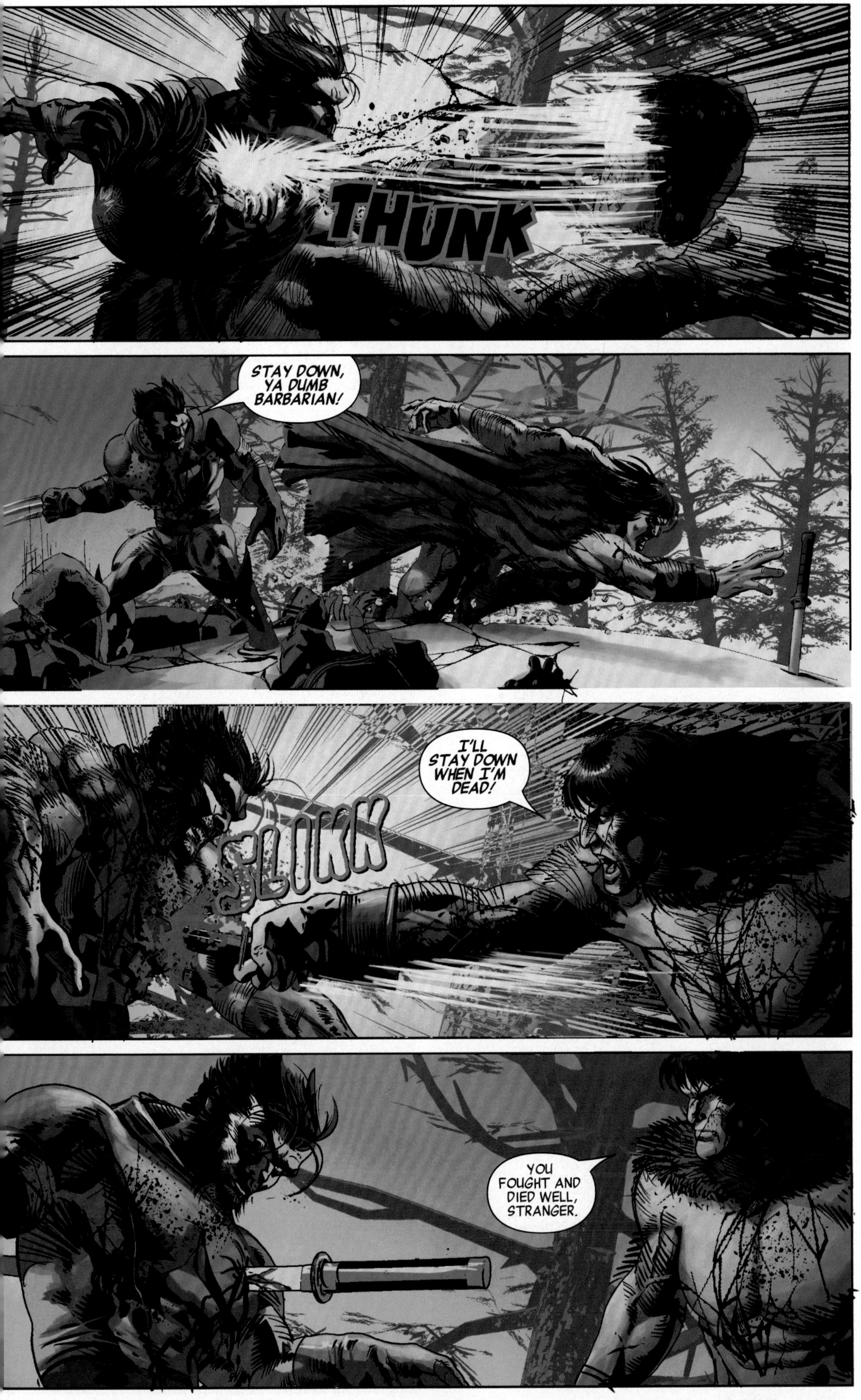
THUNK
STAY DOWN, YA DUMB BARBARIAN!
I'LL STAY DOWN WHEN I'M DEAD!
SLIKK
YOU FOUGHT AND DIED WELL, STRANGER.

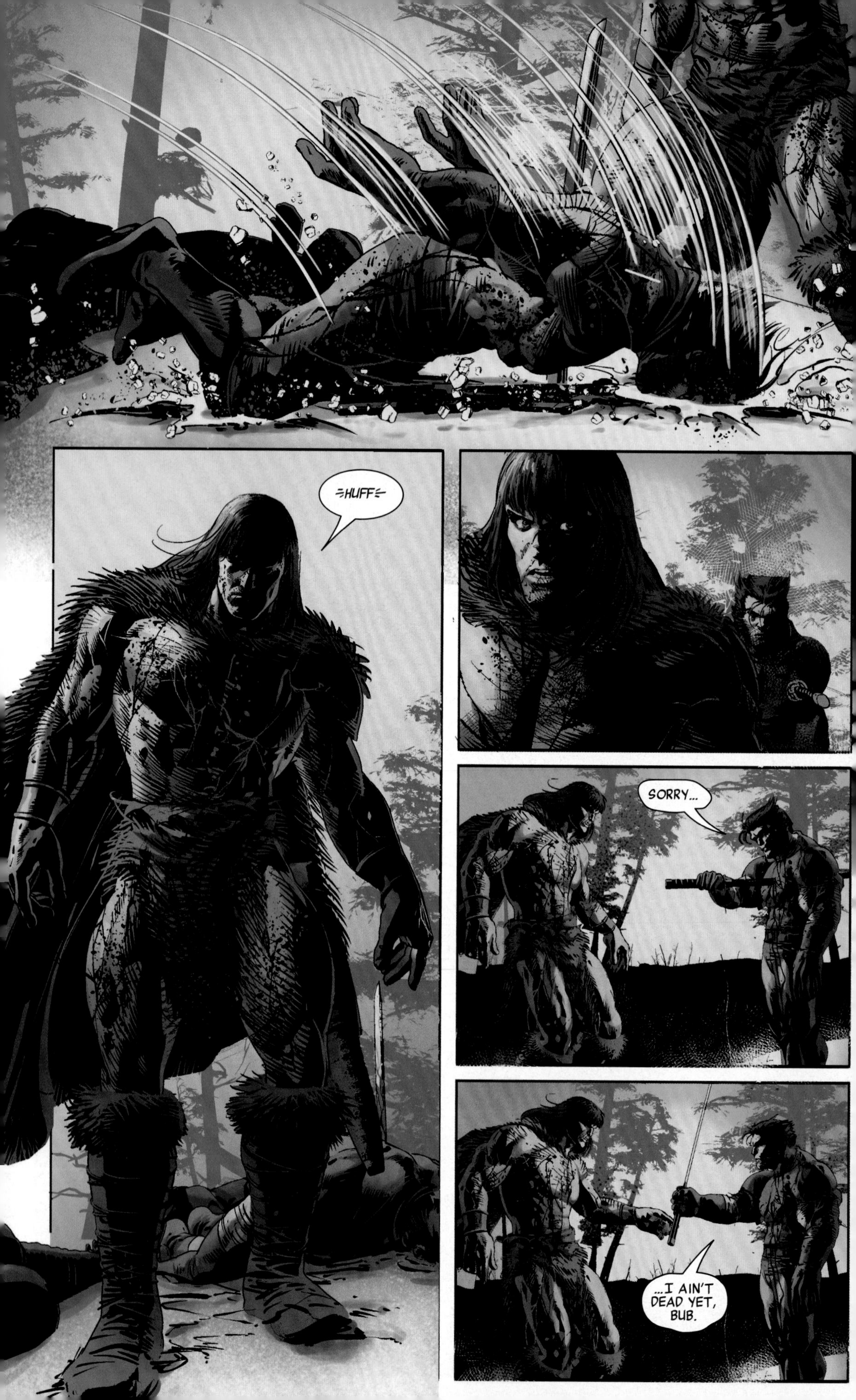

HUFF
SORRY...
...I AIN'T DEAD YET, BUB.

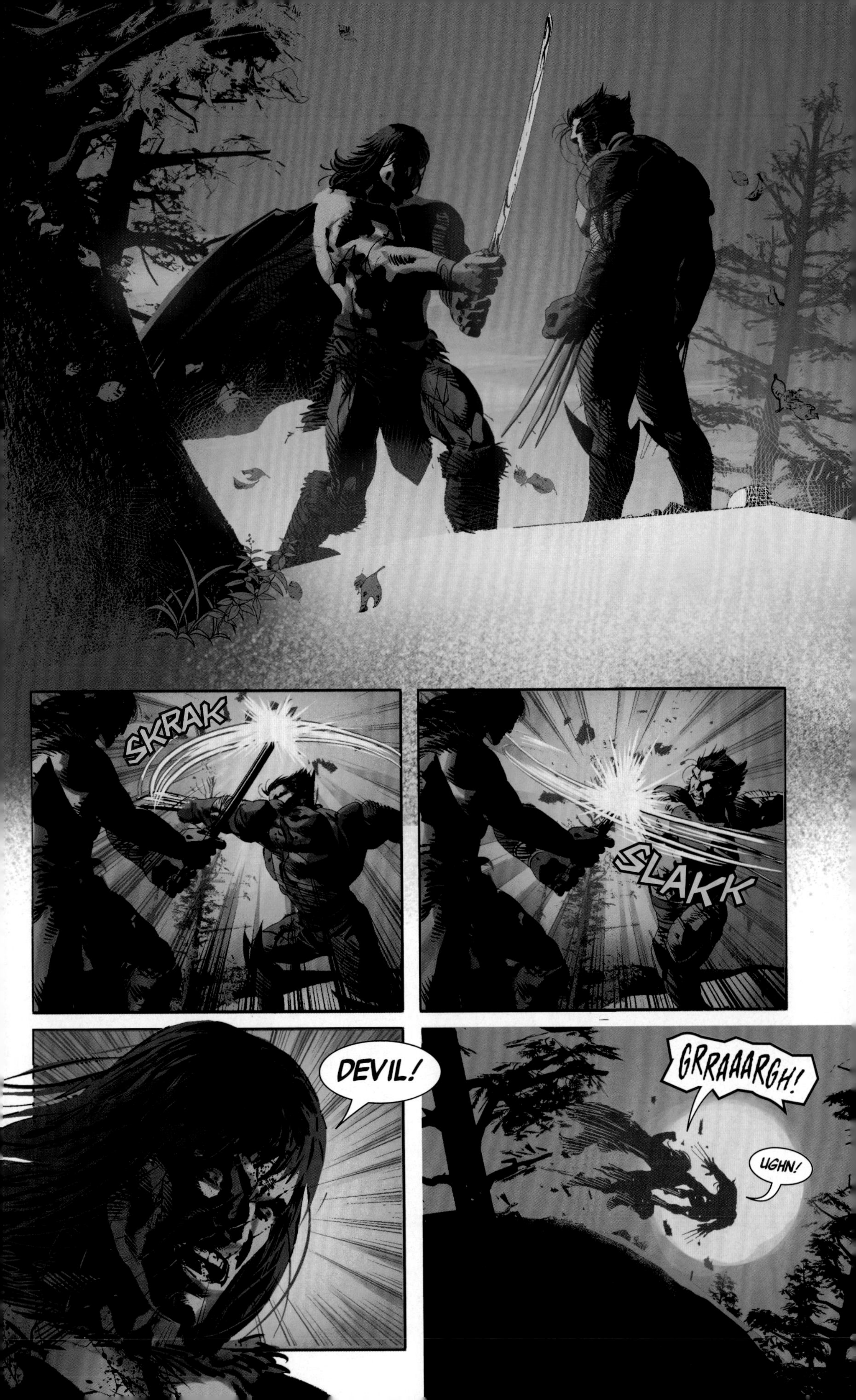
SKRAK
SLAKK
DEVIL!
GRRAAARGH!
UGHN!

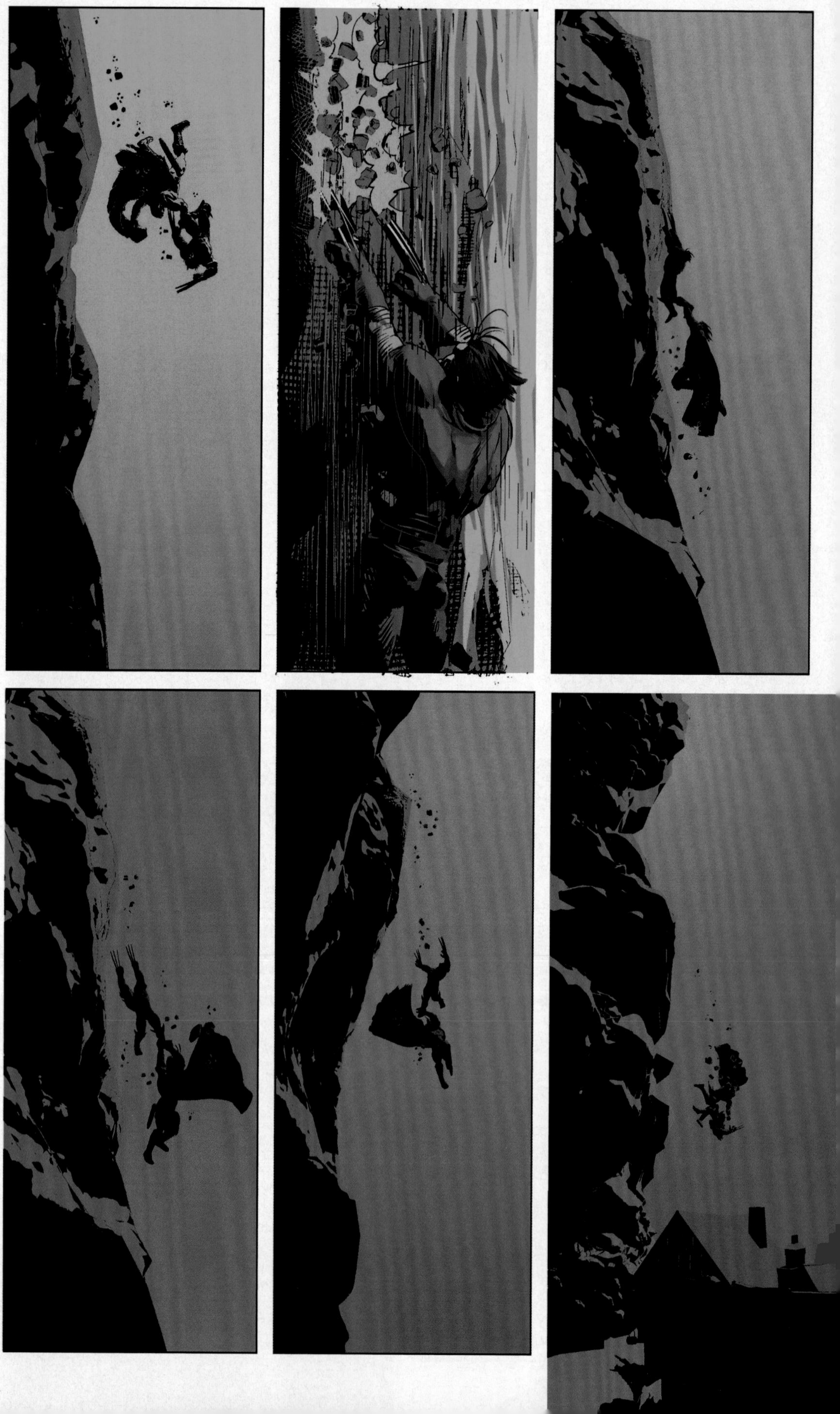

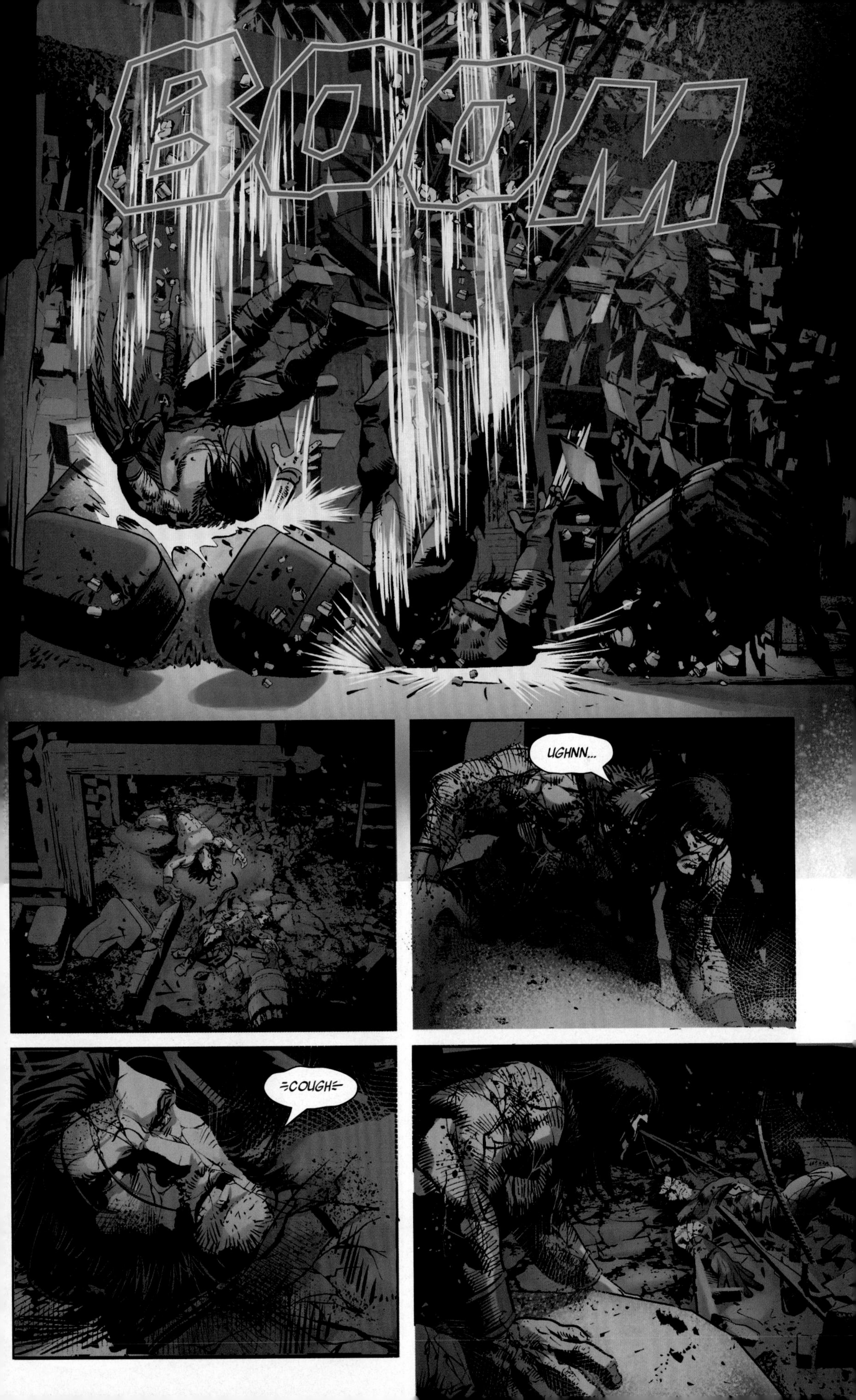
BOOM
UGHNN...
=COUGH=

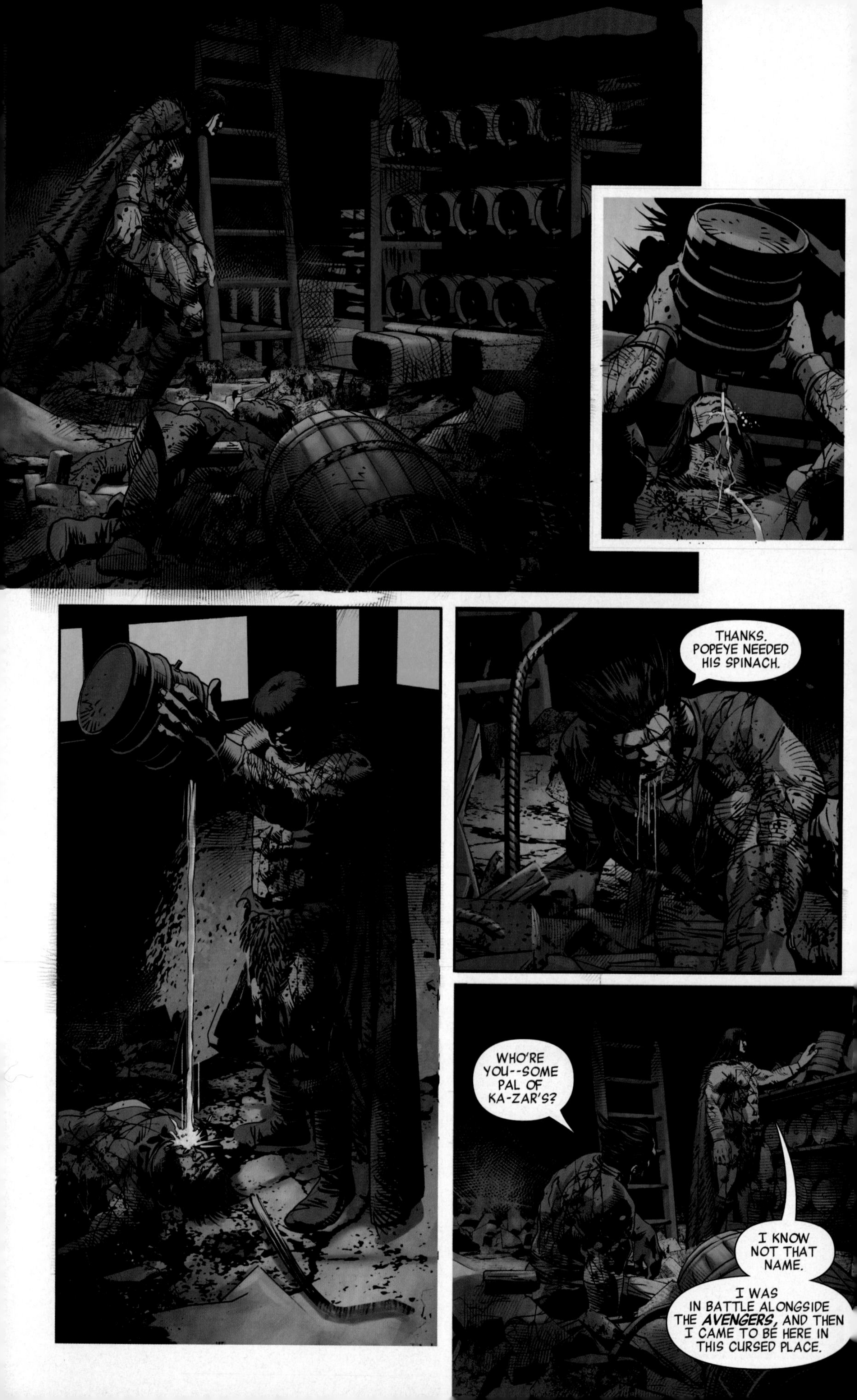
THANKS. POPEYE NEEDED HIS SPINACH.
WHO'RE YOU--SOME PAL OF KA-ZAR'S?
I KNOW NOT THAT NAME.
I WAS IN BATTLE ALONGSIDE THE AVENGERS, AND THEN I CAME TO BE HERE IN THIS CURSED PLACE.

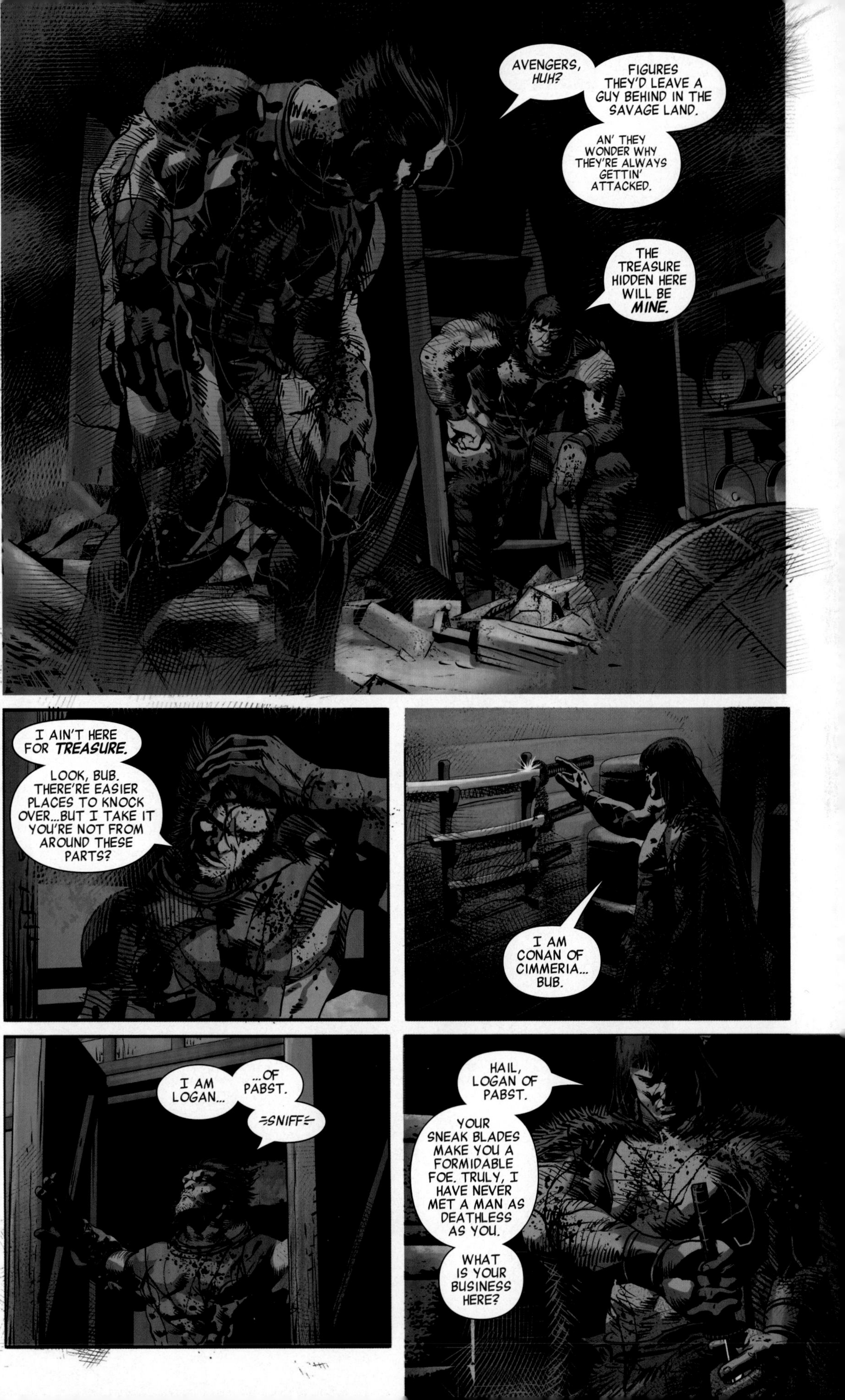
AVENGERS, HUH?
FIGURES THEY'D LEAVE A GUY BEHIND IN THE SAVAGE LAND.
AN' THEY WONDER WHY THEY'RE ALWAYS GETTIN' ATTACKED.
THE TREASURE HIDDEN HERE WILL BE MINE.
I AIN'T HERE FOR TREASURE.
LOOK, BUB. THERE'RE EASIER PLACES TO KNOCK OVER...BUT I TAKE IT YOU'RE NOT FROM AROUND THESE PARTS?
I AM CONAN OF CIMMERIA... BUB.
I AM LOGAN...
...OF PABST.
SNIFF
HAIL, LOGAN OF PABST.
YOUR SNEAK BLADES MAKE YOU A FORMIDABLE FOE. TRULY, I HAVE NEVER MET A MAN AS DEATHLESS AS YOU.
WHAT IS YOUR BUSINESS HERE?

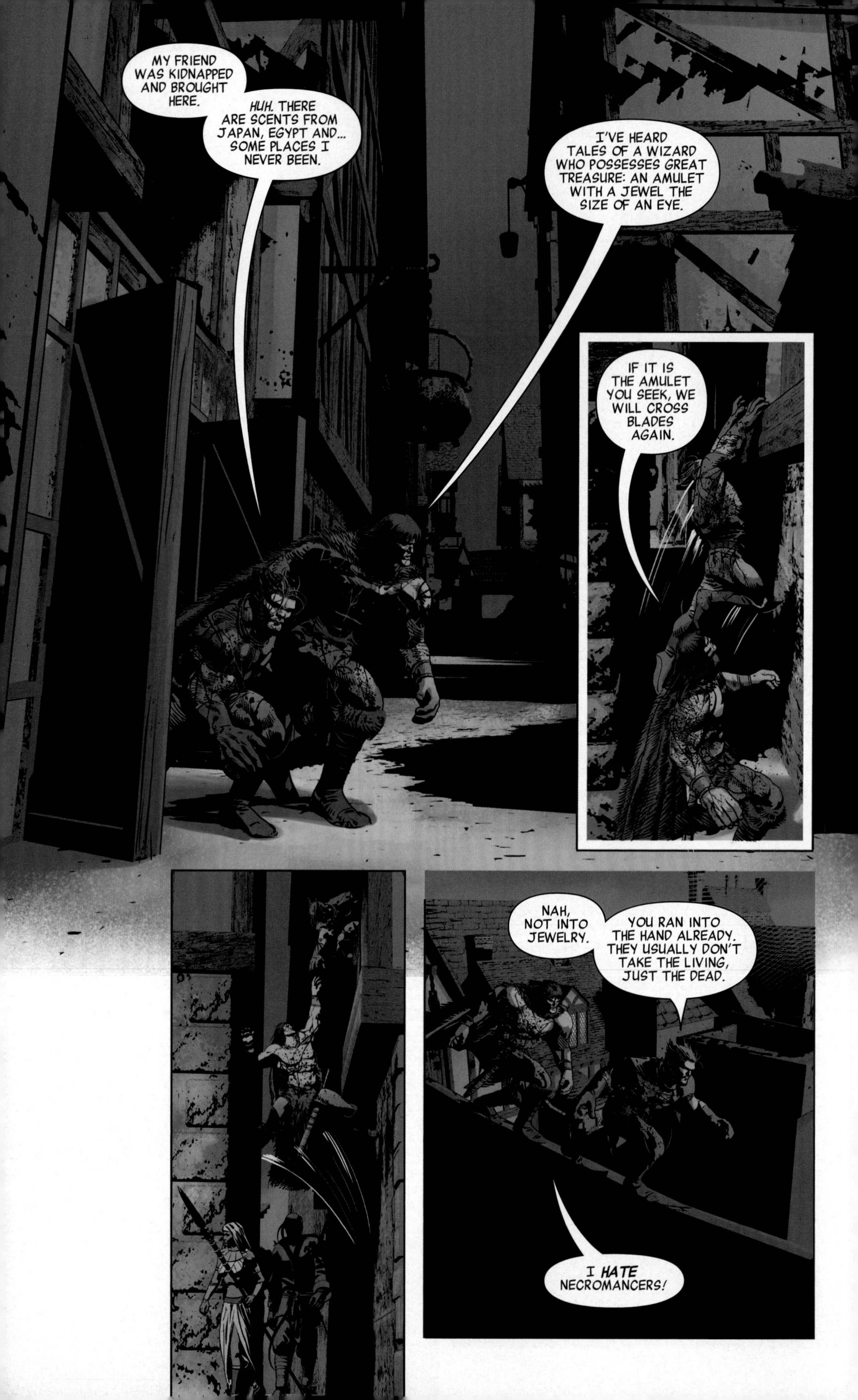
MY FRIEND WAS KIDNAPPED AND BROUGHT HERE.
HUH. THERE ARE SCENTS FROM JAPAN, EGYPT AND... SOME PLACES I NEVER BEEN.
I'VE HEARD TALES OF A WIZARD WHO POSSESSES GREAT TREASURE: AN AMULET WITH A JEWEL THE SIZE OF AN EYE.
IF IT IS THE AMULET YOU SEEK, WE WILL CROSS BLADES AGAIN.
NAH, NOT INTO JEWELRY.
YOU RAN INTO THE HAND ALREADY. THEY USUALLY DON'T TAKE THE LIVING, JUST THE DEAD.
I ***HATE*** NECROMANCERS!

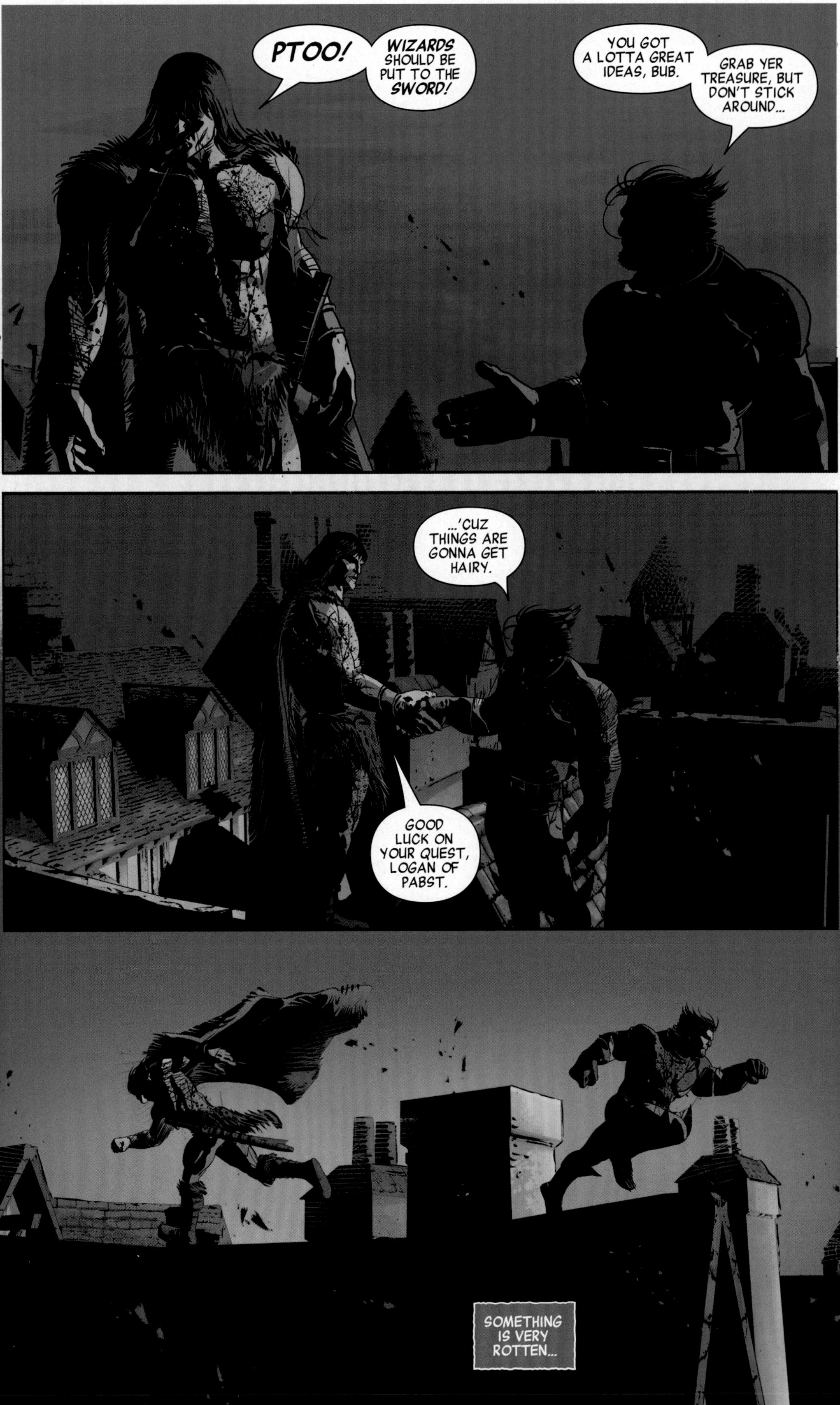
PTOO!
WIZARDS SHOULD BE PUT TO THE SWORD!
YOU GOT A LOTTA GREAT IDEAS, BUB.
GRAB YER TREASURE, BUT DON'T STICK AROUND...
...'CUZ THINGS ARE GONNA GET HAIRY.
GOOD LUCK ON YOUR QUEST, LOGAN OF PABST.
SOMETHING IS VERY ROTTEN...

MADRIPOOR.

WELL, SOMETHING IS *ALWAYS* ROTTEN HERE, BUT NEVER MORE SO THAN NOW.

SOME OF THE MOST POWERFUL GANGSTERS ON THE ISLAND HAVE *DISAPPEARED.*

EVEN CRIME BOSSES HAVE MOTHERS WHO LOVE THEM.

I'M HERE TO SEE MA.

I'M SORRY ABOUT YOUR SON, YUN.

YOU WERE RIGHT TO CALL ME. HE COULDN'T JUST DISAPPEAR FROM BEHIND ALL THIS SECURITY...

=SNIFF=

I'M GETTING THE SENSE THAT THERE'S SOMETHING... *SUPERNATURAL* ABOUT IT.

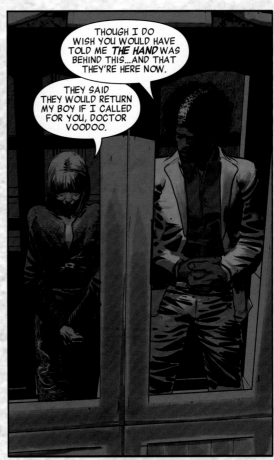

THOUGH I DO WISH YOU WOULD HAVE TOLD ME *THE HAND* WAS BEHIND THIS...AND THAT THEY'RE HERE NOW.

THEY SAID THEY WOULD RETURN MY BOY IF I CALLED FOR YOU, DOCTOR VOODOO.

THE HAND ONLY *TAKES,* YUN.

DID YOU THINK I WOULD COME TO MADRIPOOR--

--UNPREPARED?

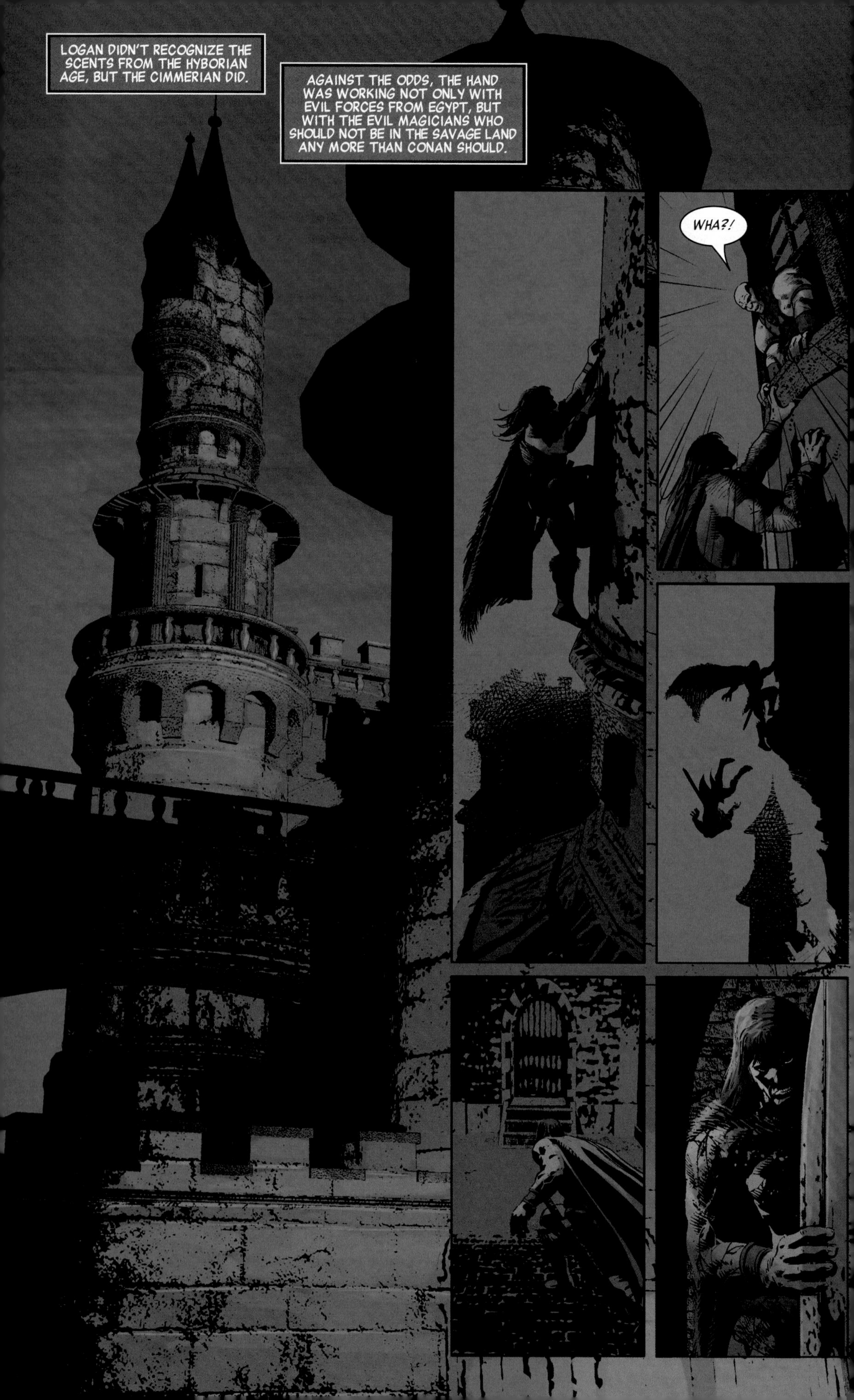
LOGAN DIDN'T RECOGNIZE THE SCENTS FROM THE HYBORIAN AGE, BUT THE CIMMERIAN DID.
AGAINST THE ODDS, THE HAND WAS WORKING NOT ONLY WITH EVIL FORCES FROM EGYPT, BUT WITH THE EVIL MAGICIANS WHO SHOULD NOT BE IN THE SAVAGE LAND ANY MORE THAN CONAN SHOULD.
WHA?!

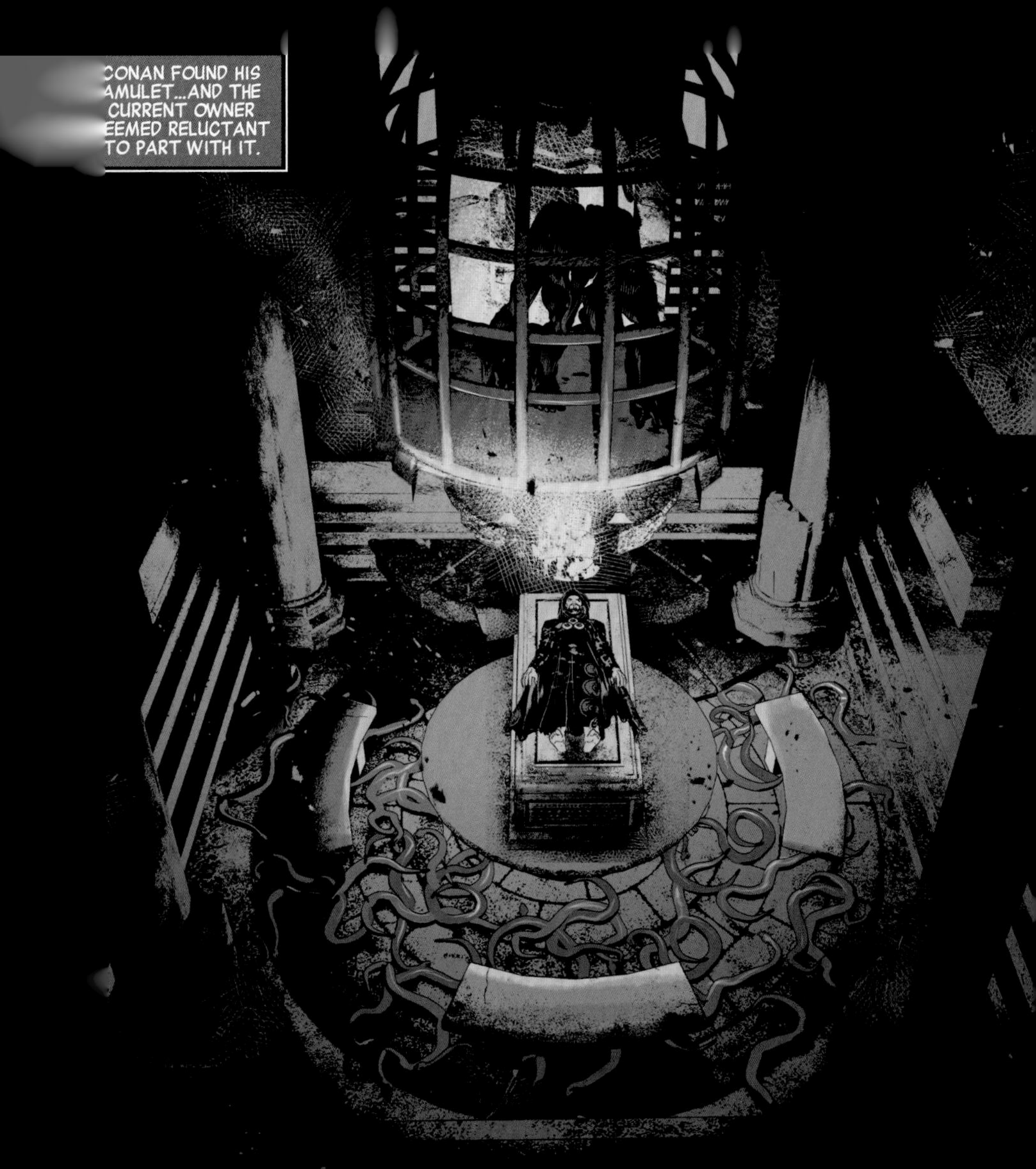
CONAN FOUND HIS AMULET...AND THE CURRENT OWNER EEMED RELUCTANT TO PART WITH IT.

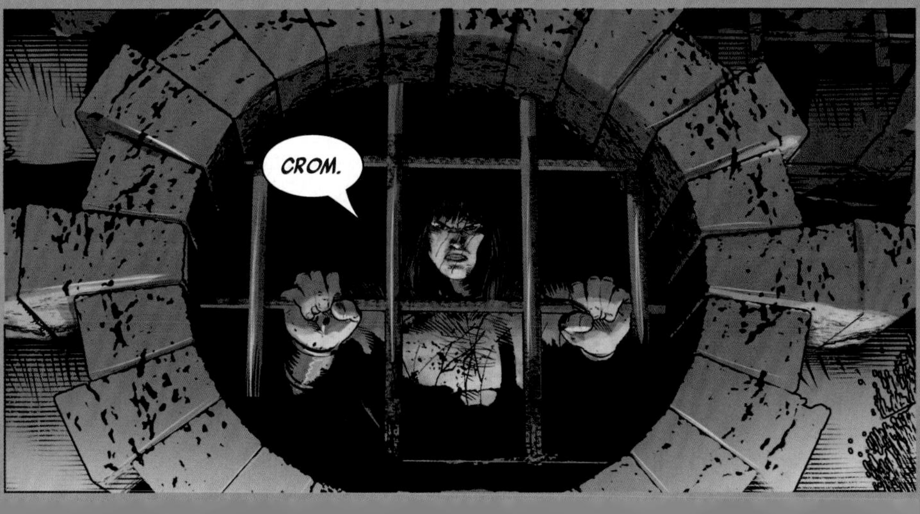
CROM.

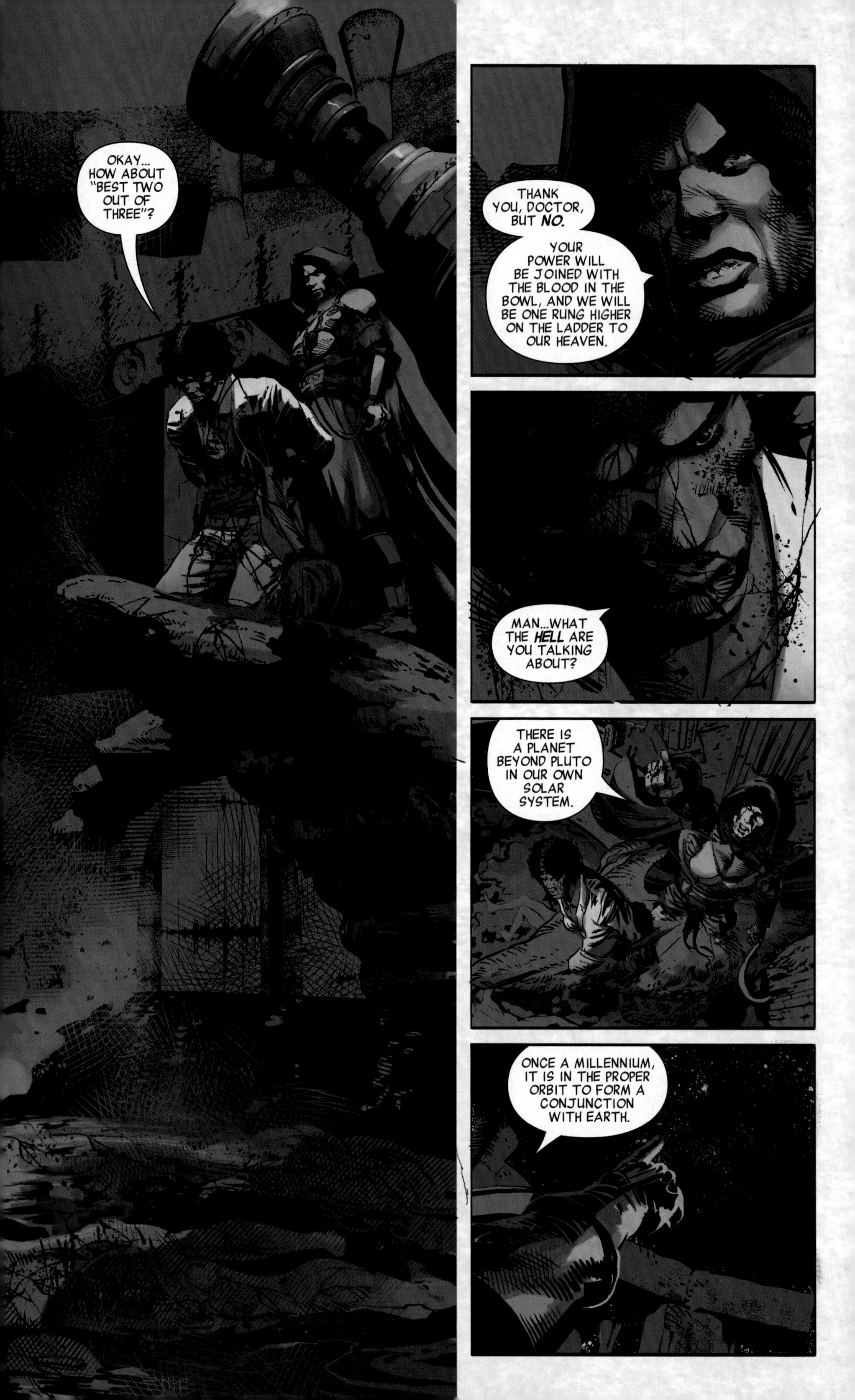
OKAY... HOW ABOUT "BEST TWO OUT OF THREE"?
THANK YOU, DOCTOR, BUT NO.
YOUR POWER WILL BE JOINED WITH THE BLOOD IN THE BOWL, AND WE WILL BE ONE RUNG HIGHER ON THE LADDER TO OUR HEAVEN.
MAN...WHAT THE HELL ARE YOU TALKING ABOUT?
THERE IS A PLANET BEYOND PLUTO IN OUR OWN SOLAR SYSTEM.
ONCE A MILLENNIUM, IT IS IN THE PROPER ORBIT TO FORM A CONJUNCTION WITH EARTH.

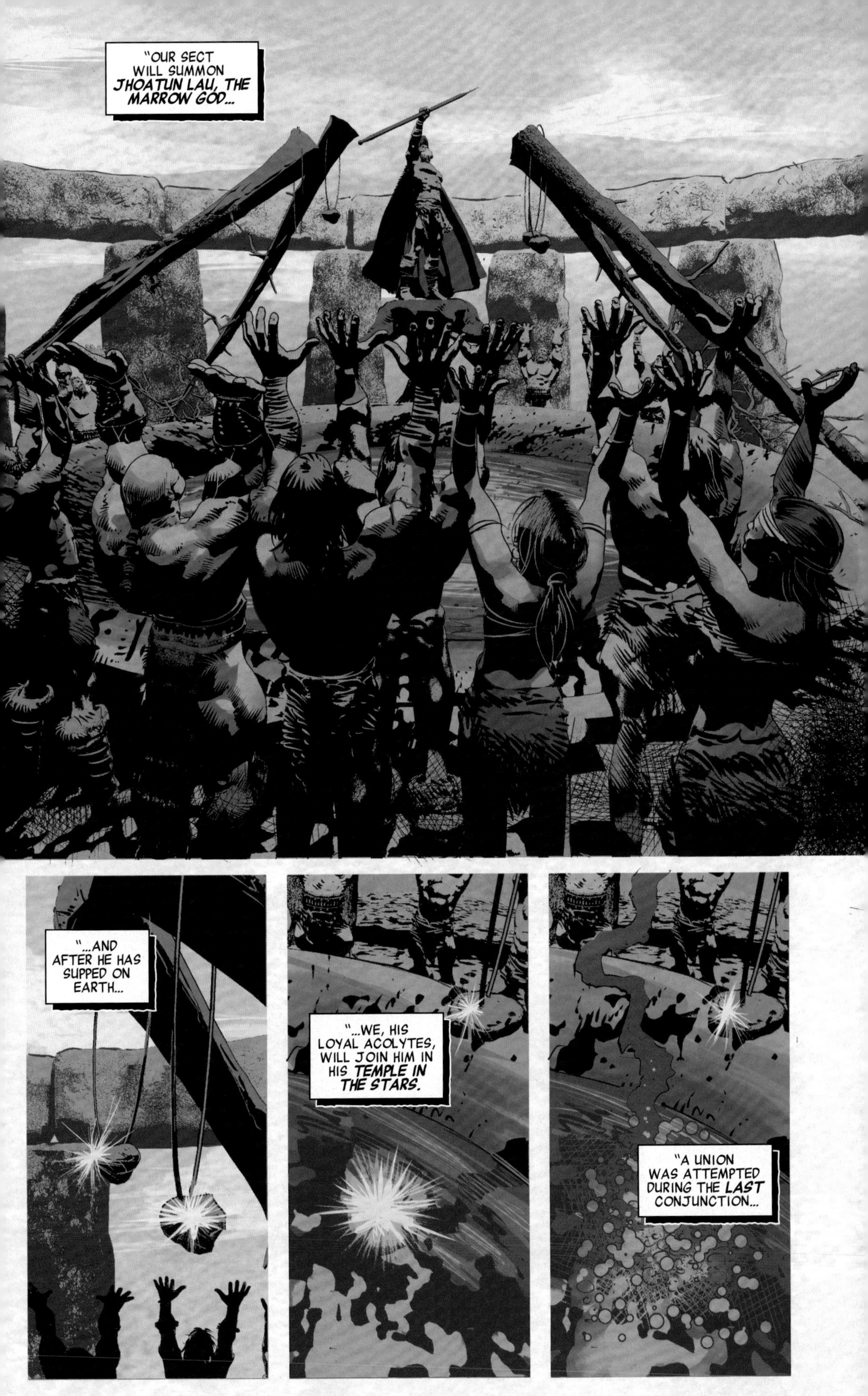
"OUR SECT WILL SUMMON JHOATUN LAU, THE MARROW GOD...
"...AND AFTER HE HAS SUPPED ON EARTH...
"...WE, HIS LOYAL ACOLYTES, WILL JOIN HIM IN HIS TEMPLE IN THE STARS.
"A UNION WAS ATTEMPTED DURING THE LAST CONJUNCTION...

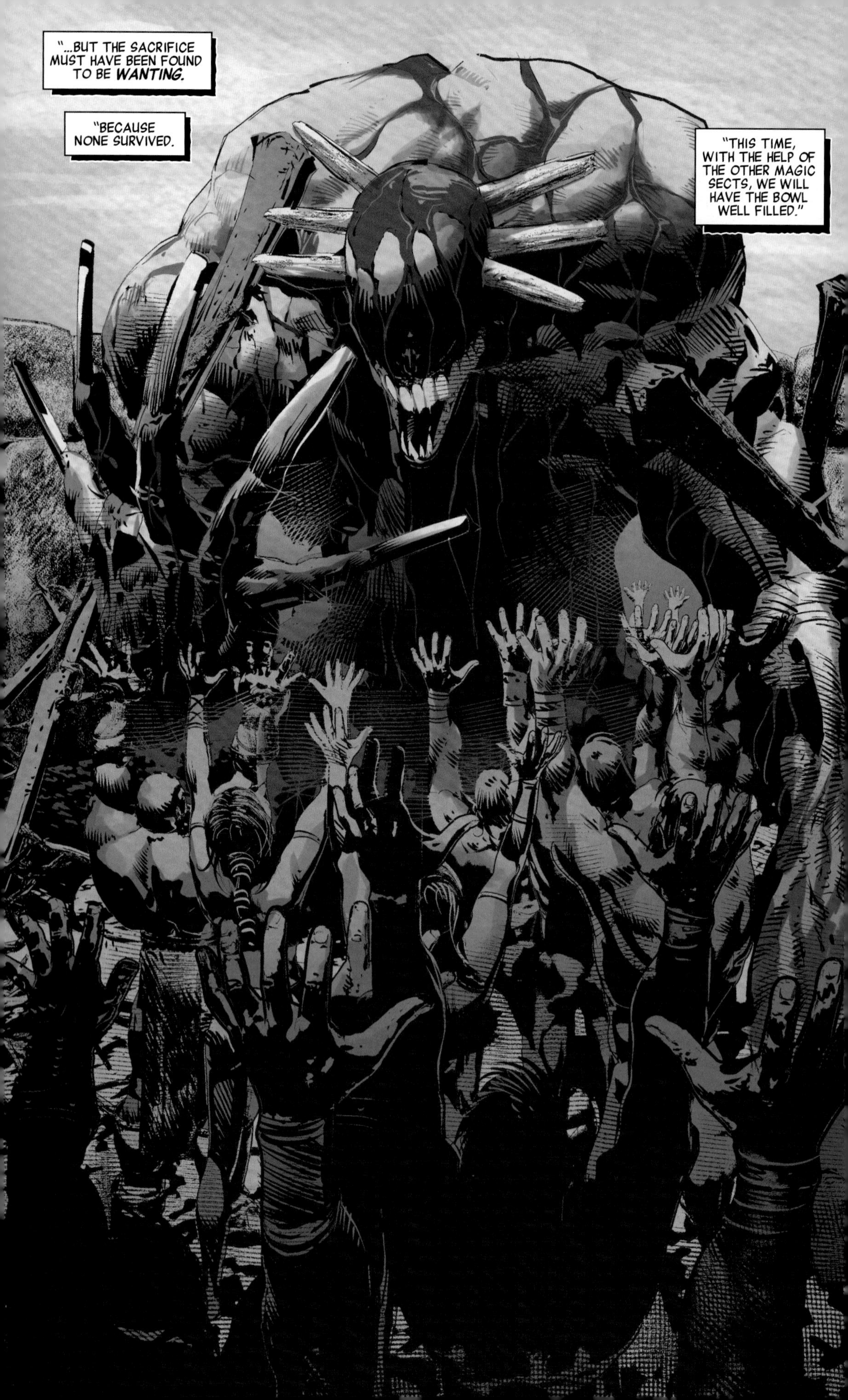
"...BUT THE SACRIFICE MUST HAVE BEEN FOUND TO BE WANTING.
"BECAUSE NONE SURVIVED.
"THIS TIME, WITH THE HELP OF THE OTHER MAGIC SECTS, WE WILL HAVE THE BOWL WELL FILLED."

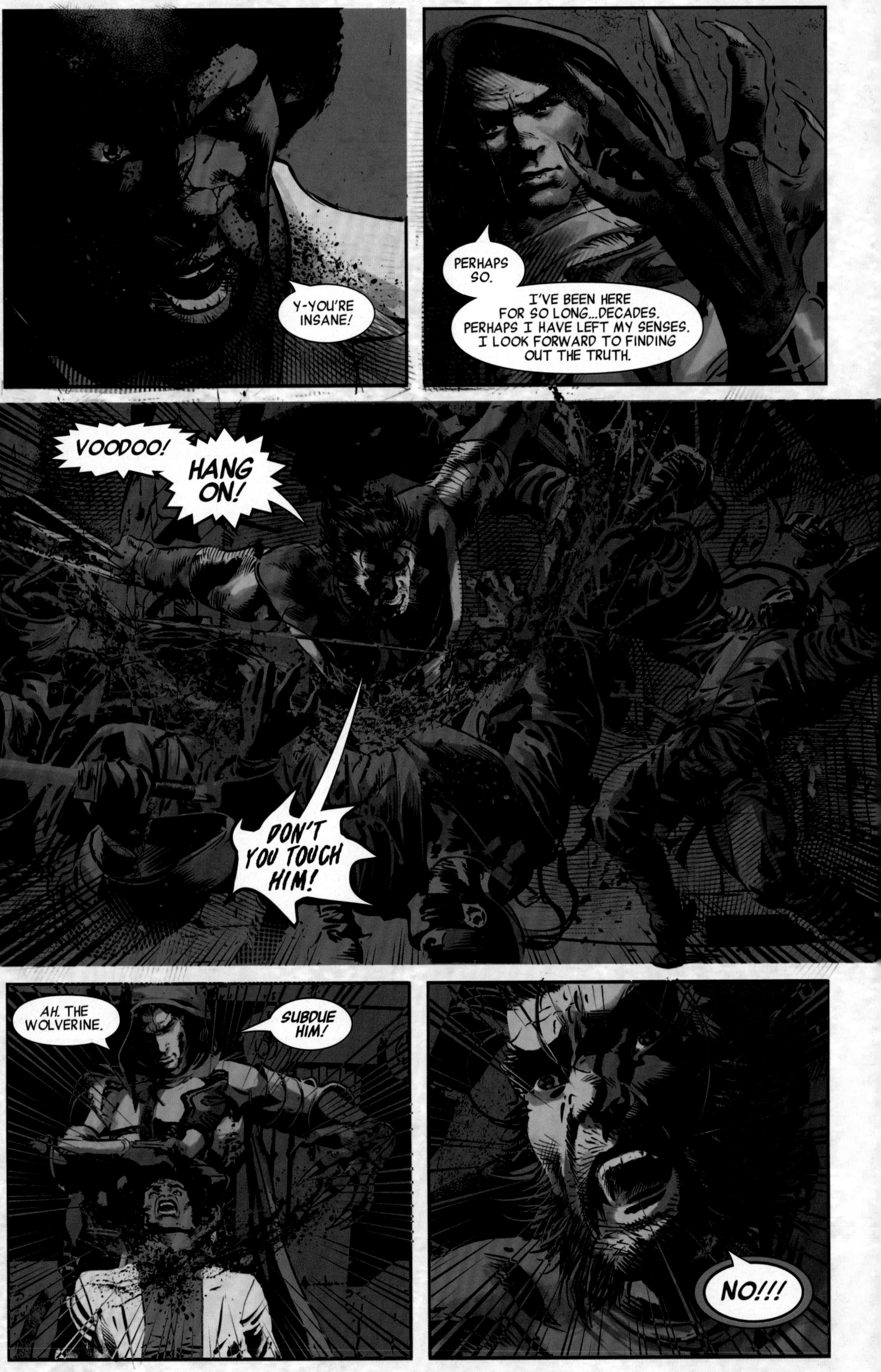
Y-YOU'RE INSANE!
PERHAPS SO.
I'VE BEEN HERE FOR SO LONG...DECADES. PERHAPS I HAVE LEFT MY SENSES. I LOOK FORWARD TO FINDING OUT THE TRUTH.
VOODOO!
HANG ON!
DON'T YOU TOUCH HIM!
AH. THE WOLVERINE.
SUBDUE HIM!
NO!!!

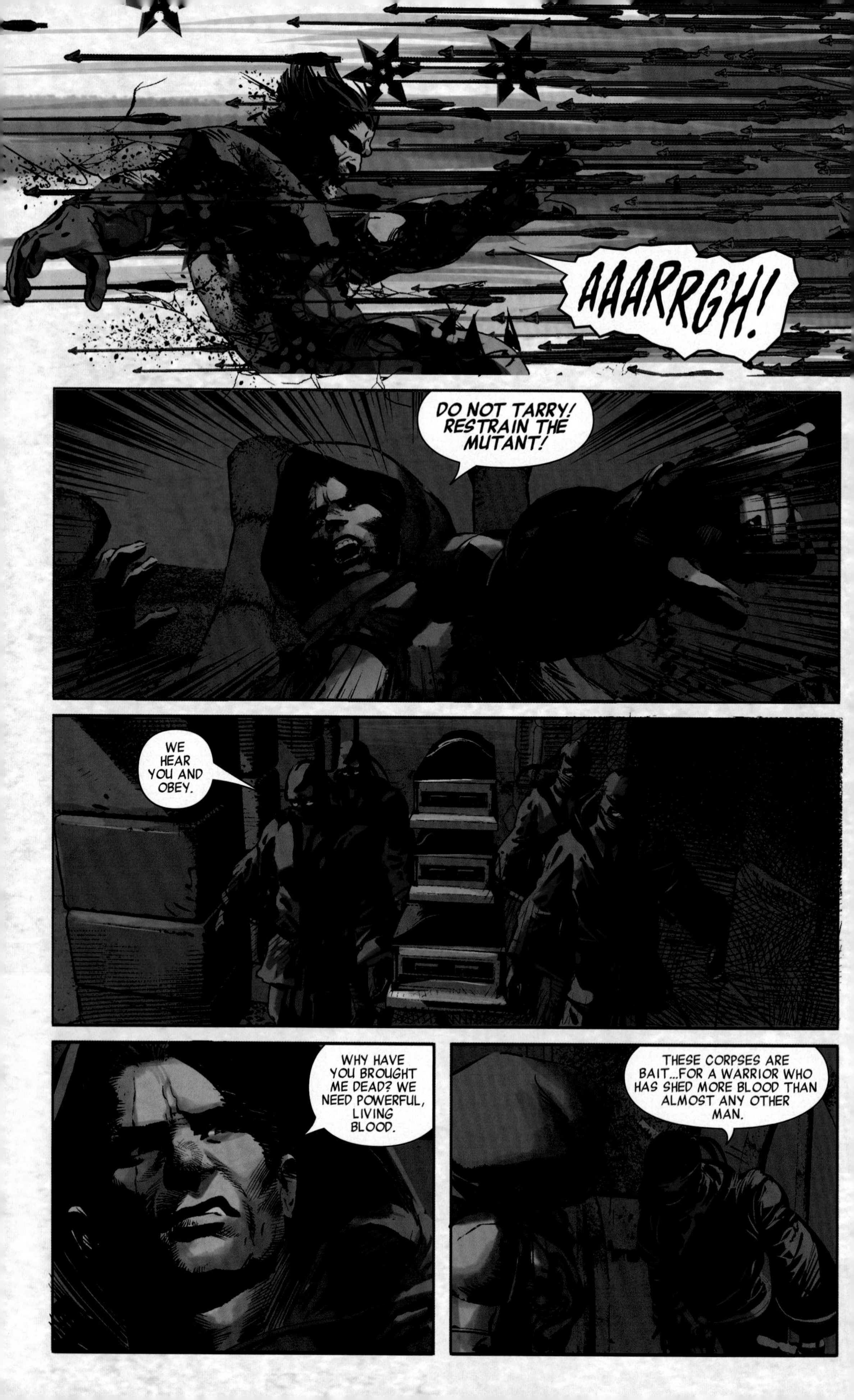
AAARRGH!
DO NOT TARRY! RESTRAIN THE MUTANT!
WE HEAR YOU AND OBEY.
WHY HAVE YOU BROUGHT ME DEAD? WE NEED POWERFUL, LIVING BLOOD.
THESE CORPSES ARE BAIT...FOR A WARRIOR WHO HAS SHED MORE BLOOD THAN ALMOST ANY OTHER MAN.

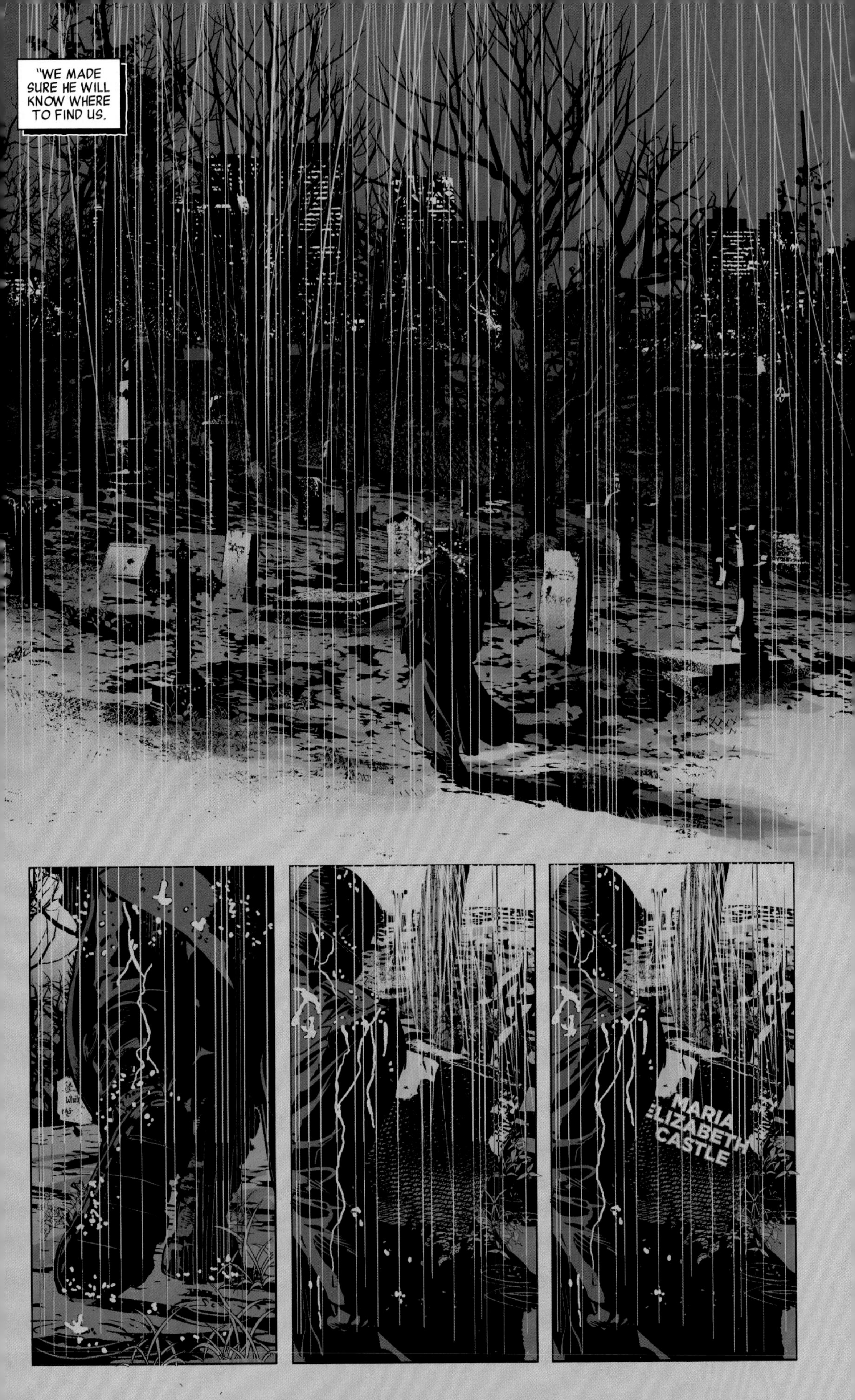
"WE MADE SURE HE WILL KNOW WHERE TO FIND US.
MARIA ELIZABETH CASTLE

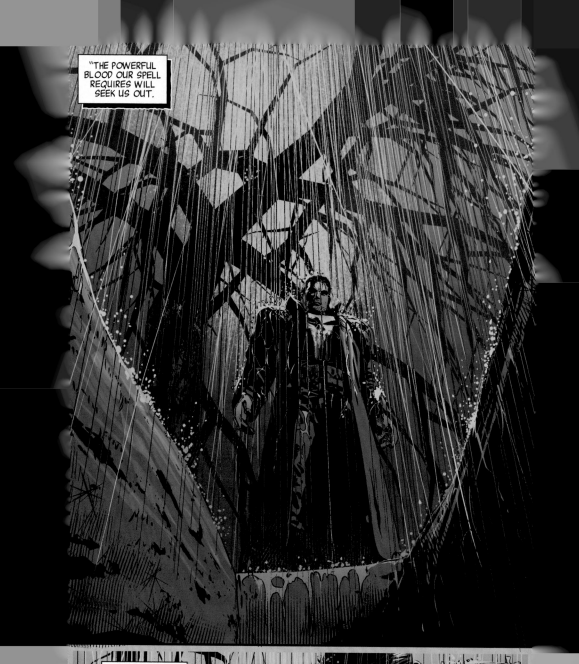

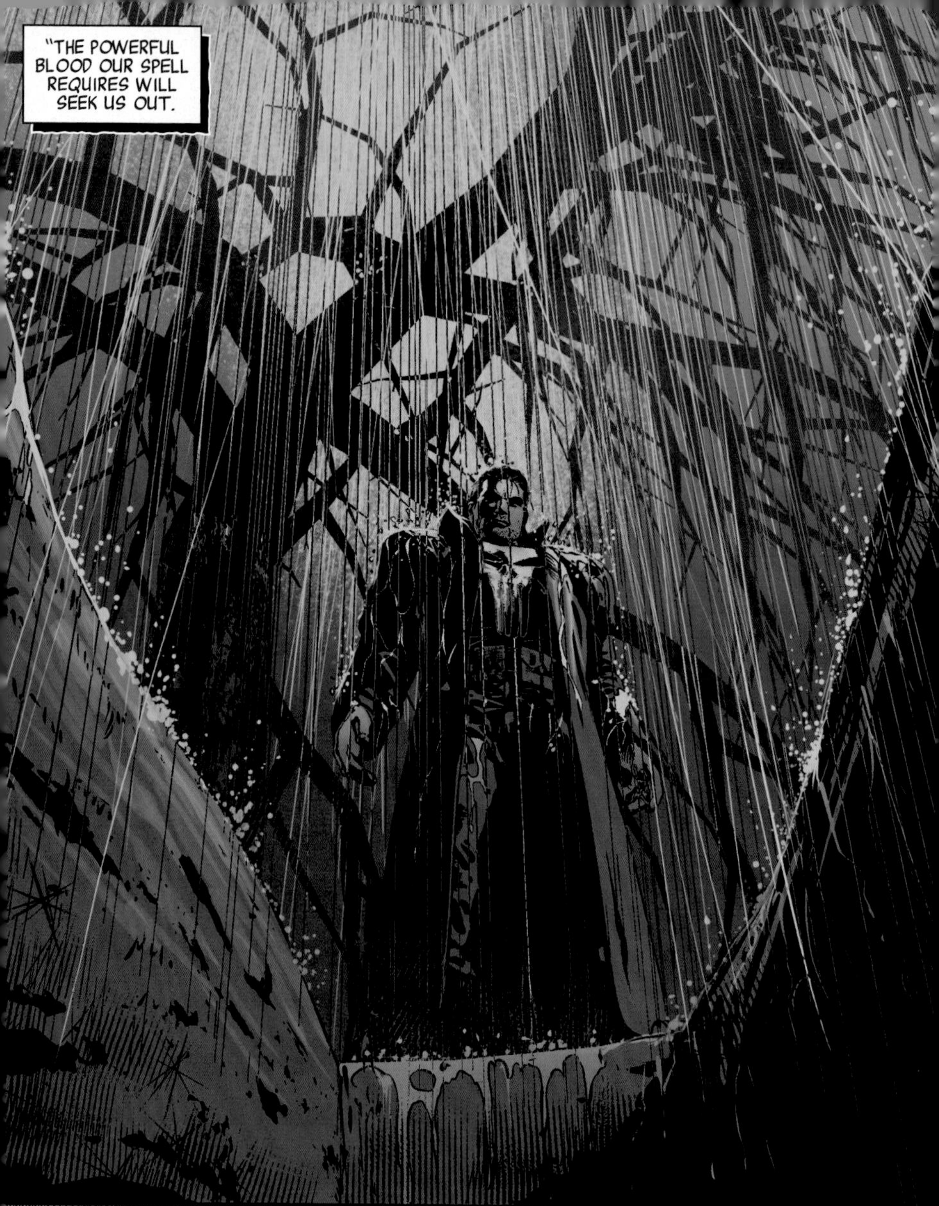
"THE POWERFUL BLOOD OUR SPELL REQUIRES WILL SEEK US OUT.

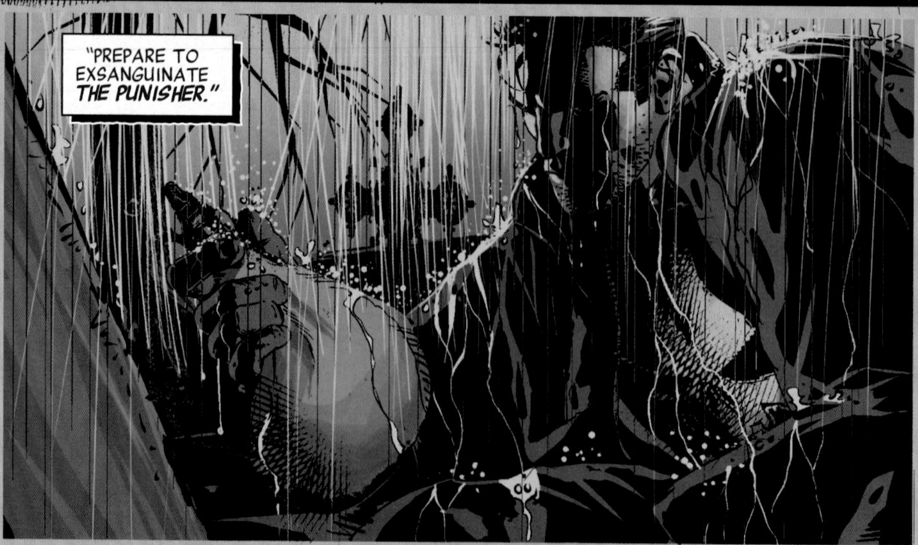
"PREPARE TO EXSANGUINATE THE PUNISHER."

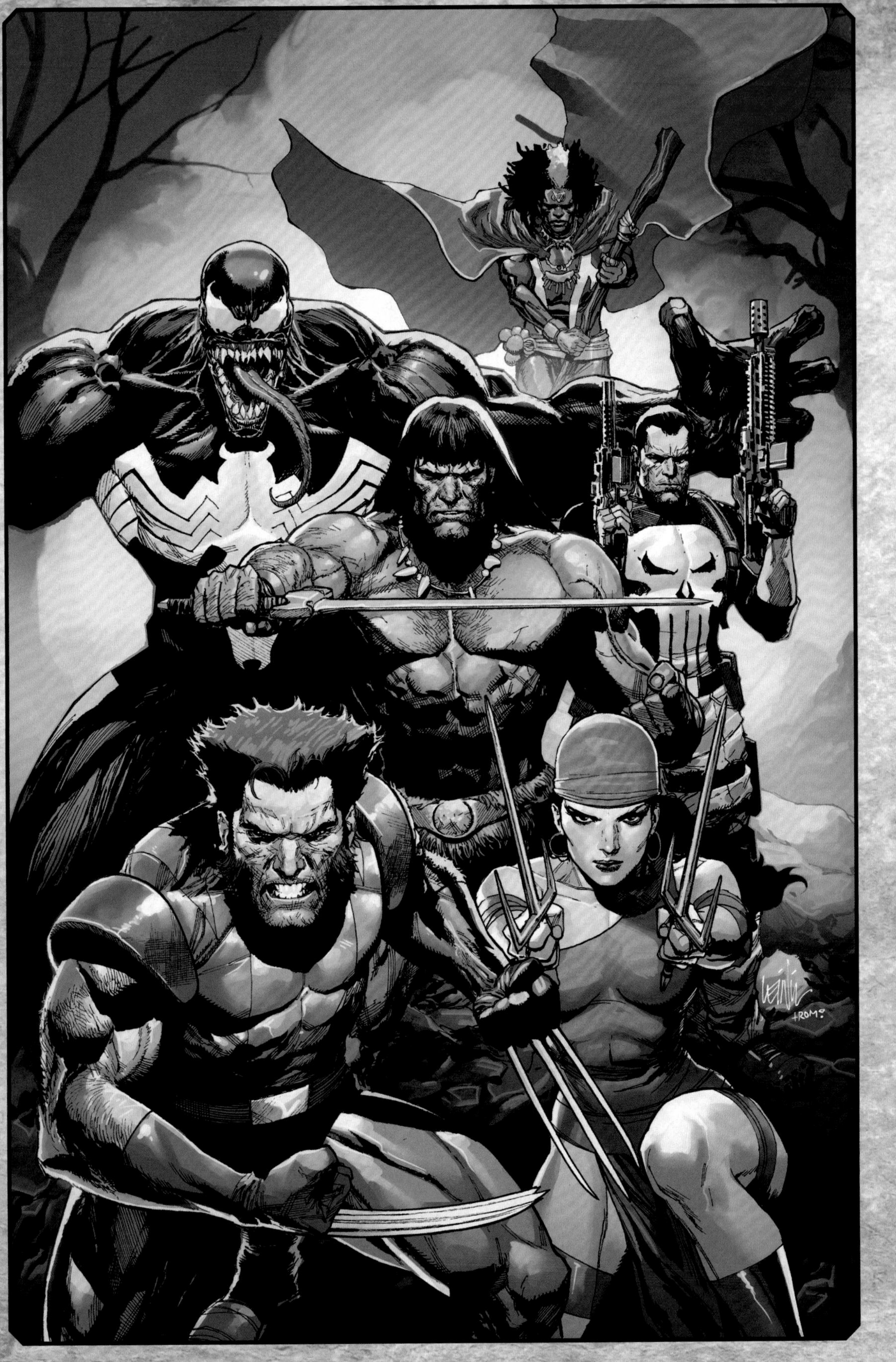

Leinil Francis Yu & Romulo Fajardo Jr.
1 VARIANT

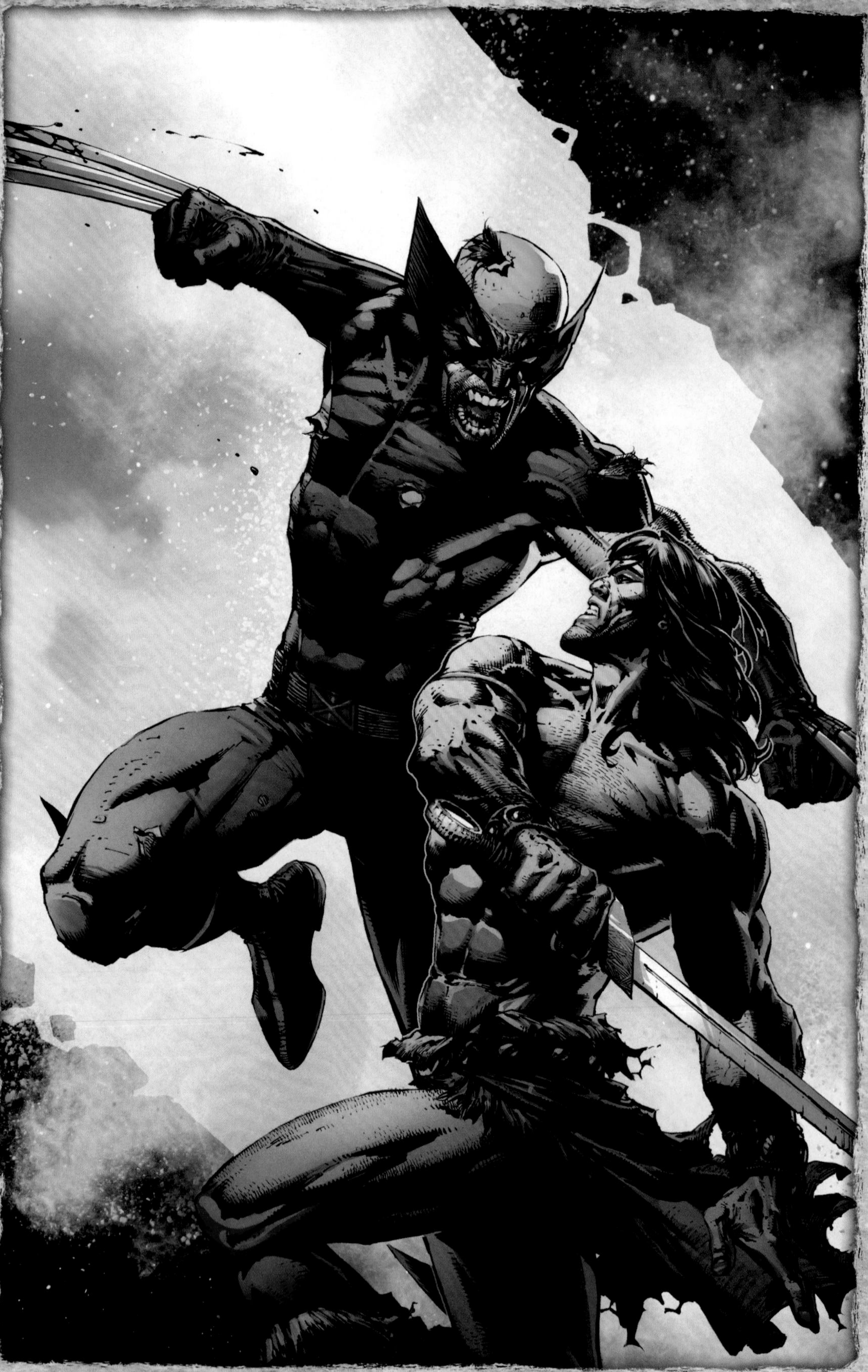

2: DEATH PROOF

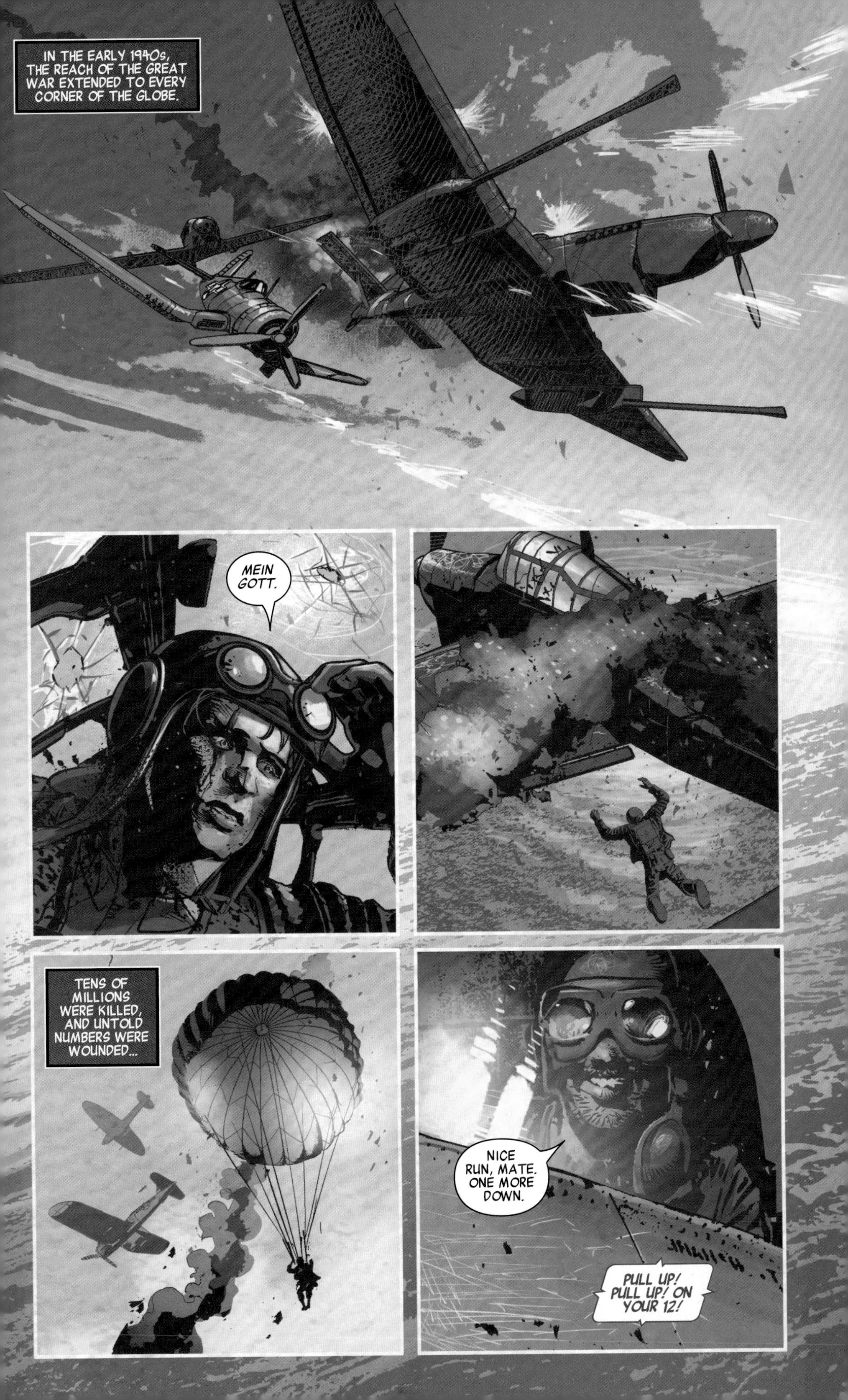
IN THE EARLY 1940s, THE REACH OF THE GREAT WAR EXTENDED TO EVERY CORNER OF THE GLOBE.
MEIN GOTT.
TENS OF MILLIONS WERE KILLED, AND UNTOLD NUMBERS WERE WOUNDED...
NICE RUN, MATE. ONE MORE DOWN.
PULL UP! PULL UP! ON YOUR 12!

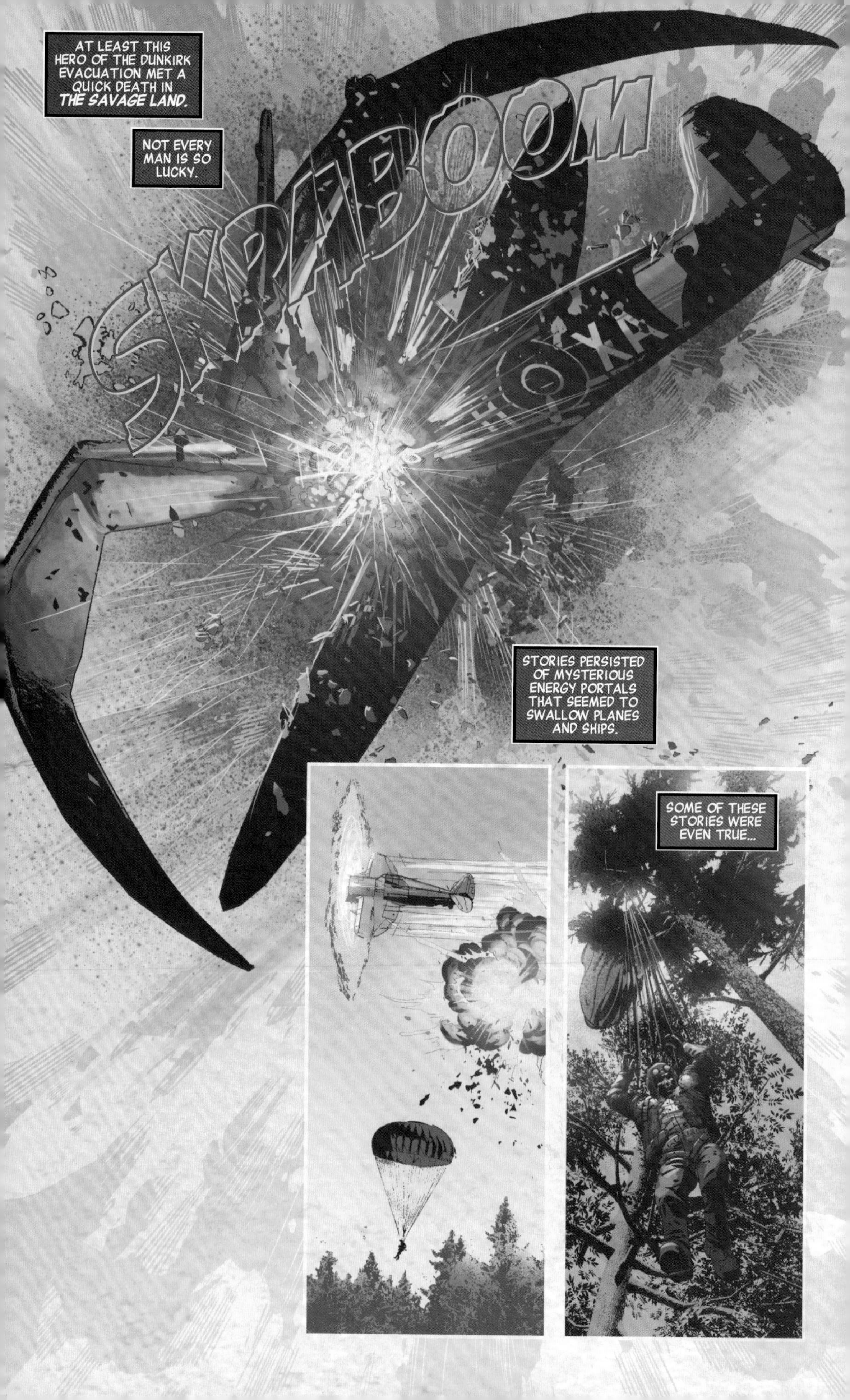
AT LEAST THIS HERO OF THE DUNKIRK EVACUATION MET A QUICK DEATH IN THE SAVAGE LAND.
NOT EVERY MAN IS SO LUCKY.
SKRABOOM
STORIES PERSISTED OF MYSTERIOUS ENERGY PORTALS THAT SEEMED TO SWALLOW PLANES AND SHIPS.
SOME OF THESE STORIES WERE EVEN TRUE...

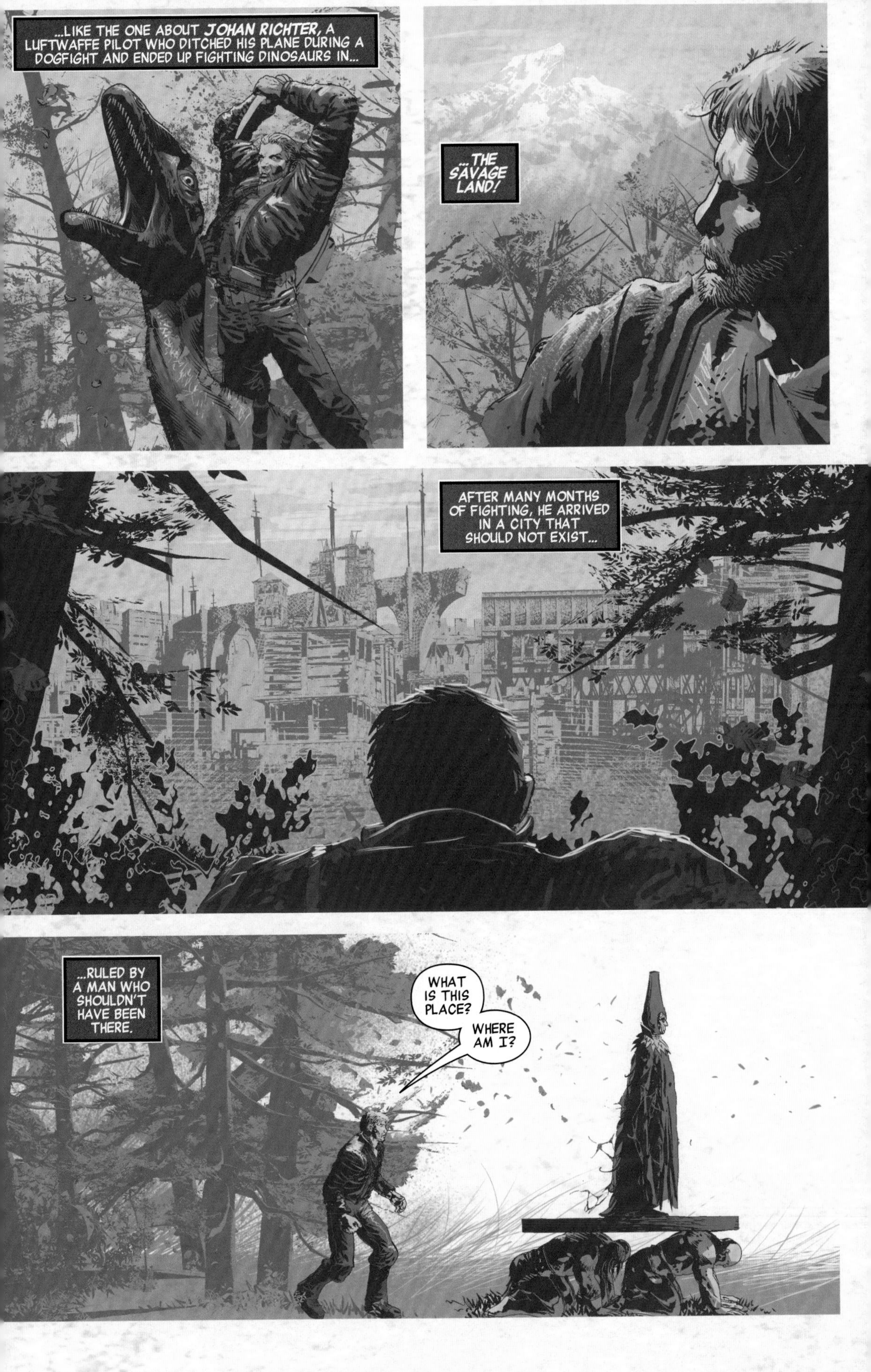

...LIKE THE ONE ABOUT JOHAN RICHTER, A LUFTWAFFE PILOT WHO DITCHED HIS PLANE DURING A DOGFIGHT AND ENDED UP FIGHTING DINOSAURS IN...
...THE SAVAGE LAND!
AFTER MANY MONTHS OF FIGHTING, HE ARRIVED IN A CITY THAT SHOULD NOT EXIST...
...RULED BY A MAN WHO SHOULDN'T HAVE BEEN THERE.
WHAT IS THIS PLACE?
WHERE AM I?

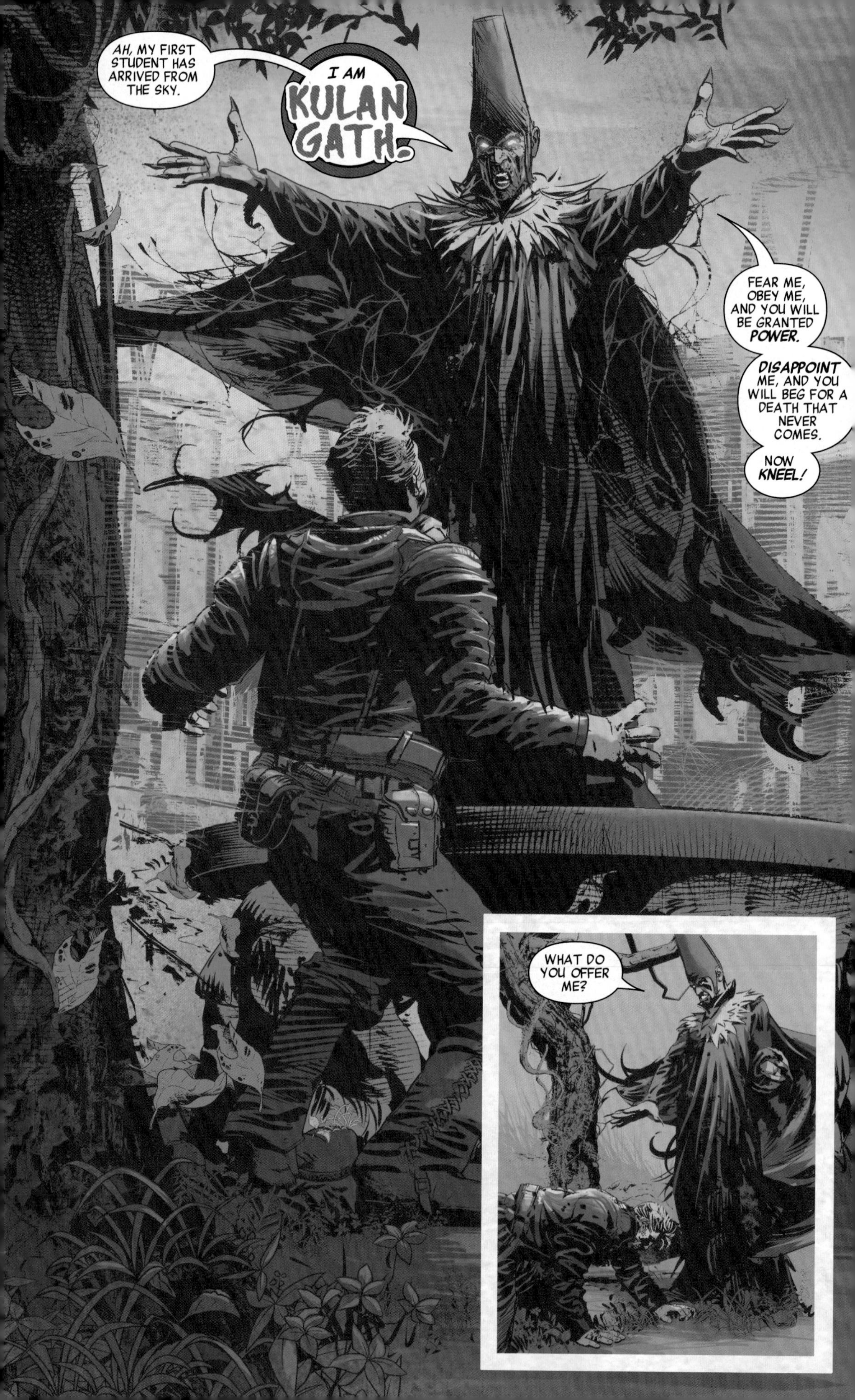
AH, MY FIRST STUDENT HAS ARRIVED FROM THE SKY.
I AM KULAN GATH.
FEAR ME, OBEY ME, AND YOU WILL BE GRANTED POWER.
DISAPPOINT ME, AND YOU WILL BEG FOR A DEATH THAT NEVER COMES.
NOW KNEEL!
WHAT DO YOU OFFER ME?

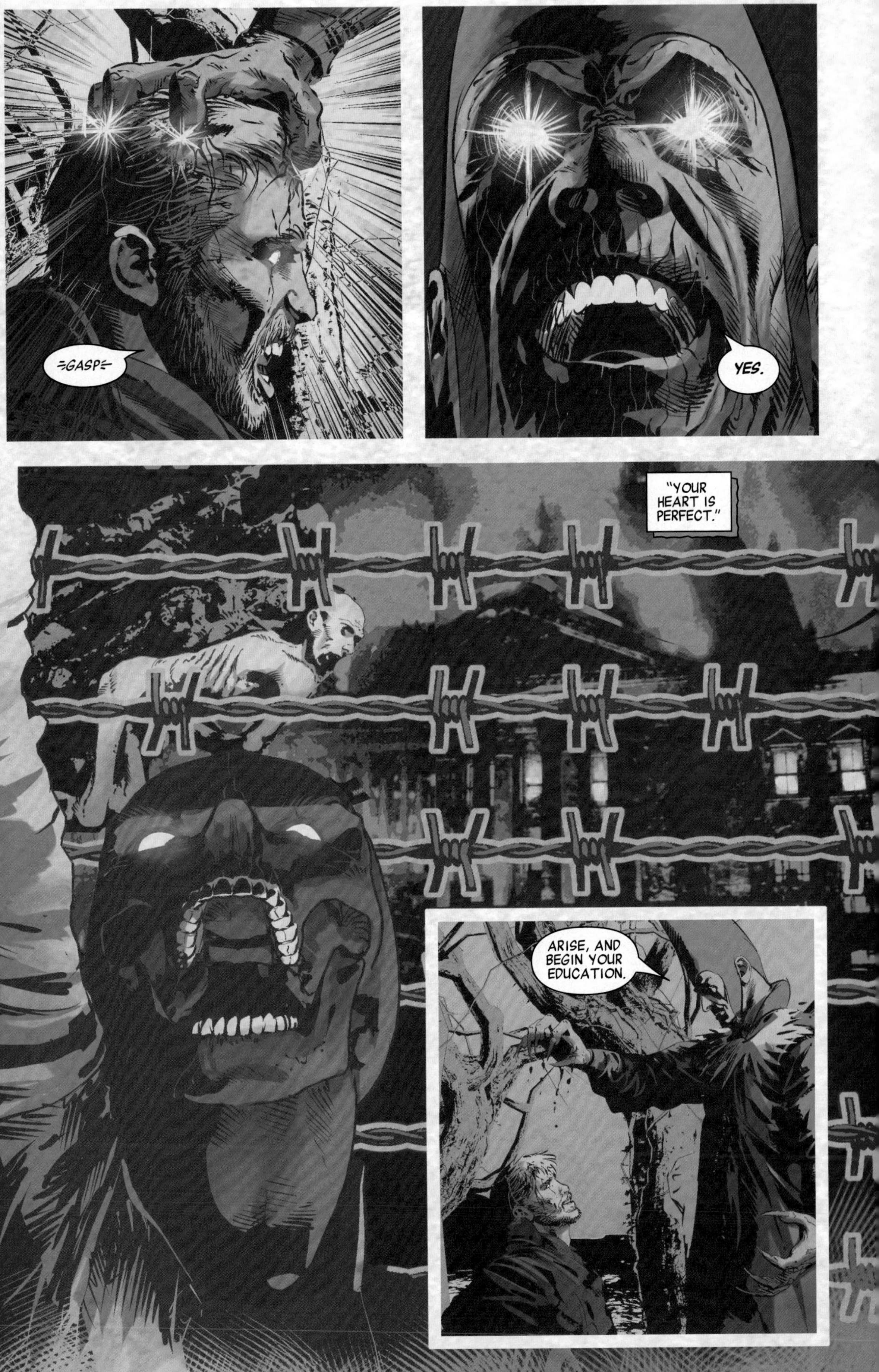

=GASP=
YES.
"YOUR HEART IS PERFECT."
ARISE, AND BEGIN YOUR EDUCATION.

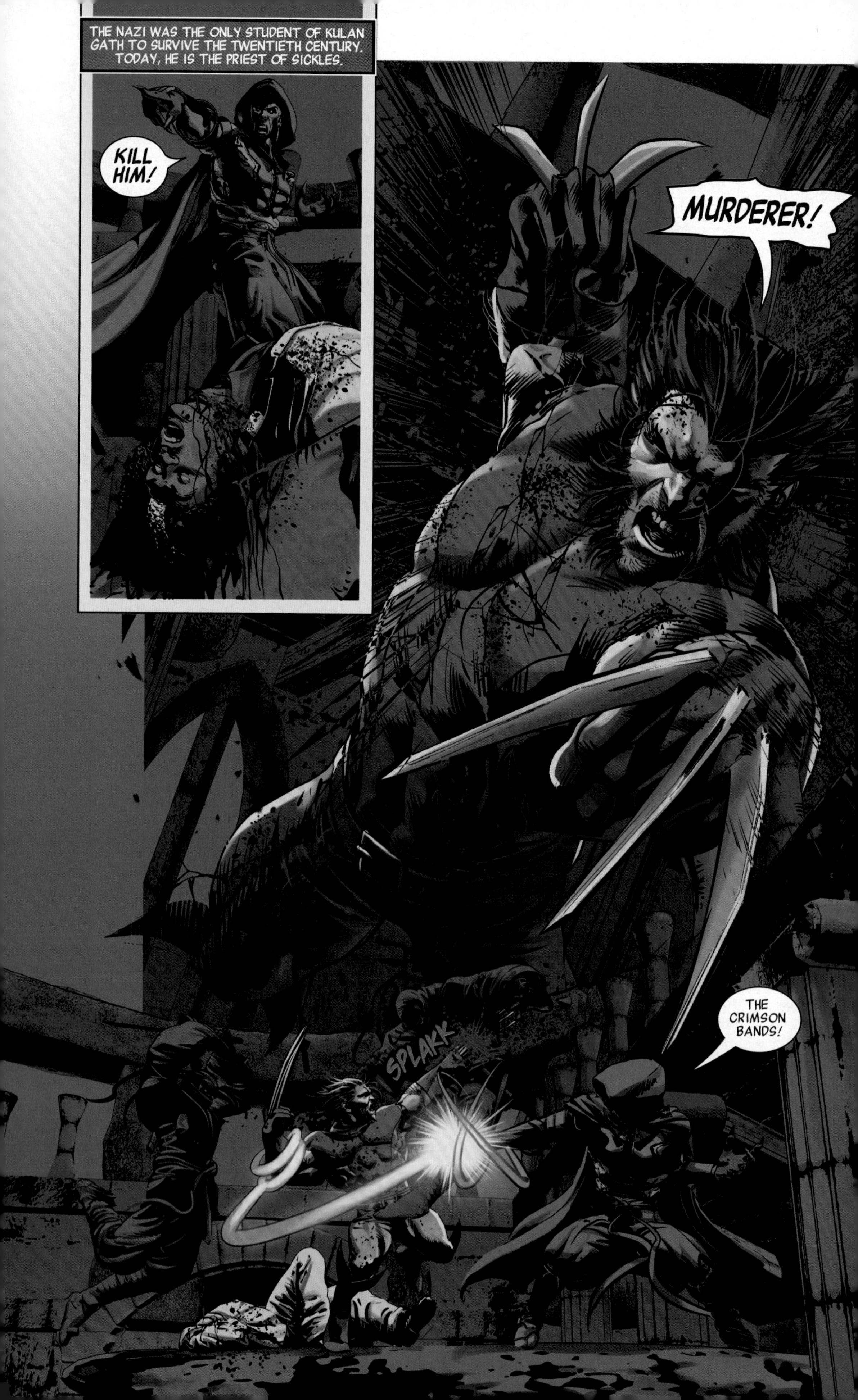
THE NAZI WAS THE ONLY STUDENT OF KULAN GATH TO SURVIVE THE TWENTIETH CENTURY. TODAY, HE IS THE PRIEST OF SICKLES.
KILL HIM!
MURDERER!
THE CRIMSON BANDS!
SPLAKK

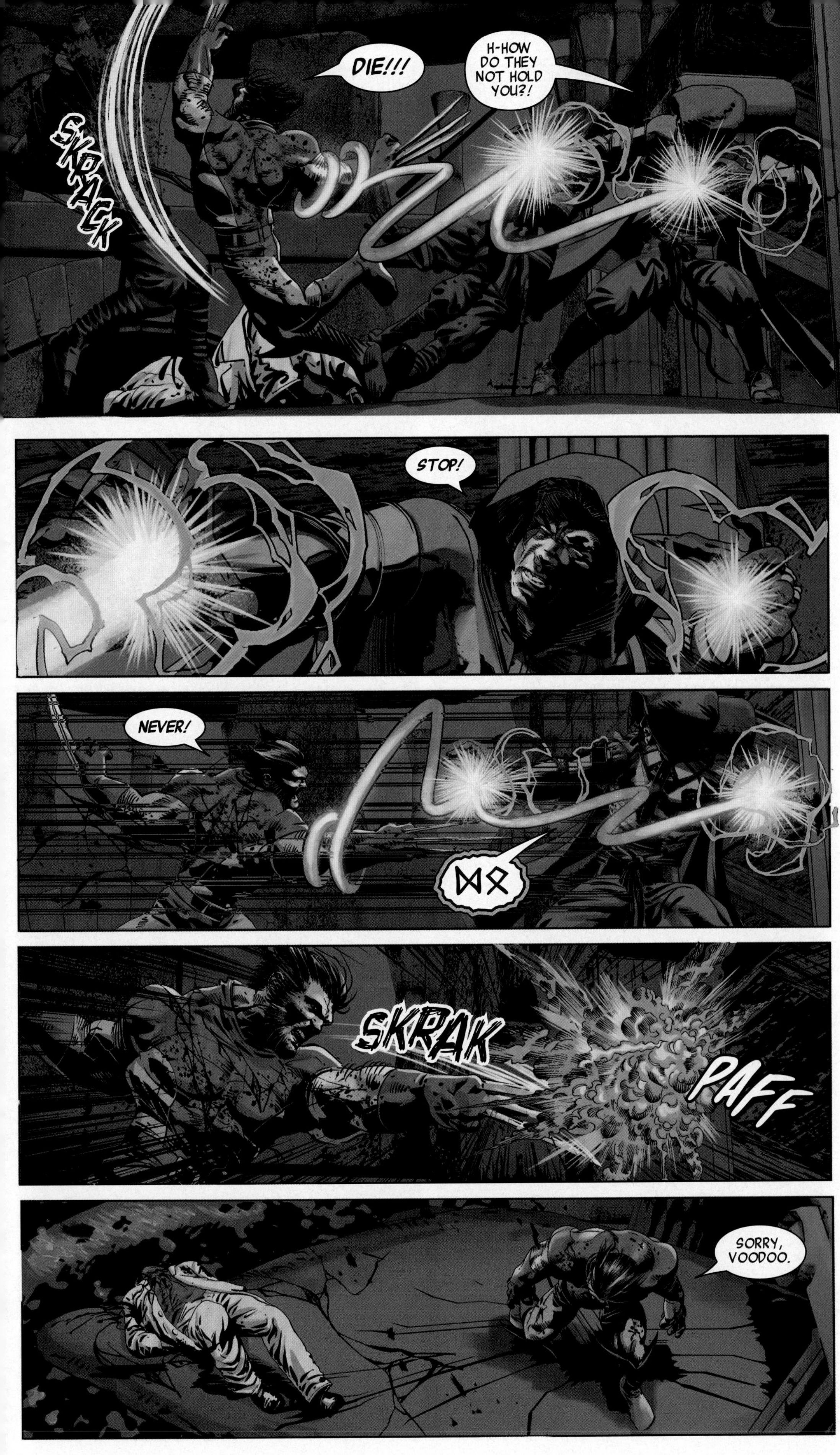
SKRACK
DIE!!!
H-HOW DO THEY NOT HOLD YOU?!
STOP!
NEVER!
SKRAK
PAFF
SORRY, VOODOO.

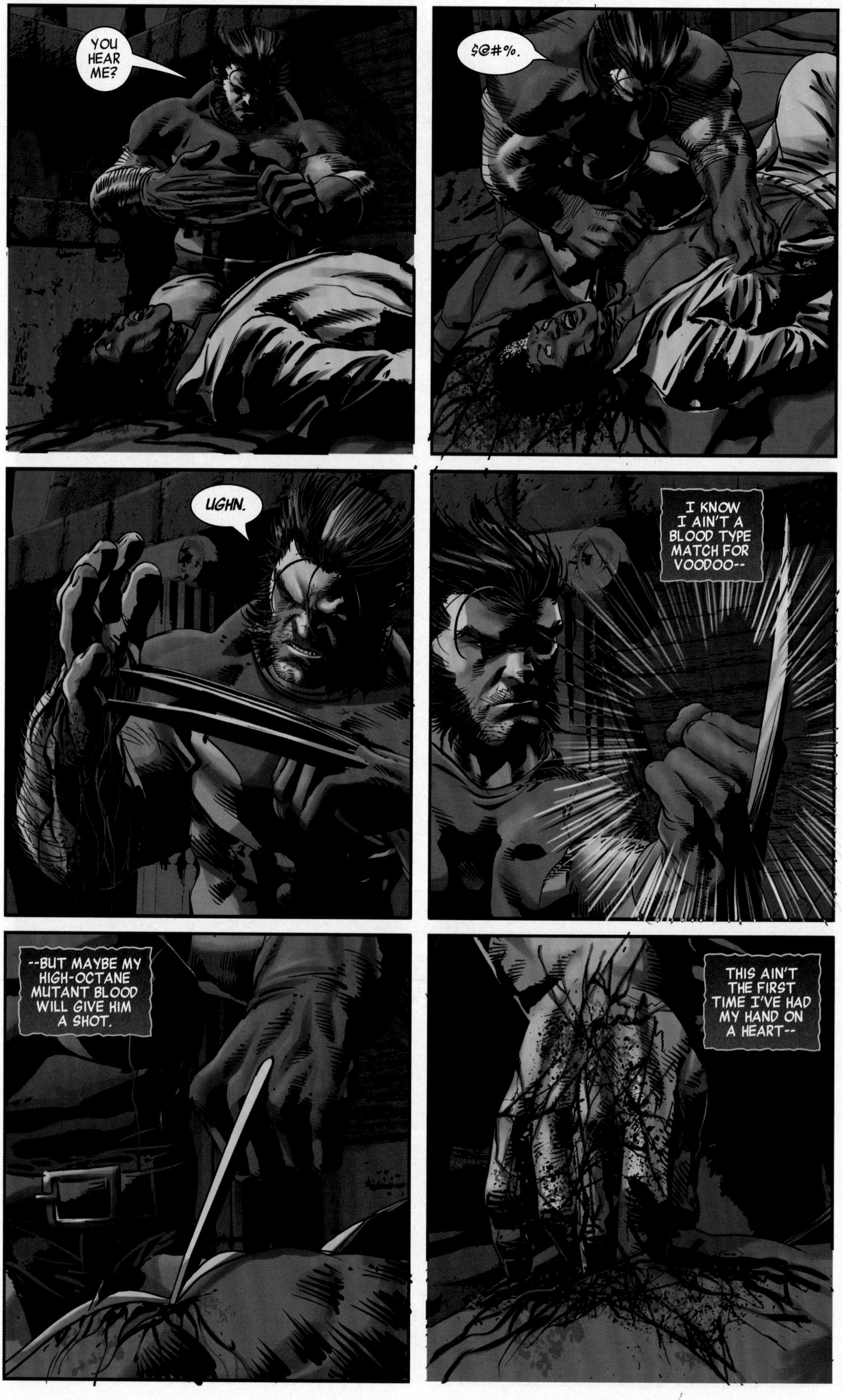

YOU HEAR ME?
$@#%.
UGHN.
I KNOW I AIN'T A BLOOD TYPE MATCH FOR VOODOO--
--BUT MAYBE MY HIGH-OCTANE MUTANT BLOOD WILL GIVE HIM A SHOT.
THIS AIN'T THE FIRST TIME I'VE HAD MY HAND ON A HEART--

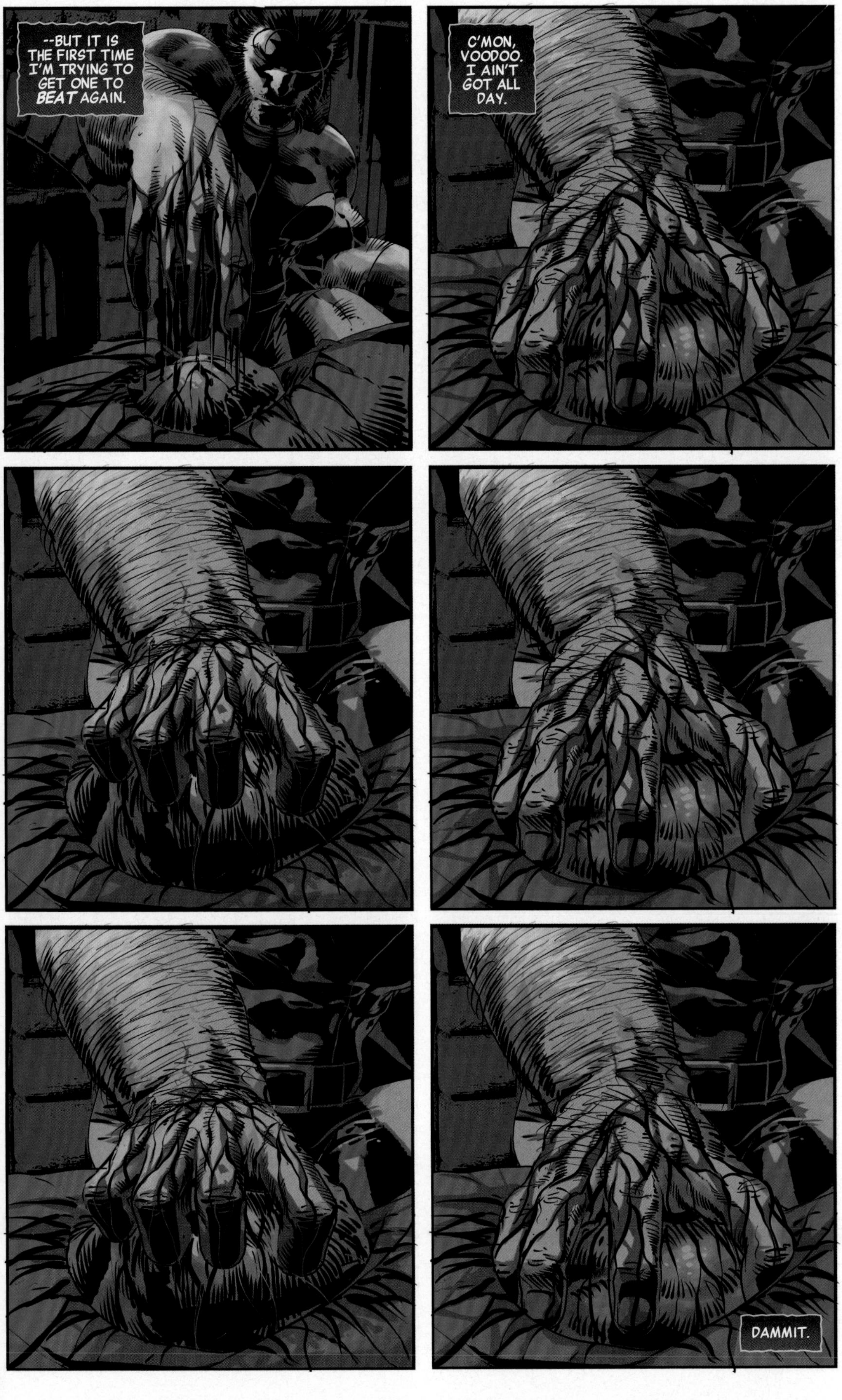
--BUT IT IS THE FIRST TIME I'M TRYING TO GET ONE TO BEAT AGAIN.
C'MON, VOODOO. I AIN'T GOT ALL DAY.
DAMMIT.

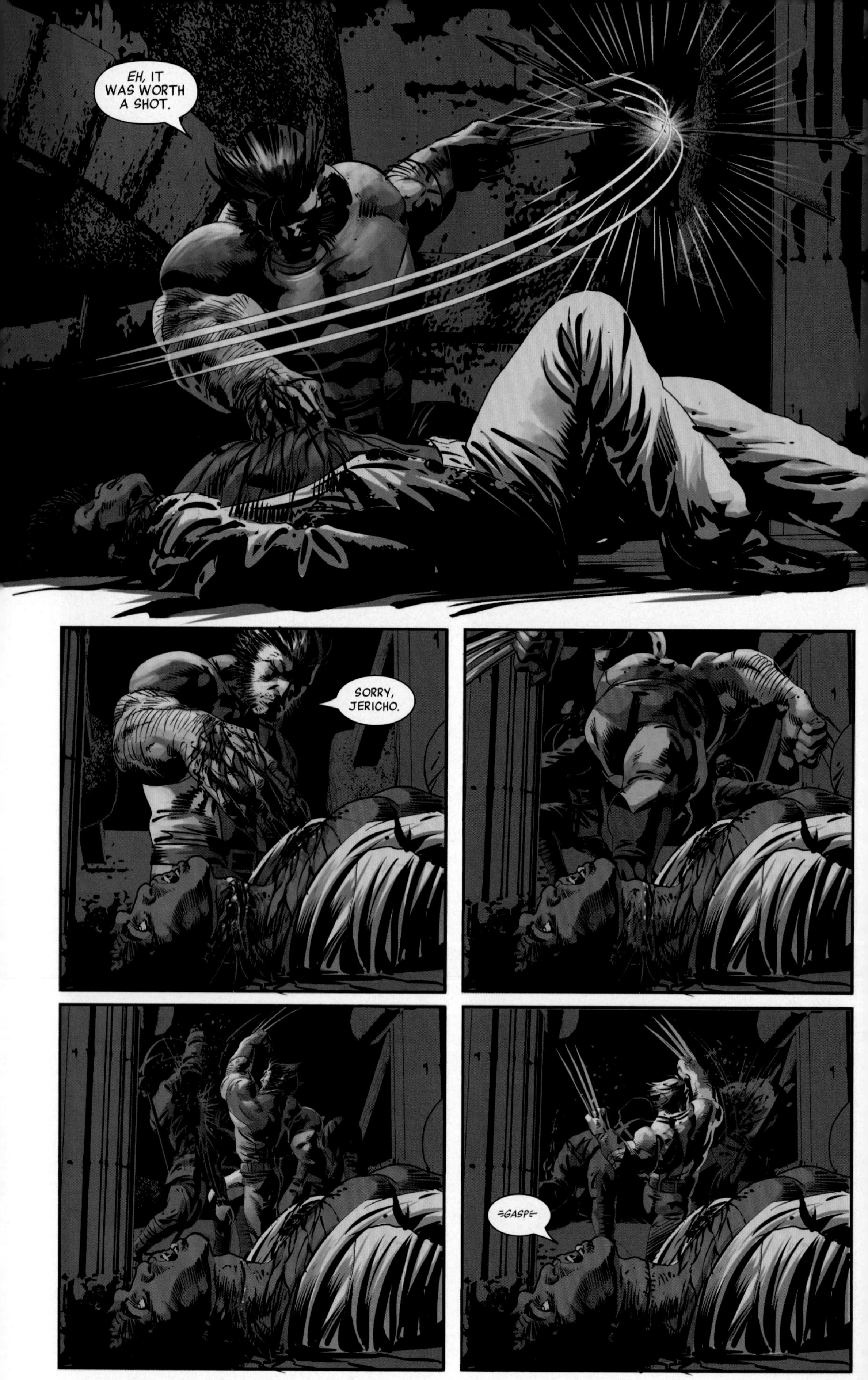
EH, IT WAS WORTH A SHOT.
SORRY, JERICHO.
=GASP=

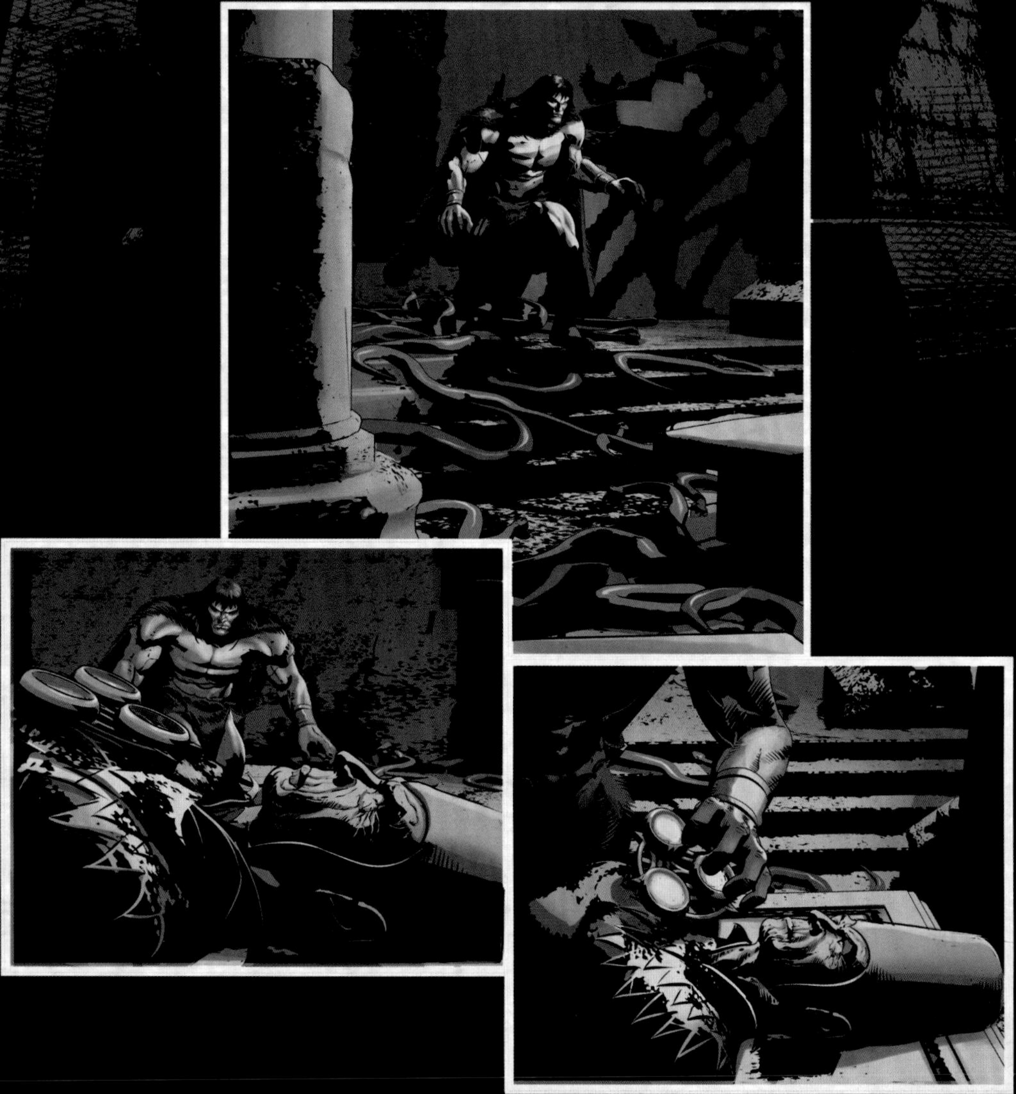

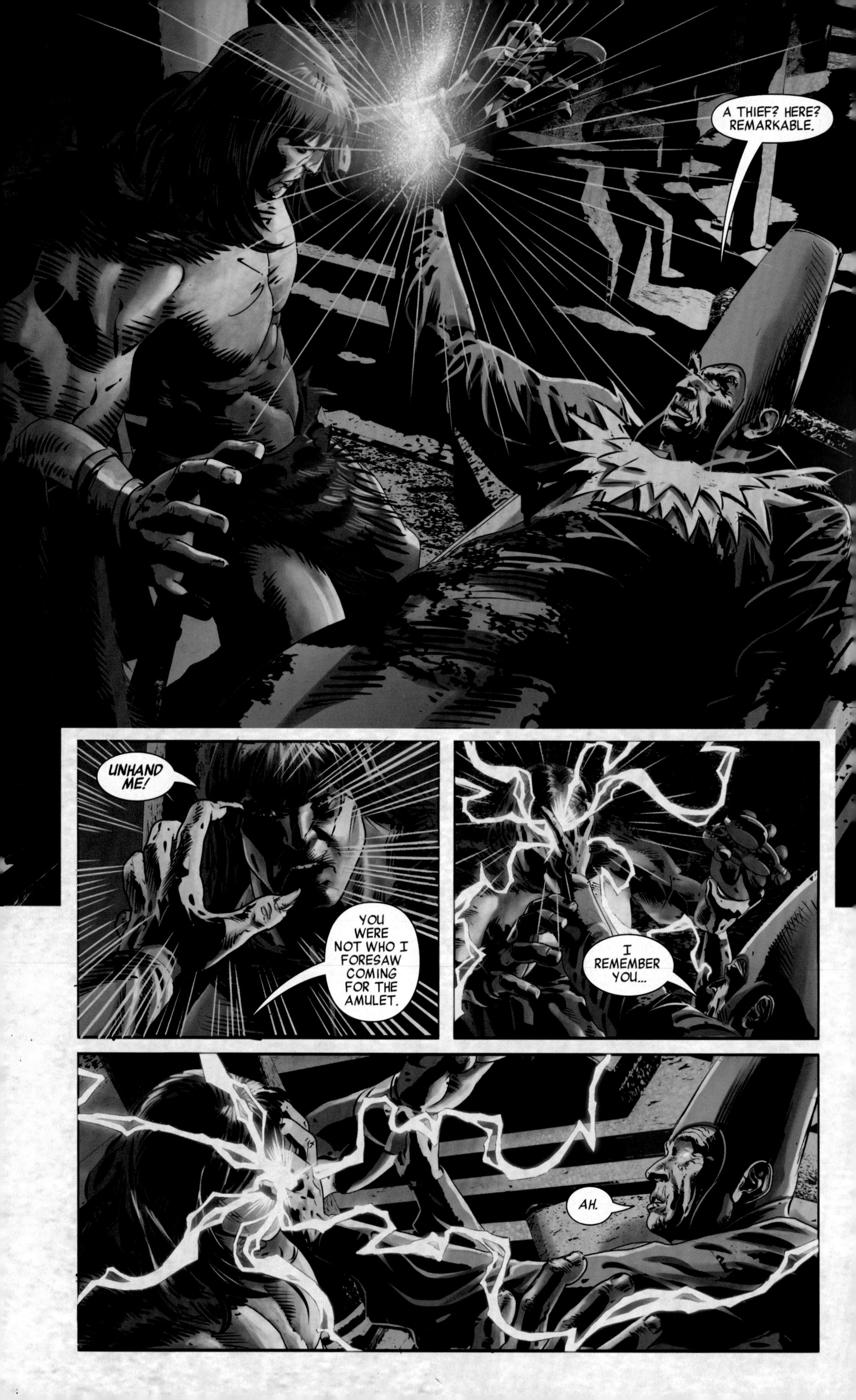
A THIEF? HERE? REMARKABLE.
UNHAND ME!
YOU WERE NOT WHO I FORESAW COMING FOR THE AMULET.
I REMEMBER YOU...
AH.

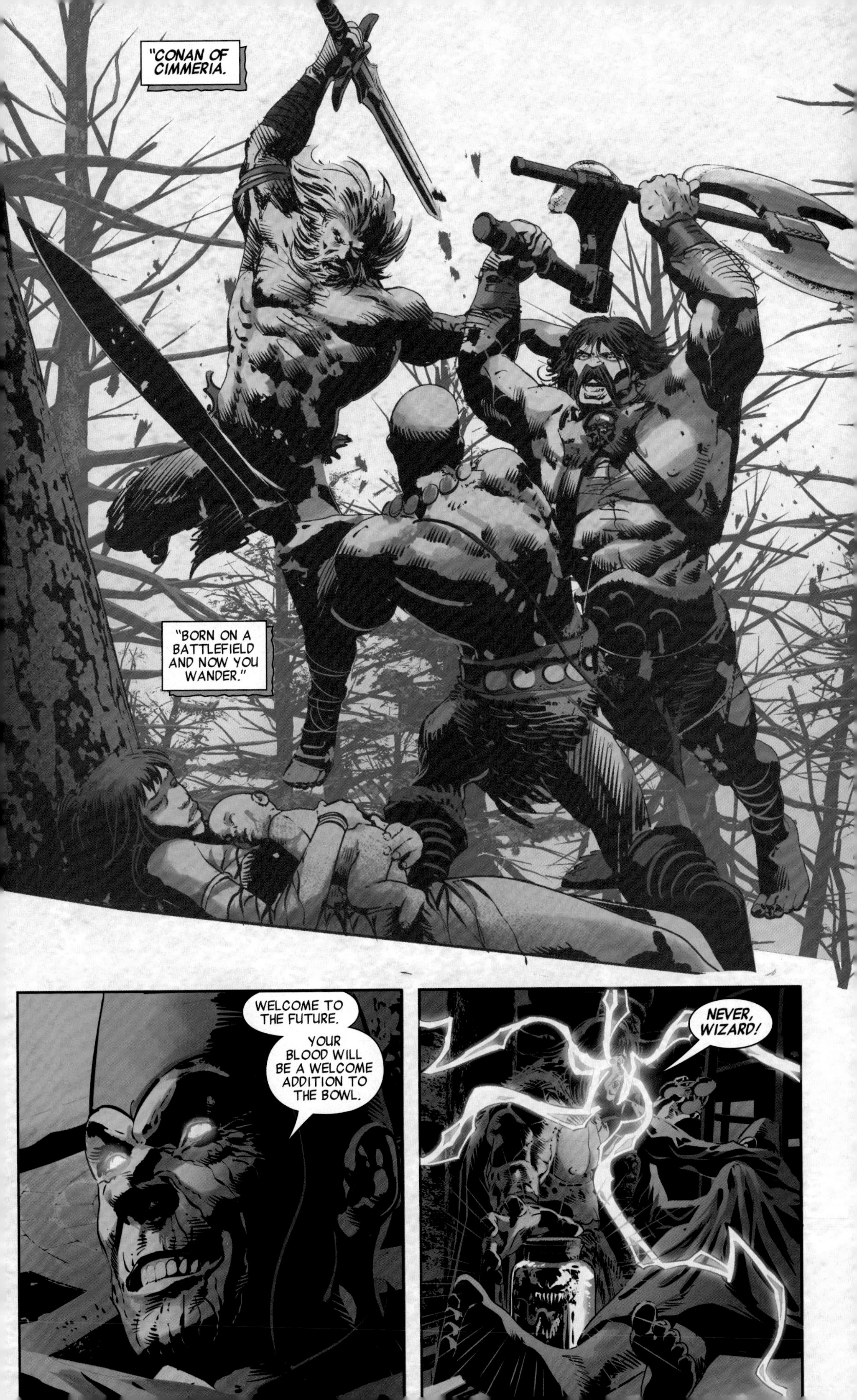
"CONAN OF CIMMERIA.
"BORN ON A BATTLEFIELD AND NOW YOU WANDER."
WELCOME TO THE FUTURE.
YOUR BLOOD WILL BE A WELCOME ADDITION TO THE BOWL.
NEVER, WIZARD!

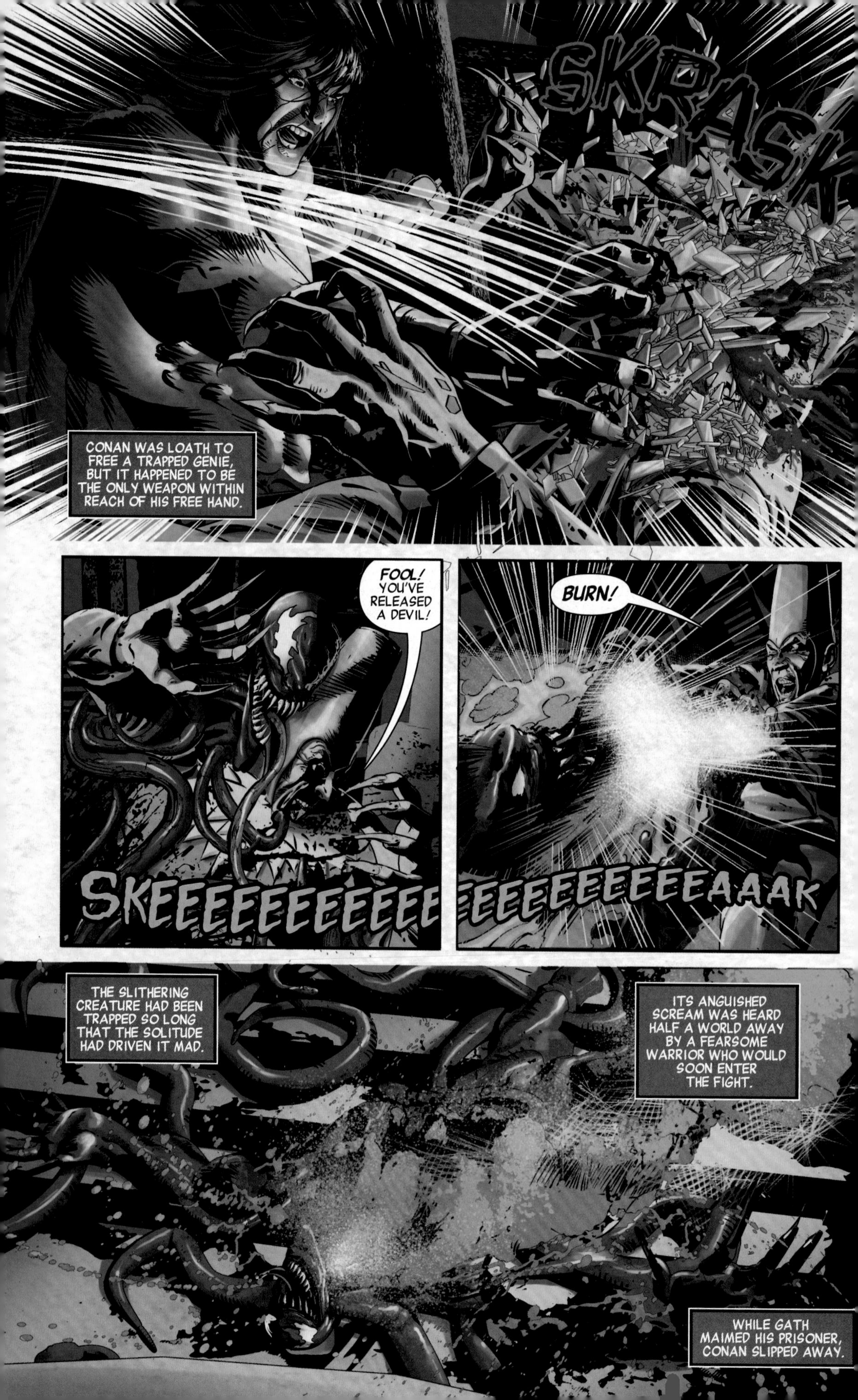
SKRASK
CONAN WAS LOATH TO FREE A TRAPPED GENIE, BUT IT HAPPENED TO BE THE ONLY WEAPON WITHIN REACH OF HIS FREE HAND.
FOOL! YOU'VE RELEASED A DEVIL!
BURN!
SKEEEEEEEEEEEEEEEEEEEEEEEAAAK
THE SLITHERING CREATURE HAD BEEN TRAPPED SO LONG THAT THE SOLITUDE HAD DRIVEN IT MAD.
ITS ANGUISHED SCREAM WAS HEARD HALF A WORLD AWAY BY A FEARSOME WARRIOR WHO WOULD SOON ENTER THE FIGHT.
WHILE GATH MAIMED HIS PRISONER, CONAN SLIPPED AWAY.

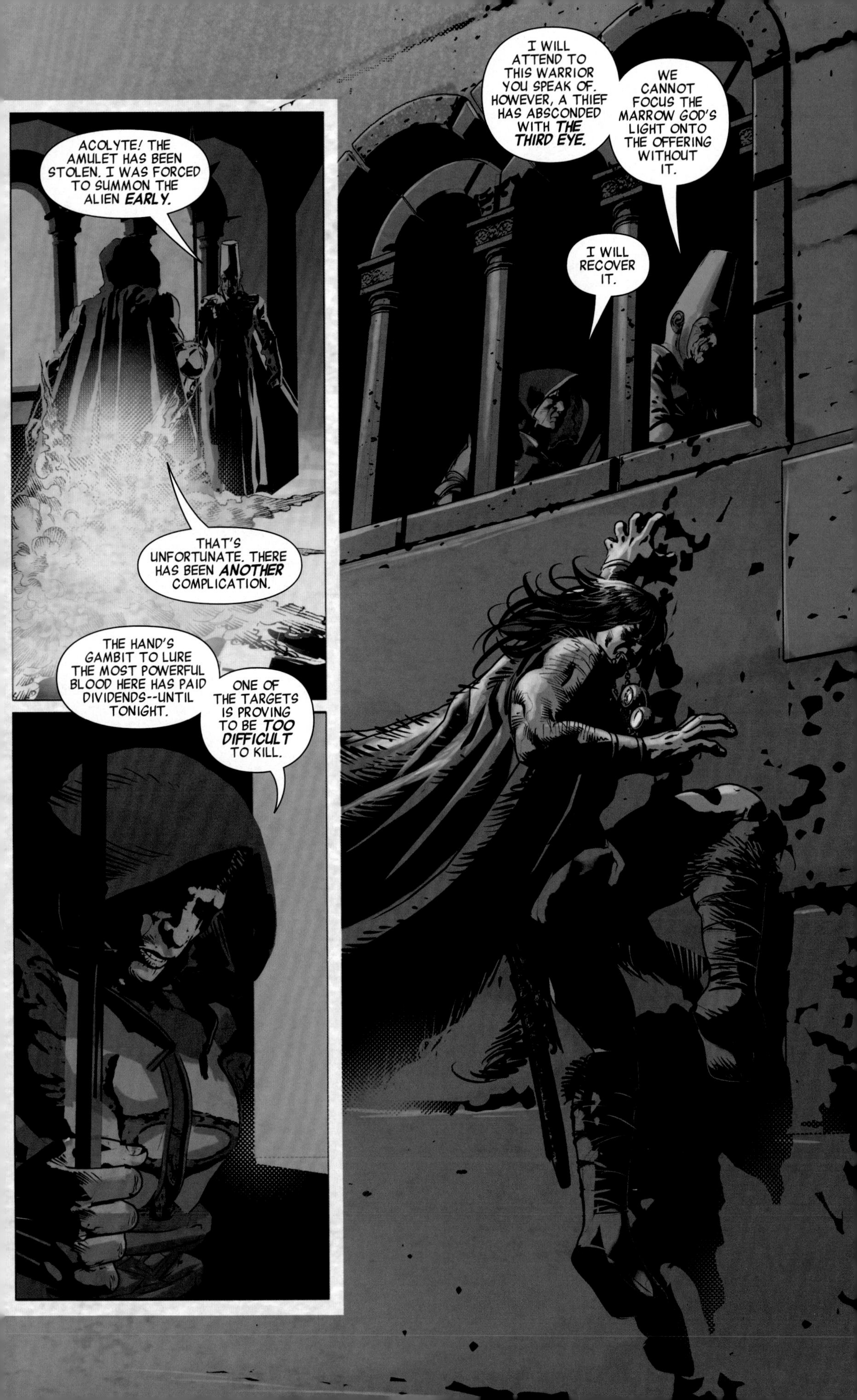
ACOLYTE! THE AMULET HAS BEEN STOLEN. I WAS FORCED TO SUMMON THE ALIEN EARLY.
THAT'S UNFORTUNATE. THERE HAS BEEN ANOTHER COMPLICATION.
THE HAND'S GAMBIT TO LURE THE MOST POWERFUL BLOOD HERE HAS PAID DIVIDENDS--UNTIL TONIGHT.
ONE OF THE TARGETS IS PROVING TO BE TOO DIFFICULT TO KILL.
I WILL ATTEND TO THIS WARRIOR YOU SPEAK OF. HOWEVER, A THIEF HAS ABSCONDED WITH THE THIRD EYE.
WE CANNOT FOCUS THE MARROW GOD'S LIGHT ONTO THE OFFERING WITHOUT IT.
I WILL RECOVER IT.

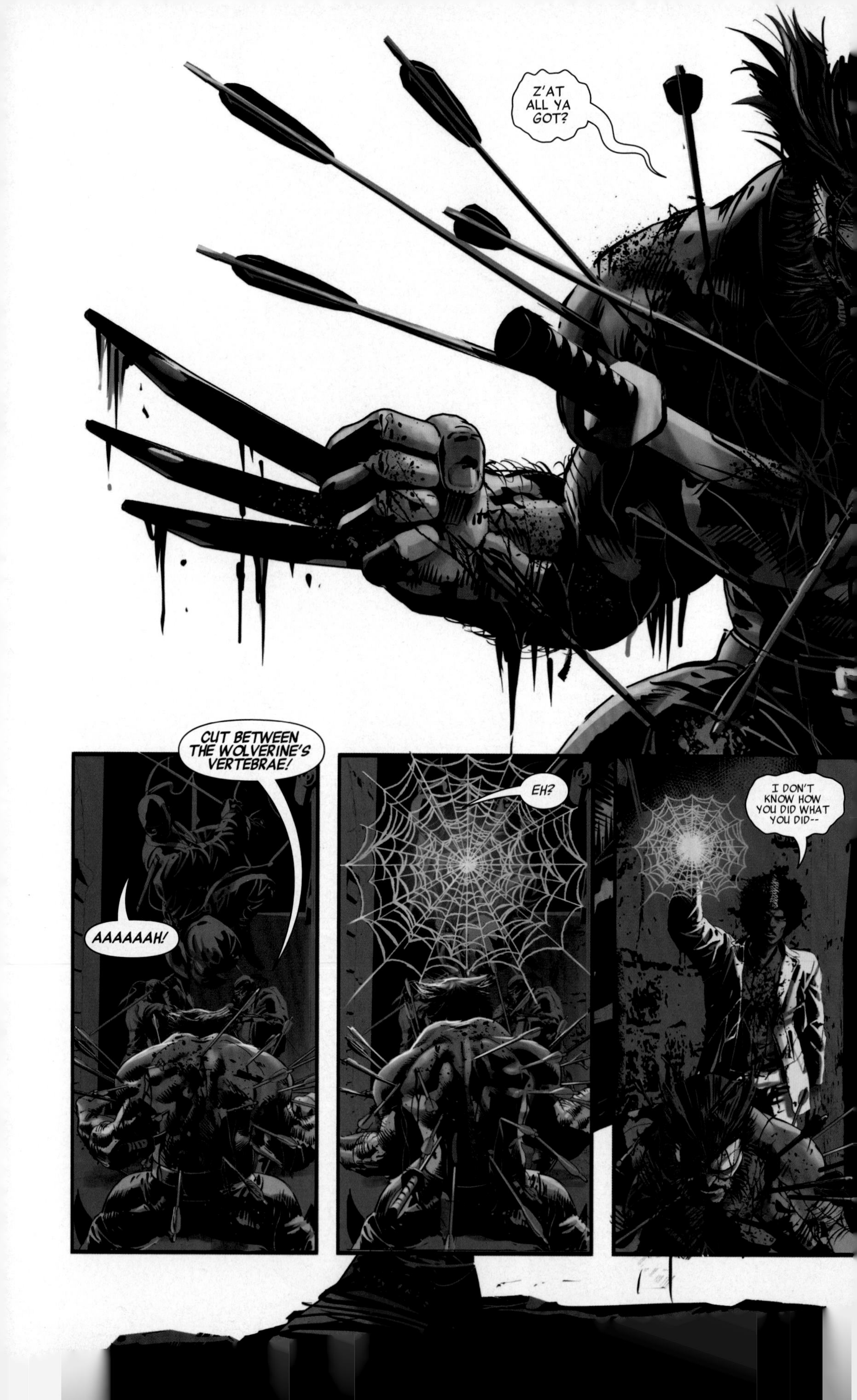

Z'AT ALL YA GOT?
CUT BETWEEN THE WOLVERINE'S VERTEBRAE!
AAAAAAH!
EH?
I DON'T KNOW HOW YOU DID WHAT YOU DID--

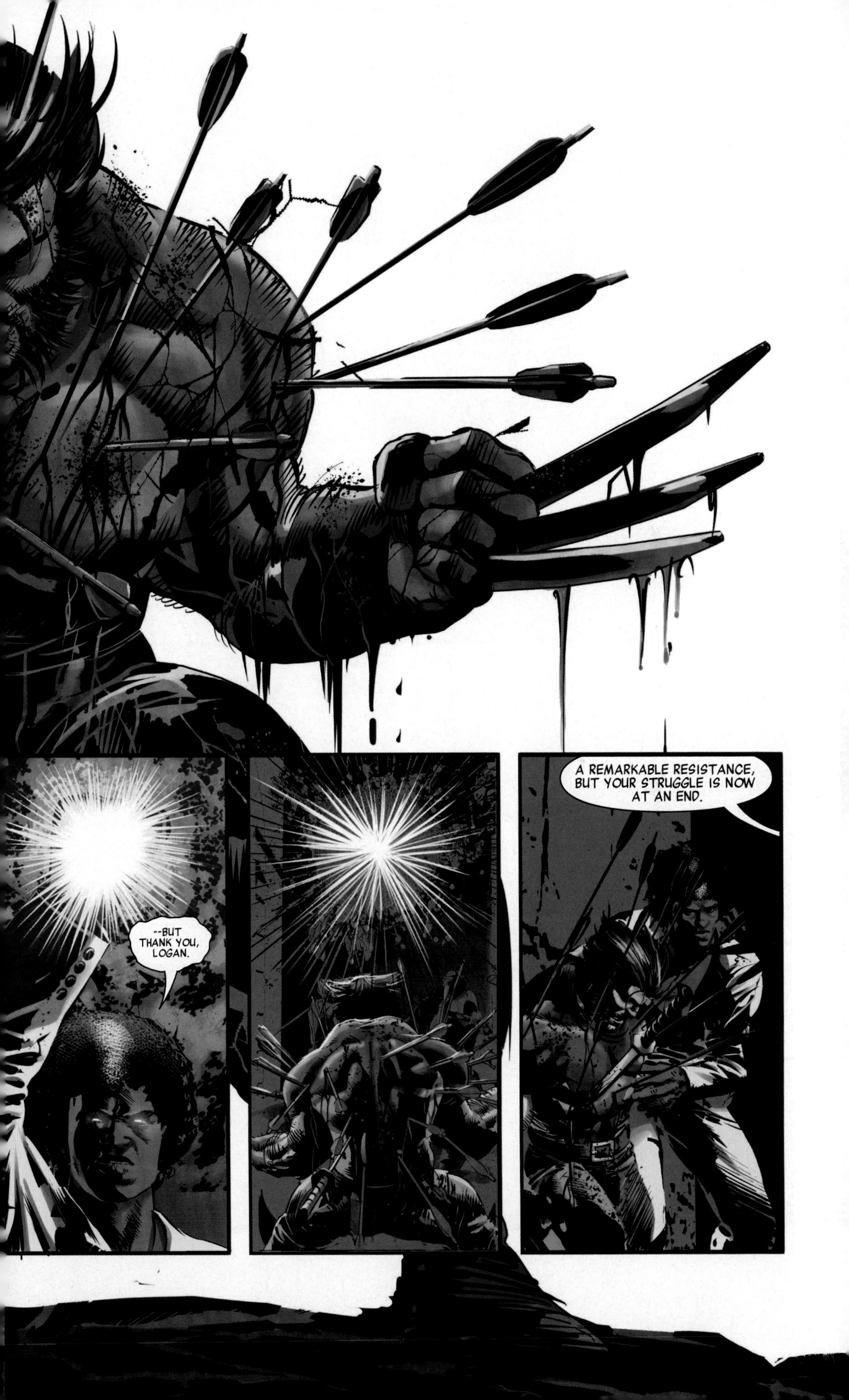
--BUT THANK YOU, LOGAN.
A REMARKABLE RESISTANCE, BUT YOUR STRUGGLE IS NOW AT AN END.

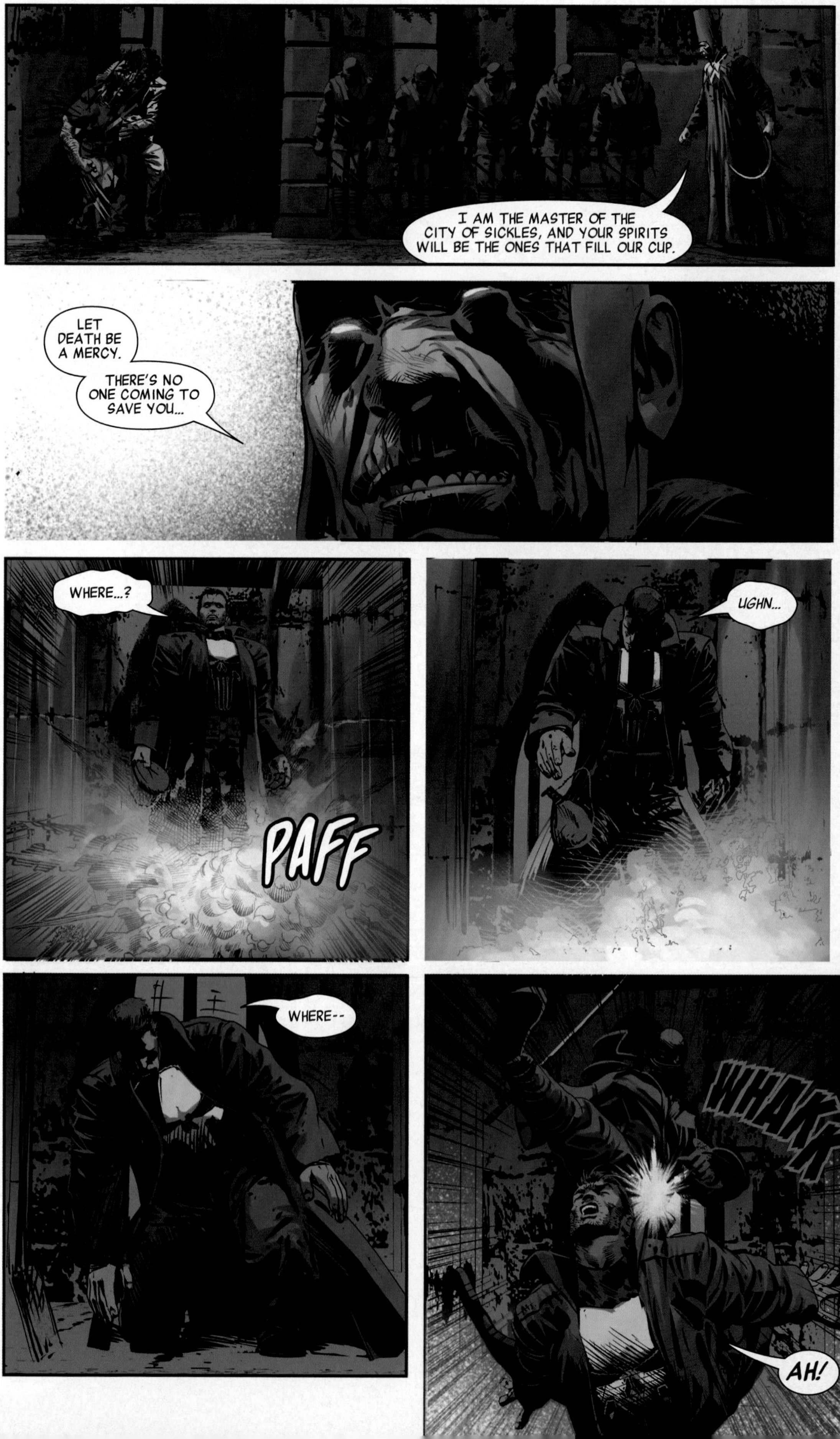
I AM THE MASTER OF THE CITY OF SICKLES, AND YOUR SPIRITS WILL BE THE ONES THAT FILL OUR CUP.
LET DEATH BE A MERCY.
THERE'S NO ONE COMING TO SAVE YOU...
WHERE...?
PAFF
UGHN...
WHERE--
WHAKK
AH!

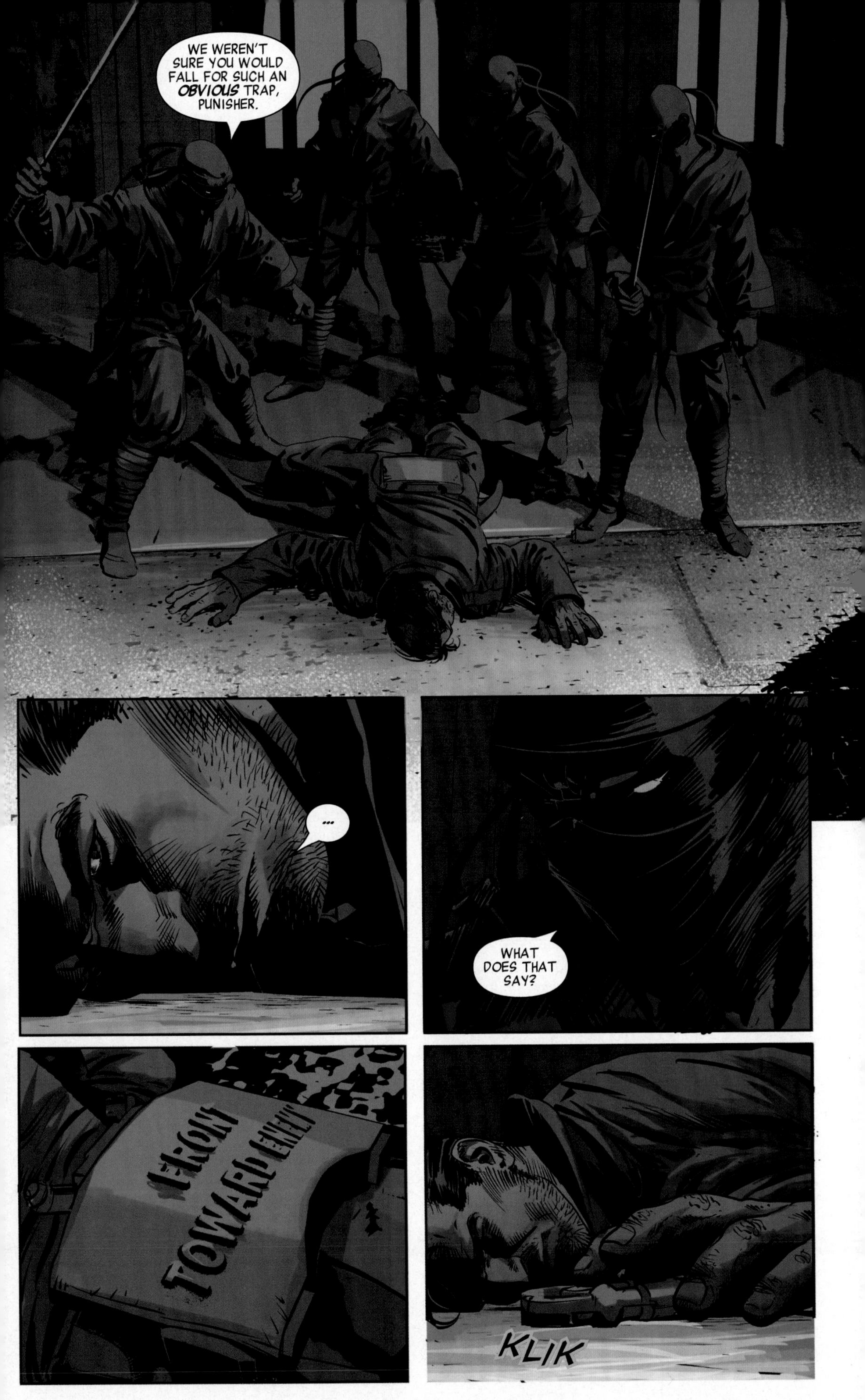
WE WEREN'T SURE YOU WOULD FALL FOR SUCH AN OBVIOUS TRAP, PUNISHER.
...
WHAT DOES THAT SAY?
FRONT TOWARD ENEMY
KLIK

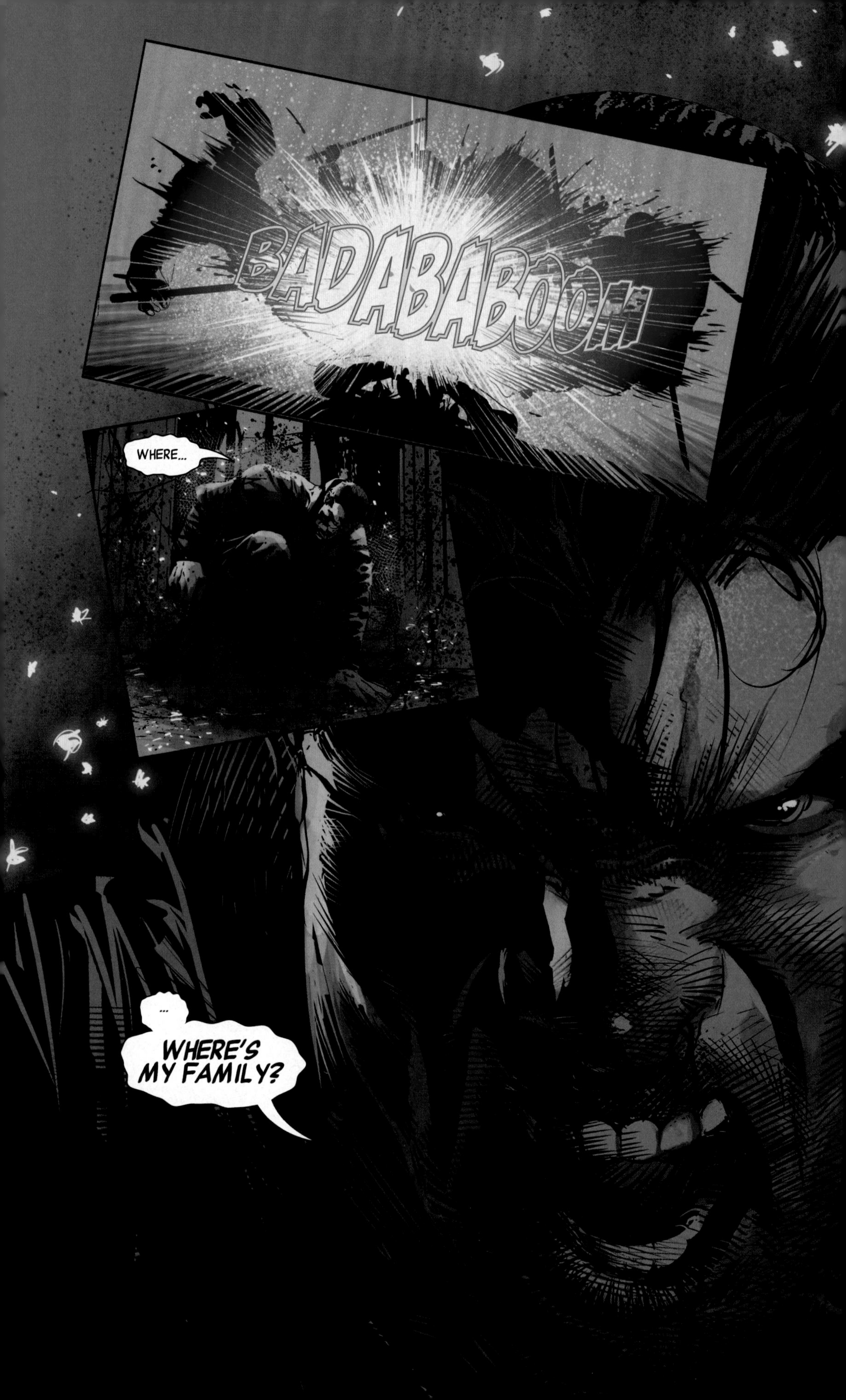
BADADABOOM
WHERE...
...
WHERE'S MY FAMILY?

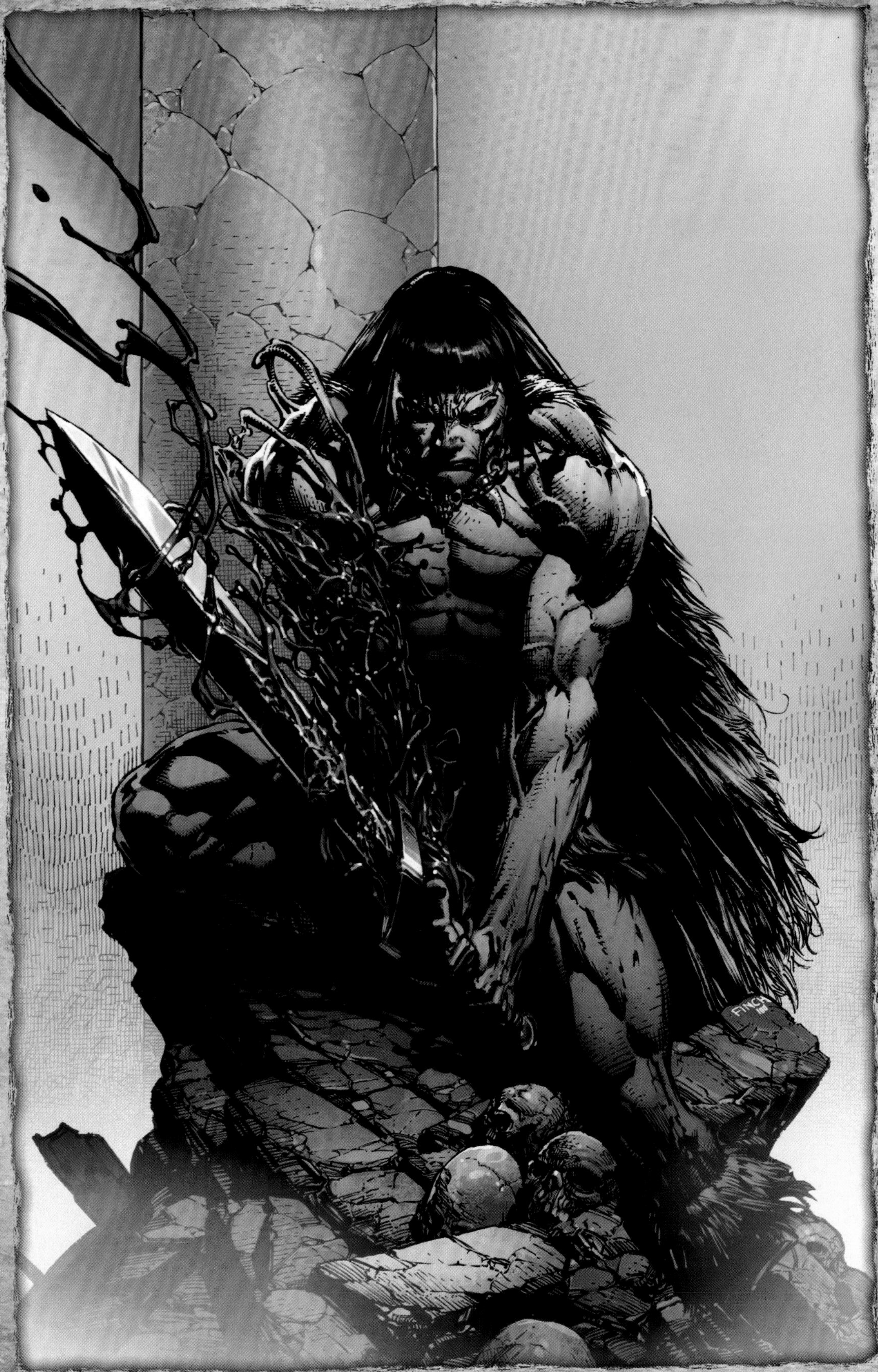
FINCH

3: CROM WHISPERS

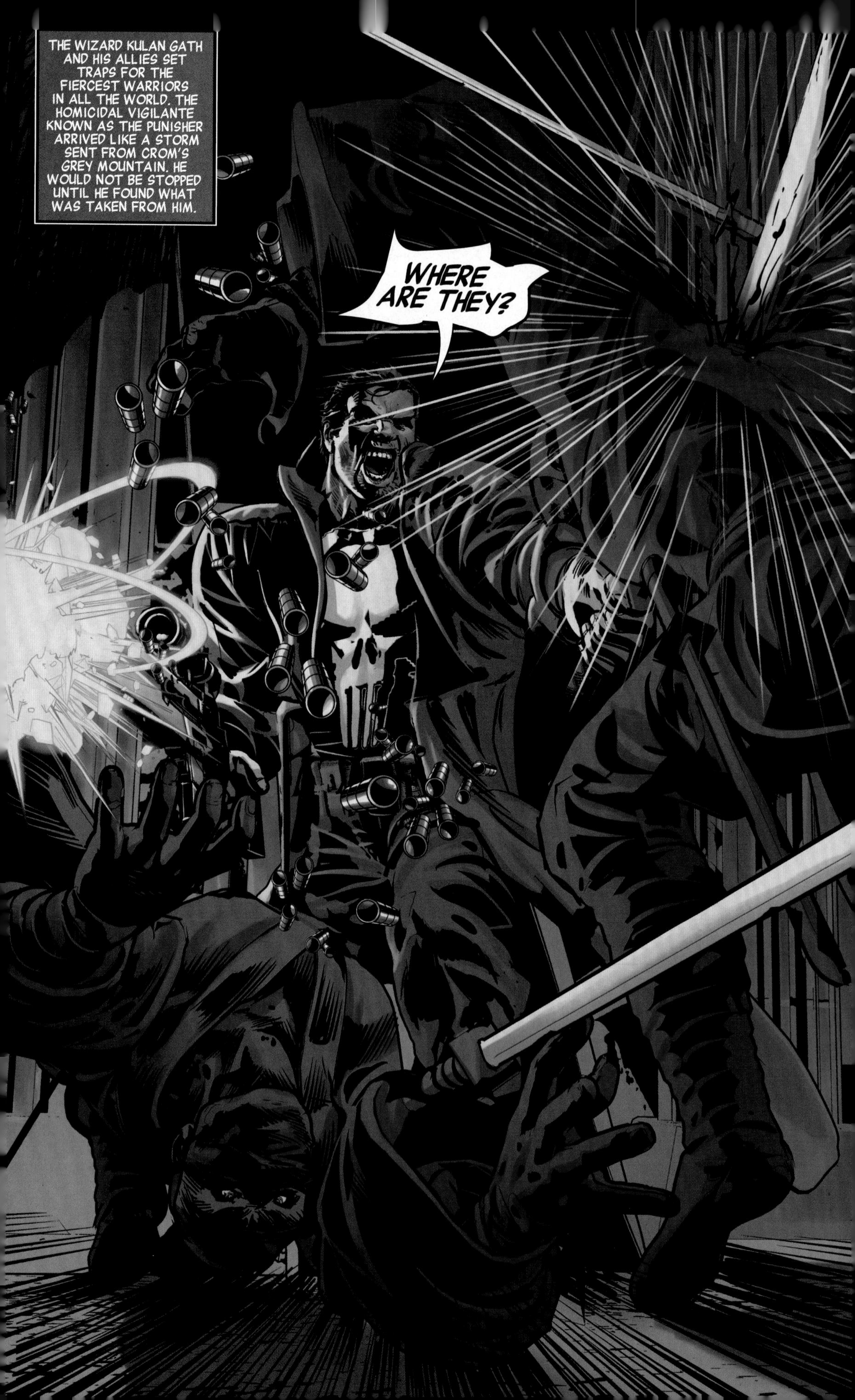
THE WIZARD KULAN GATH AND HIS ALLIES SET TRAPS FOR THE FIERCEST WARRIORS IN ALL THE WORLD. THE HOMICIDAL VIGILANTE KNOWN AS THE PUNISHER ARRIVED LIKE A STORM SENT FROM CROM'S GREY MOUNTAIN. HE WOULD NOT BE STOPPED UNTIL HE FOUND WHAT WAS TAKEN FROM HIM.
WHERE ARE THEY?

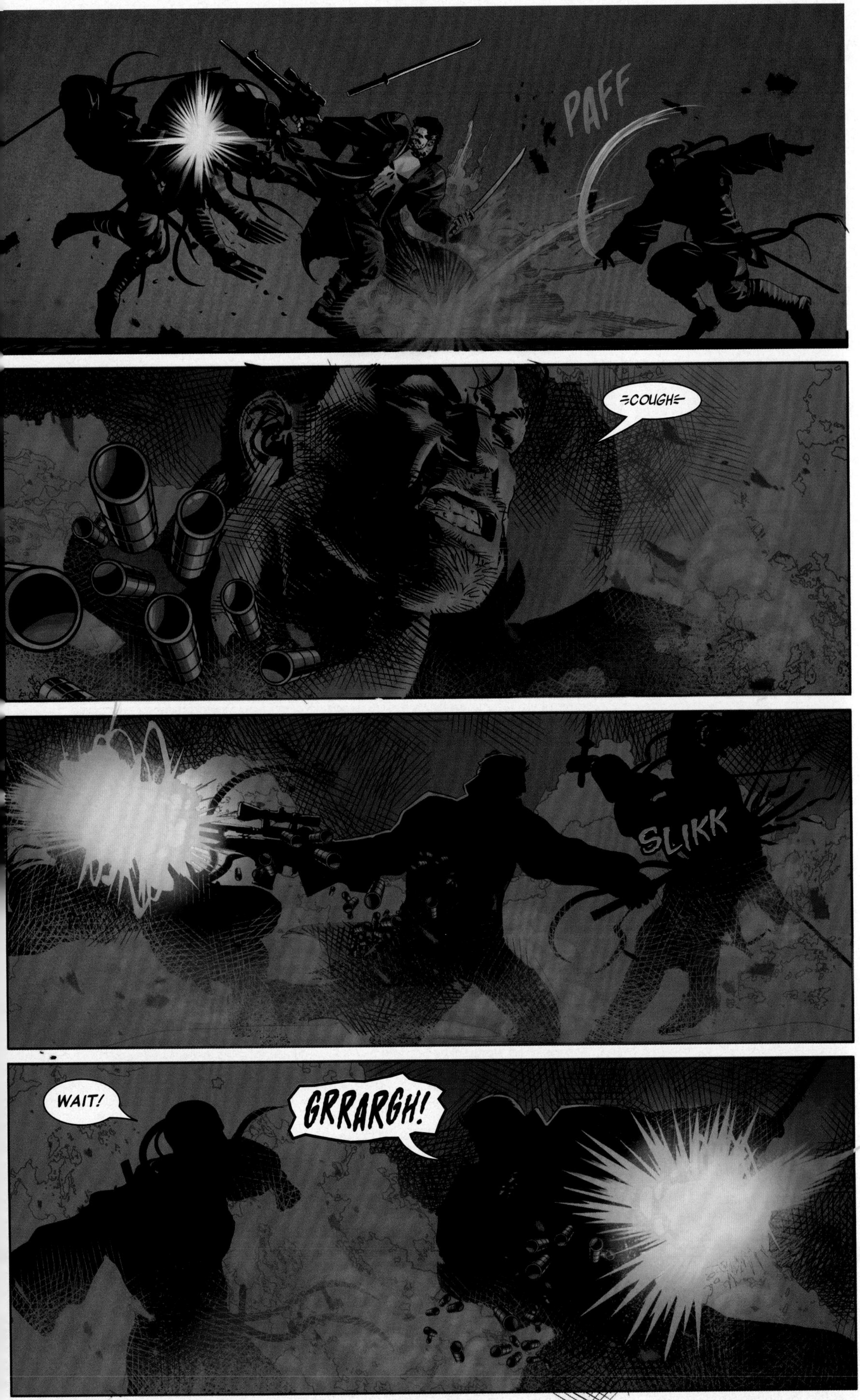
PAFF
=COUGH=
SLIKK
WAIT!
GRRARGH!

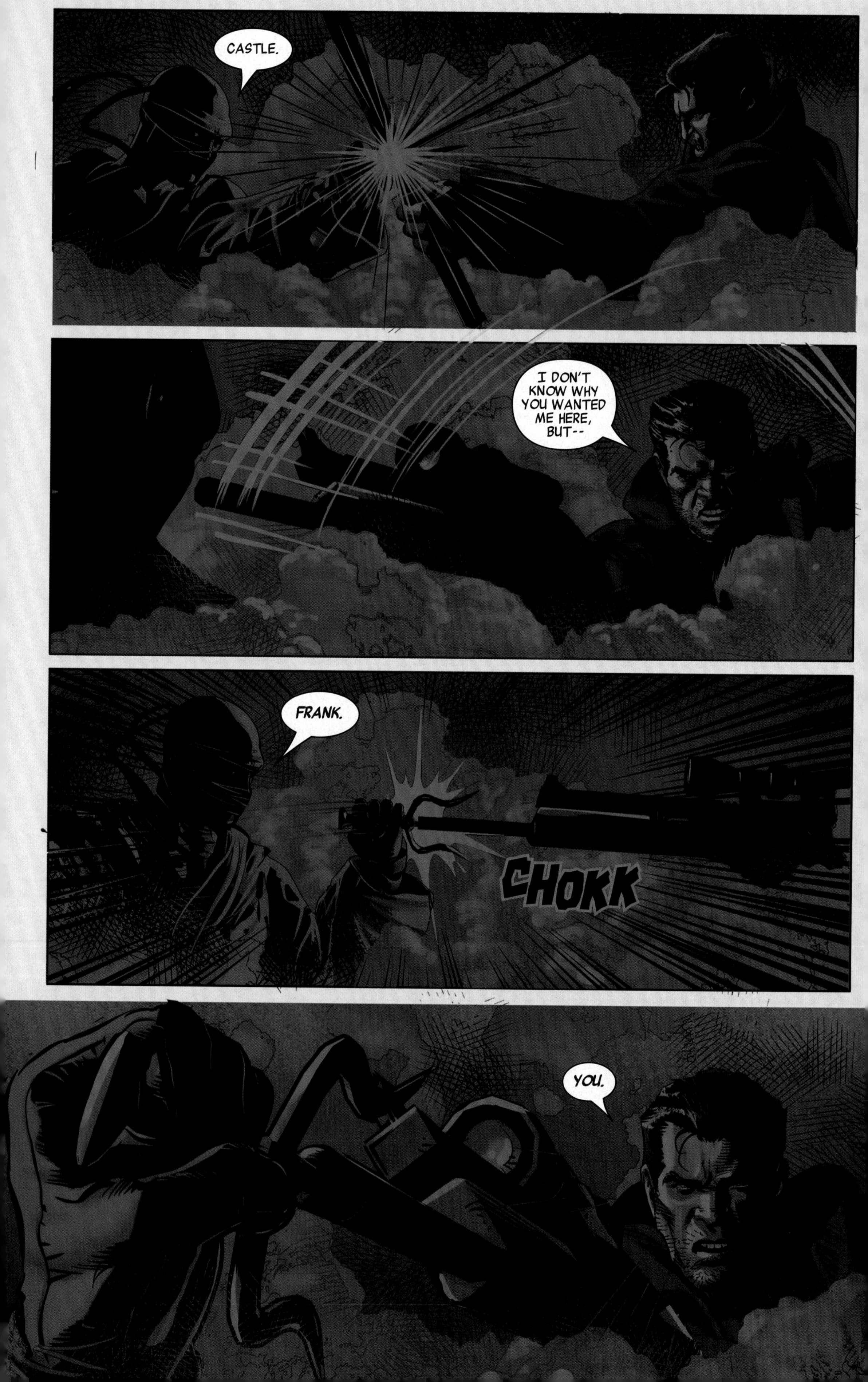
CASTLE.
I DON'T KNOW WHY YOU WANTED ME HERE, BUT--
FRANK.
CHOKK
YOU.

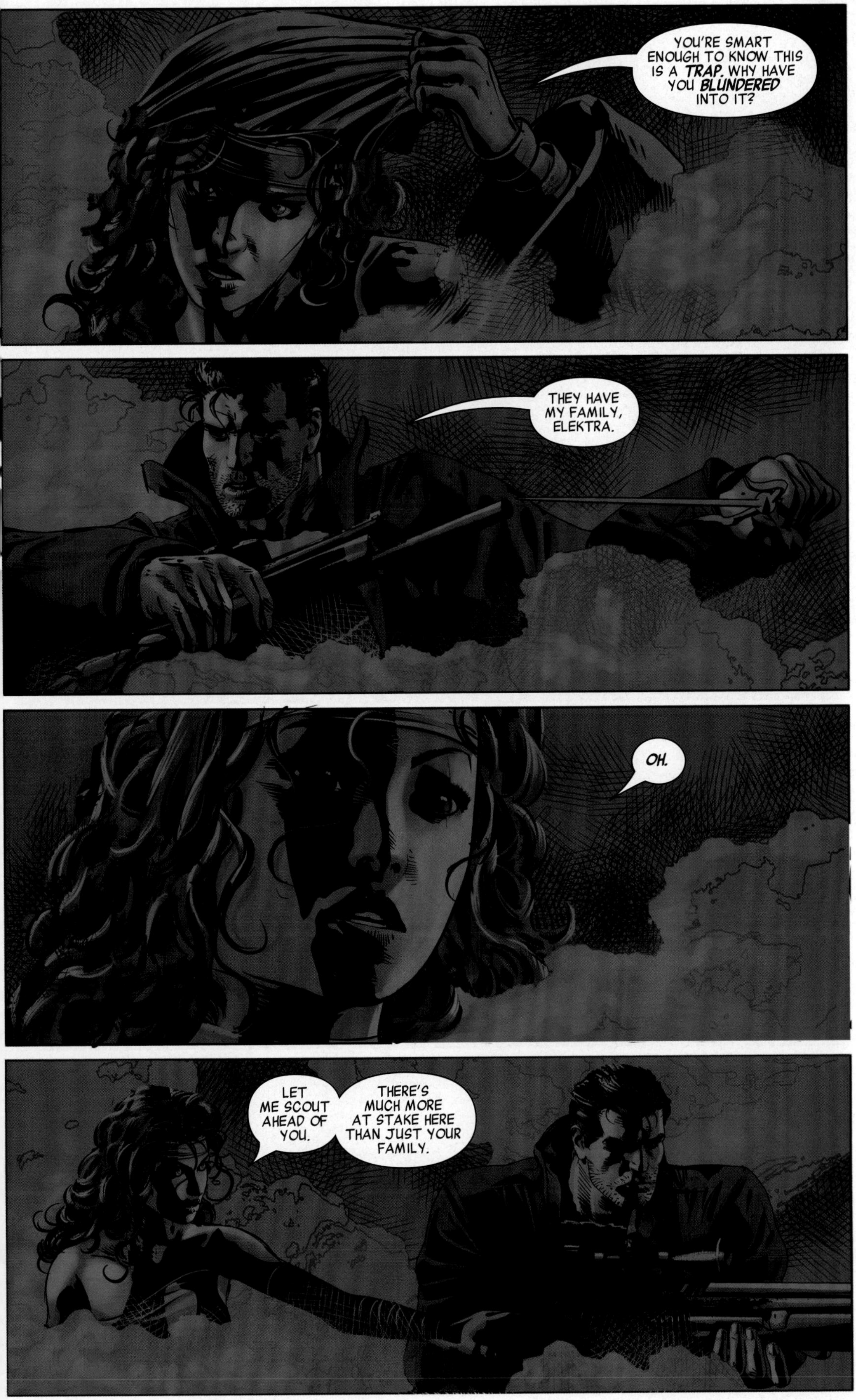
YOU'RE SMART ENOUGH TO KNOW THIS IS A TRAP. WHY HAVE YOU BLUNDERED INTO IT?
THEY HAVE MY FAMILY, ELEKTRA.
OH.
LET ME SCOUT AHEAD OF YOU.
THERE'S MUCH MORE AT STAKE HERE THAN JUST YOUR FAMILY.

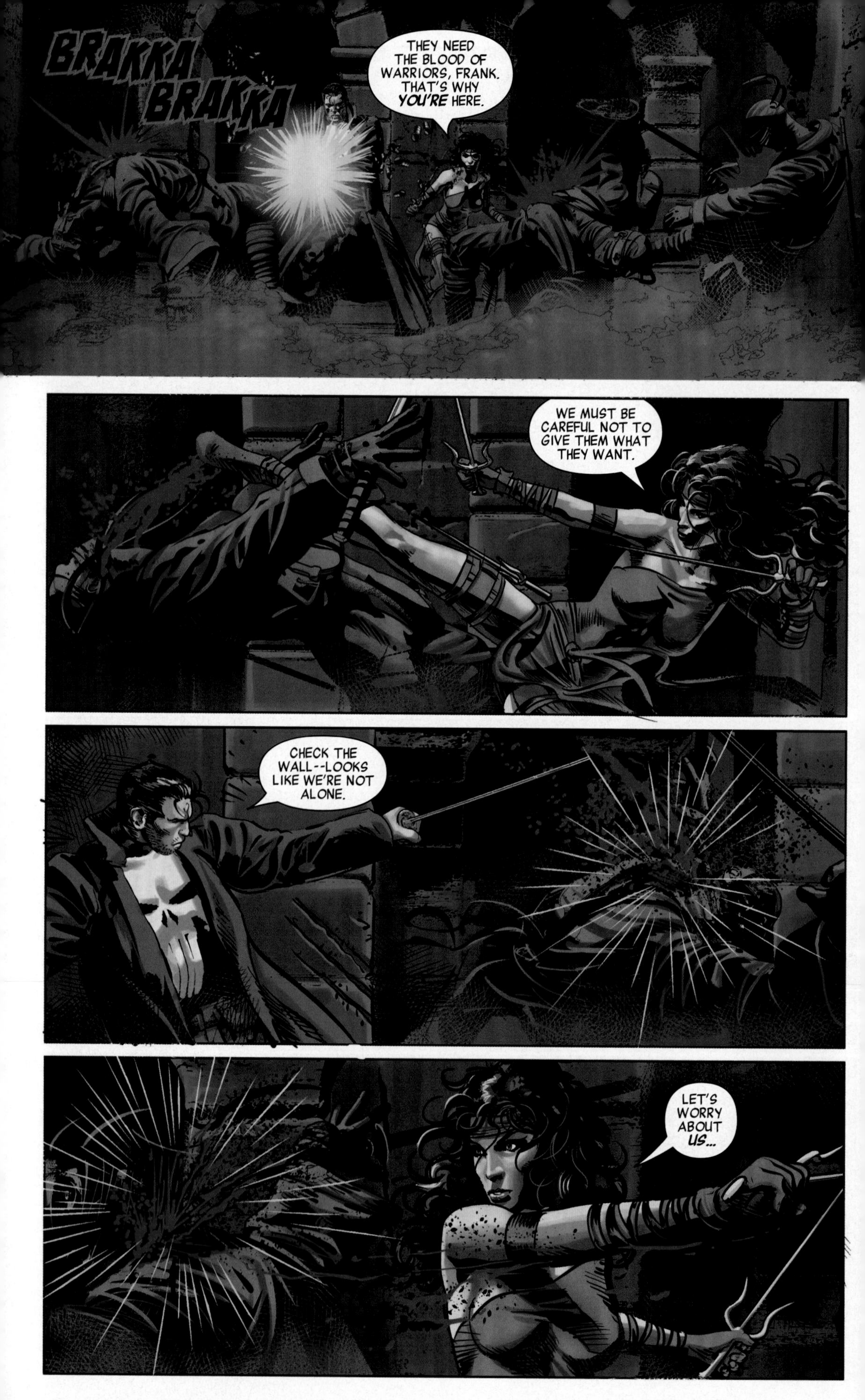
BRAKKA BRAKKA
THEY NEED THE BLOOD OF WARRIORS, FRANK. THAT'S WHY YOU'RE HERE.
WE MUST BE CAREFUL NOT TO GIVE THEM WHAT THEY WANT.
CHECK THE WALL--LOOKS LIKE WE'RE NOT ALONE.
LET'S WORRY ABOUT US...

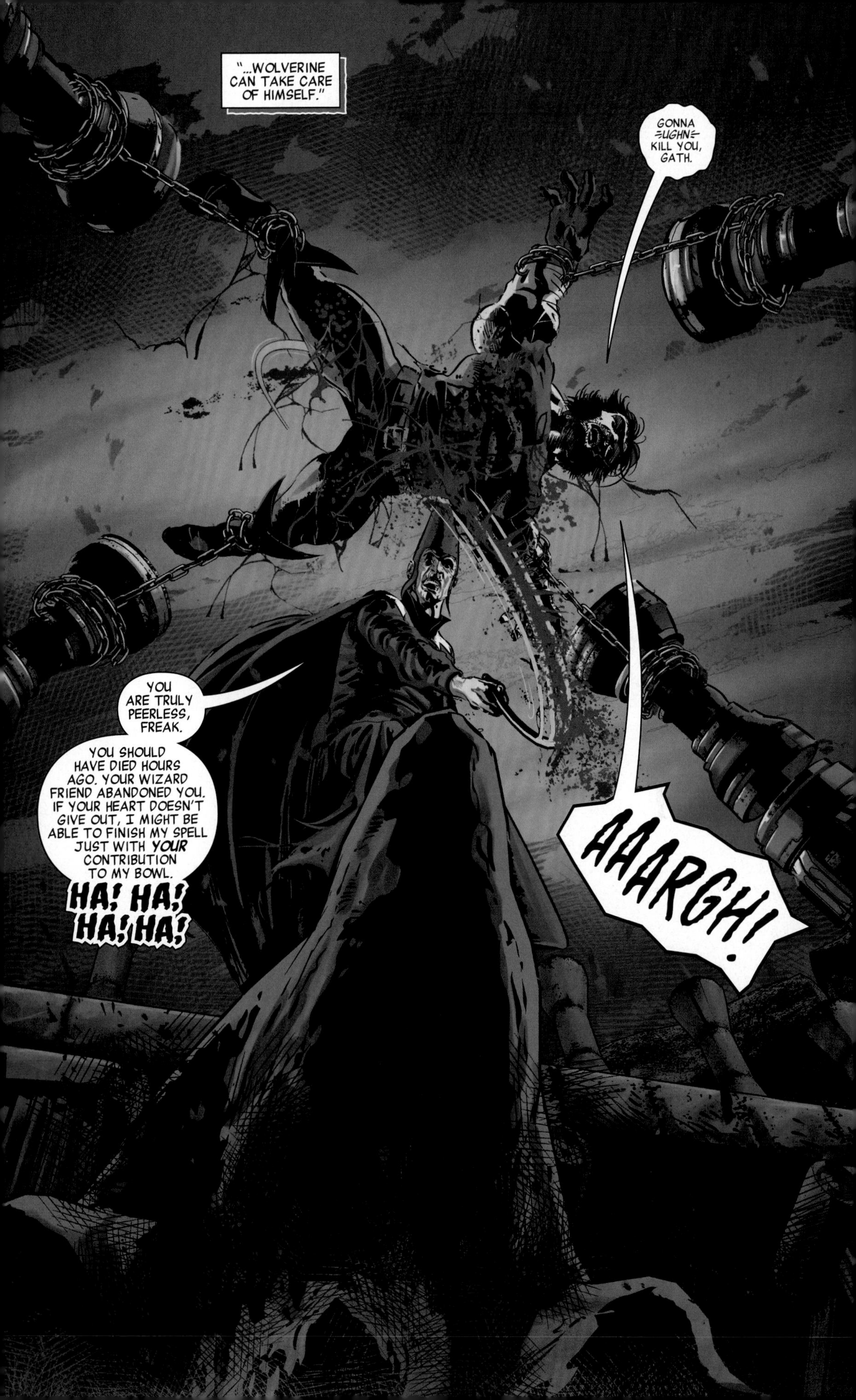
"...WOLVERINE CAN TAKE CARE OF HIMSELF."
GONNA =UGHN= KILL YOU, GATH.
YOU ARE TRULY PEERLESS, FREAK.
YOU SHOULD HAVE DIED HOURS AGO. YOUR WIZARD FRIEND ABANDONED YOU. IF YOUR HEART DOESN'T GIVE OUT, I MIGHT BE ABLE TO FINISH MY SPELL JUST WITH *YOUR* CONTRIBUTION TO MY BOWL.
HA! HA! HA! HA!
AAARGH!

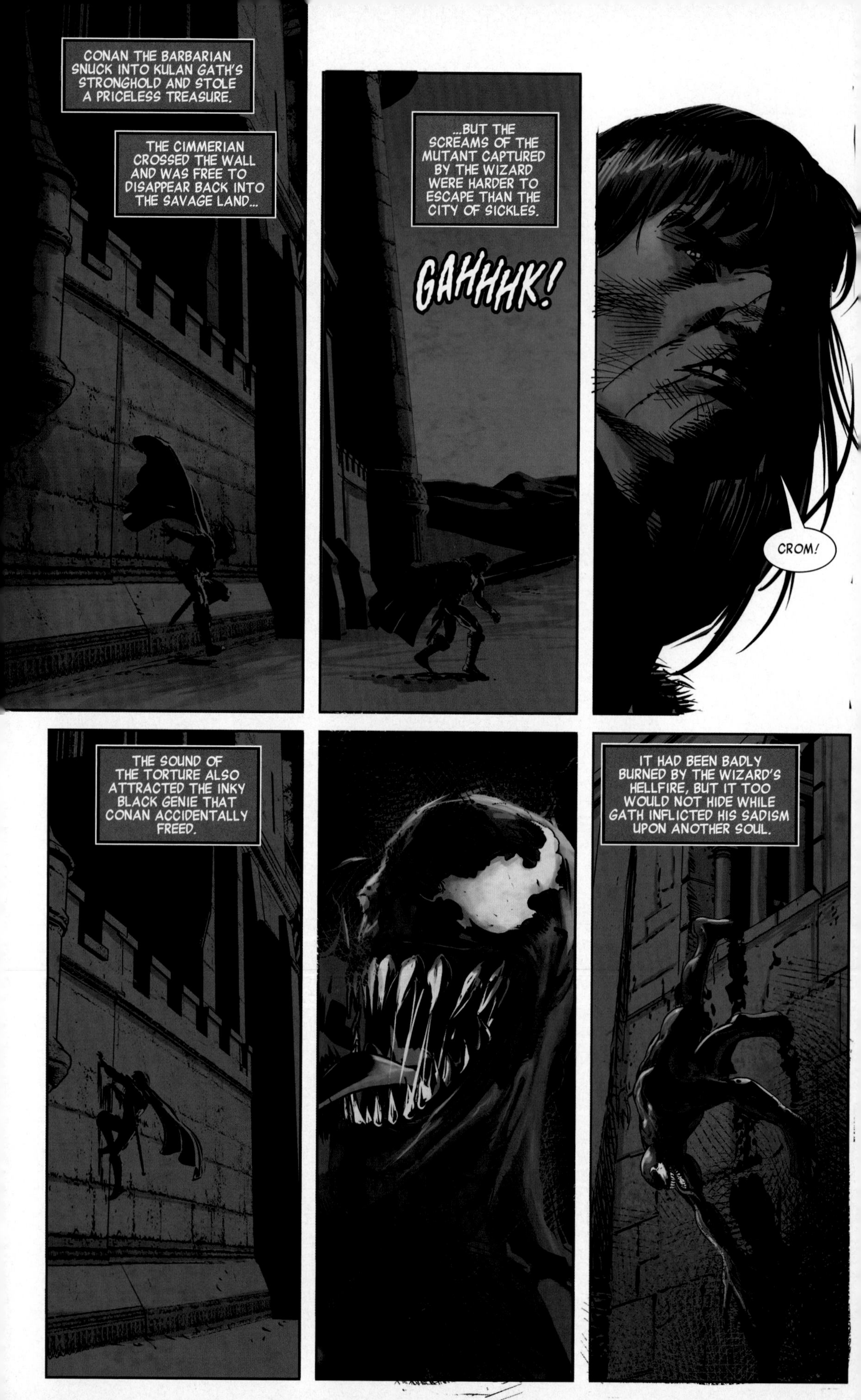
CONAN THE BARBARIAN SNUCK INTO KULAN GATH'S STRONGHOLD AND STOLE A PRICELESS TREASURE.
THE CIMMERIAN CROSSED THE WALL AND WAS FREE TO DISAPPEAR BACK INTO THE SAVAGE LAND...
...BUT THE SCREAMS OF THE MUTANT CAPTURED BY THE WIZARD WERE HARDER TO ESCAPE THAN THE CITY OF SICKLES.
GAHHHK!
CROM!
THE SOUND OF THE TORTURE ALSO ATTRACTED THE INKY BLACK GENIE THAT CONAN ACCIDENTALLY FREED.
IT HAD BEEN BADLY BURNED BY THE WIZARD'S HELLFIRE, BUT IT TOO WOULD NOT HIDE WHILE GATH INFLICTED HIS SADISM UPON ANOTHER SOUL.

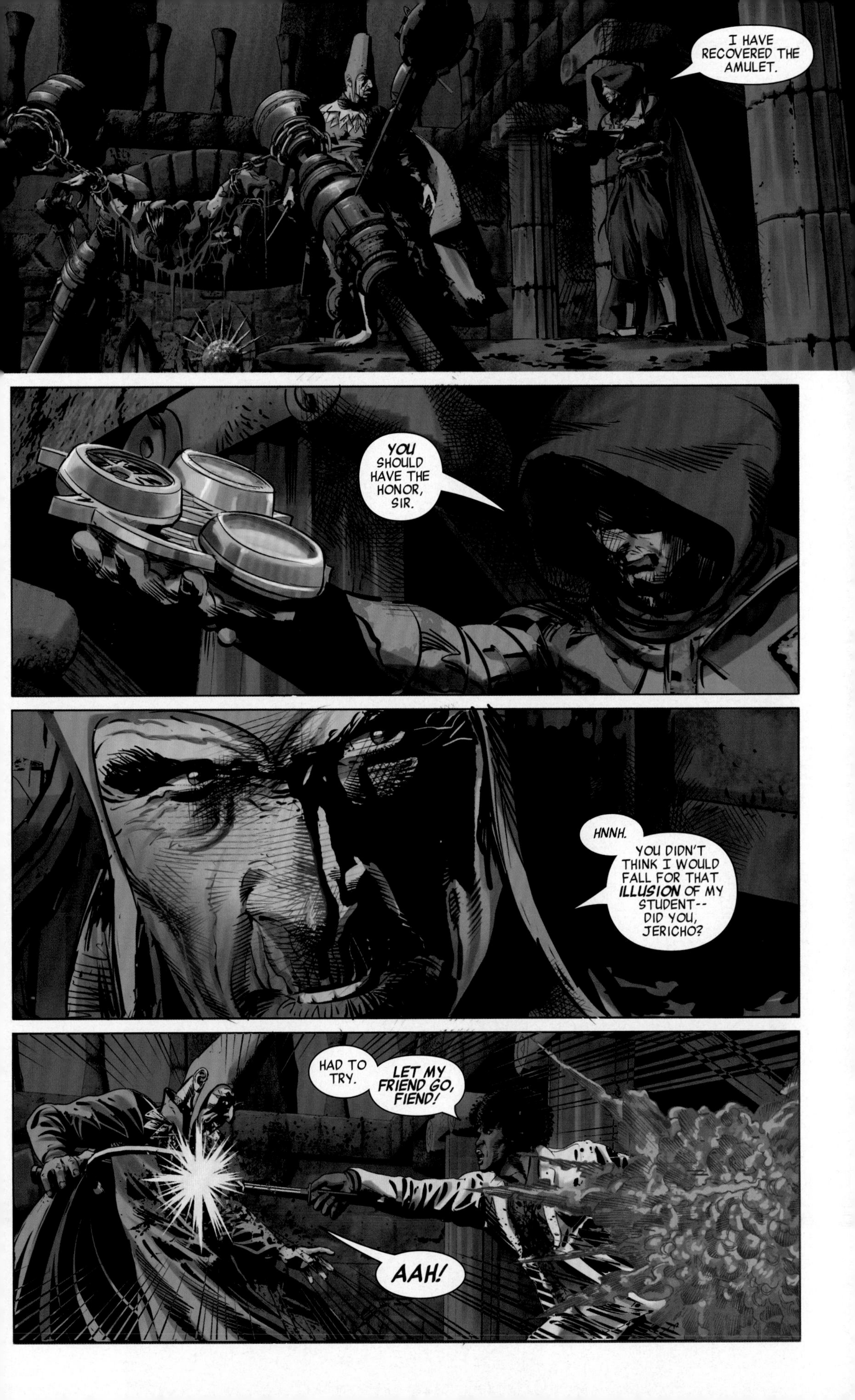
I HAVE RECOVERED THE AMULET.
YOU SHOULD HAVE THE HONOR, SIR.
HNNH.
YOU DIDN'T THINK I WOULD FALL FOR THAT ILLUSION OF MY STUDENT-- DID YOU, JERICHO?
HAD TO TRY.
LET MY FRIEND GO, FIEND!
AAH!

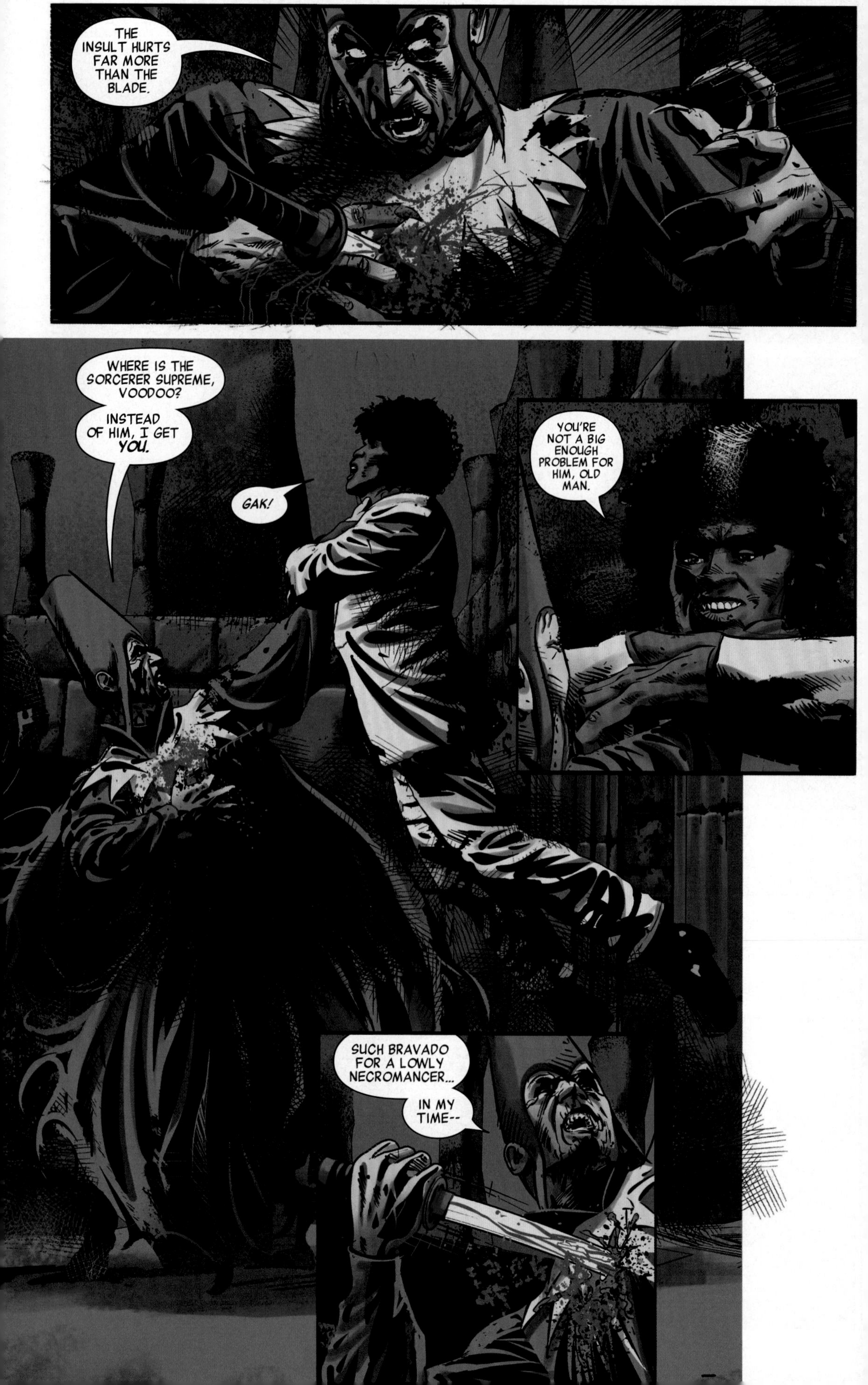
THE INSULT HURTS FAR MORE THAN THE BLADE.
WHERE IS THE SORCERER SUPREME, VOODOO?
INSTEAD OF HIM, I GET YOU.
GAK!
YOU'RE NOT A BIG ENOUGH PROBLEM FOR HIM, OLD MAN.
SUCH BRAVADO FOR A LOWLY NECROMANCER...
IN MY TIME--

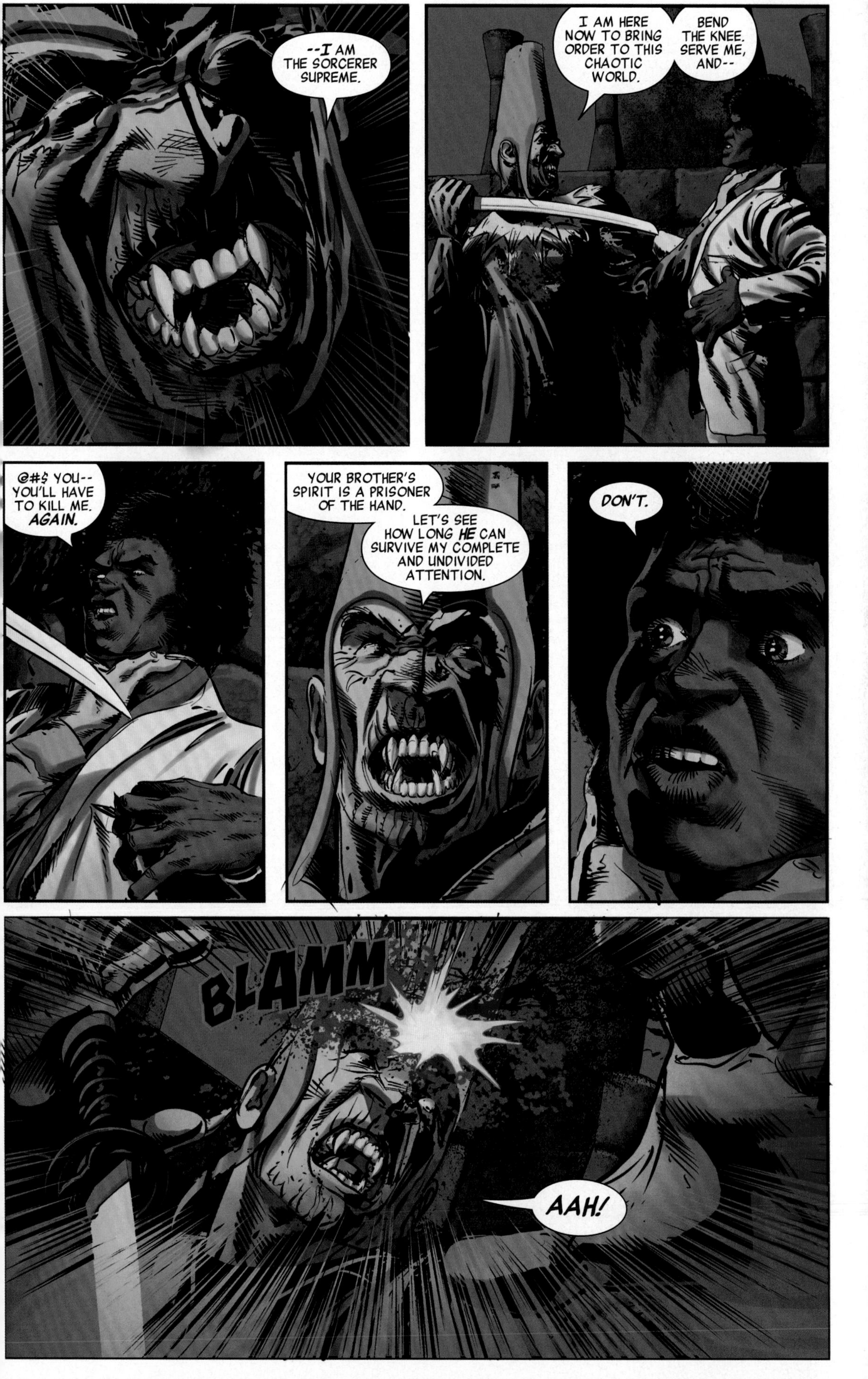
--I AM THE SORCERER SUPREME.
I AM HERE NOW TO BRING ORDER TO THIS CHAOTIC WORLD.
BEND THE KNEE. SERVE ME, AND--
@#$ YOU-- YOU'LL HAVE TO KILL ME. AGAIN.
YOUR BROTHER'S SPIRIT IS A PRISONER OF THE HAND.
LET'S SEE HOW LONG HE CAN SURVIVE MY COMPLETE AND UNDIVIDED ATTENTION.
DON'T.
BLAMM
AAH!

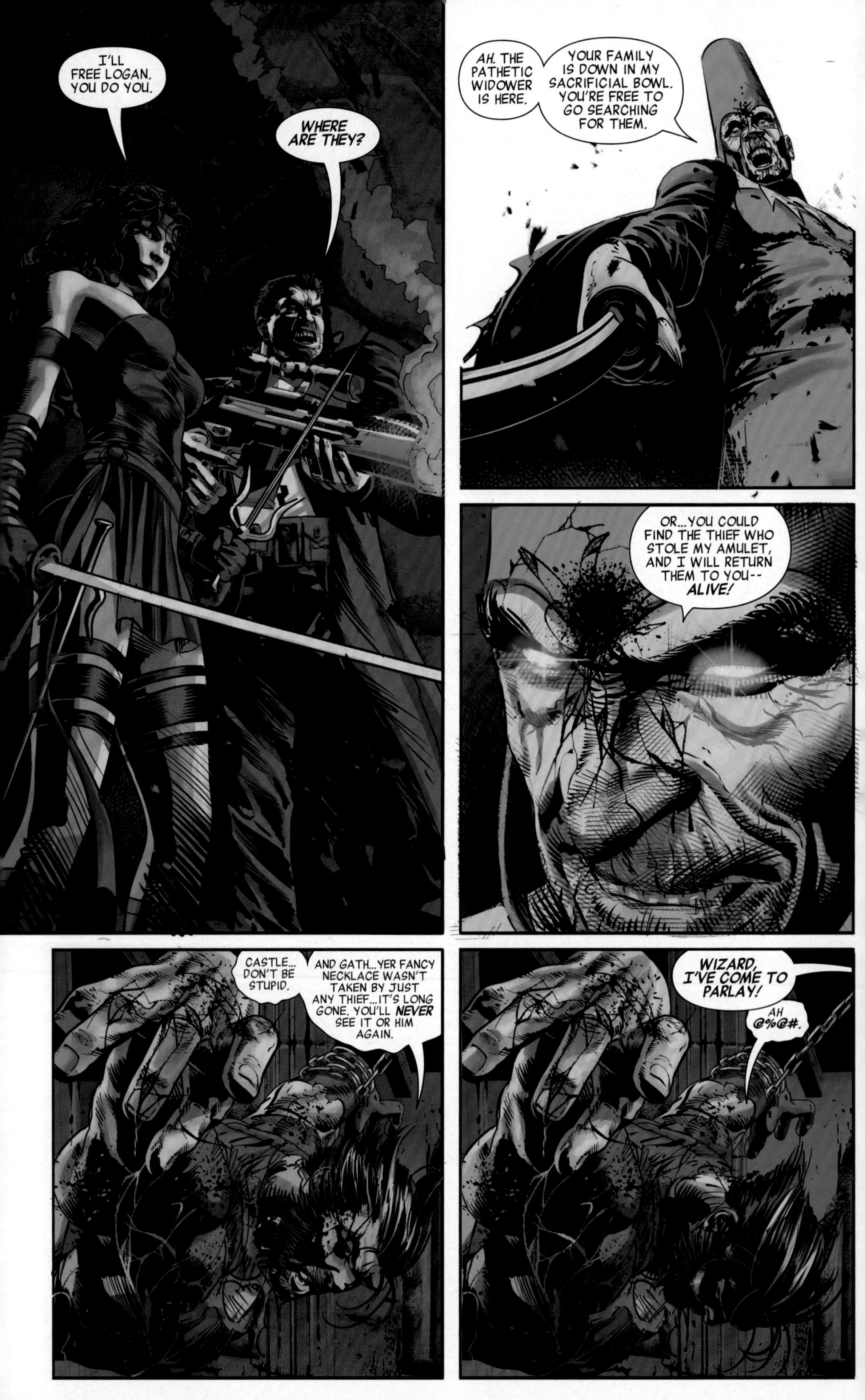
I'LL FREE LOGAN. YOU DO YOU.
WHERE ARE THEY?
AH. THE PATHETIC WIDOWER IS HERE.
YOUR FAMILY IS DOWN IN MY SACRIFICIAL BOWL. YOU'RE FREE TO GO SEARCHING FOR THEM.
OR...YOU COULD FIND THE THIEF WHO STOLE MY AMULET, AND I WILL RETURN THEM TO YOU-- ALIVE!
CASTLE... DON'T BE STUPID.
AND GATH...YER FANCY NECKLACE WASN'T TAKEN BY JUST ANY THIEF...IT'S LONG GONE. YOU'LL NEVER SEE IT OR HIM AGAIN.
WIZARD, I'VE COME TO PARLAY!
AH @%@#.

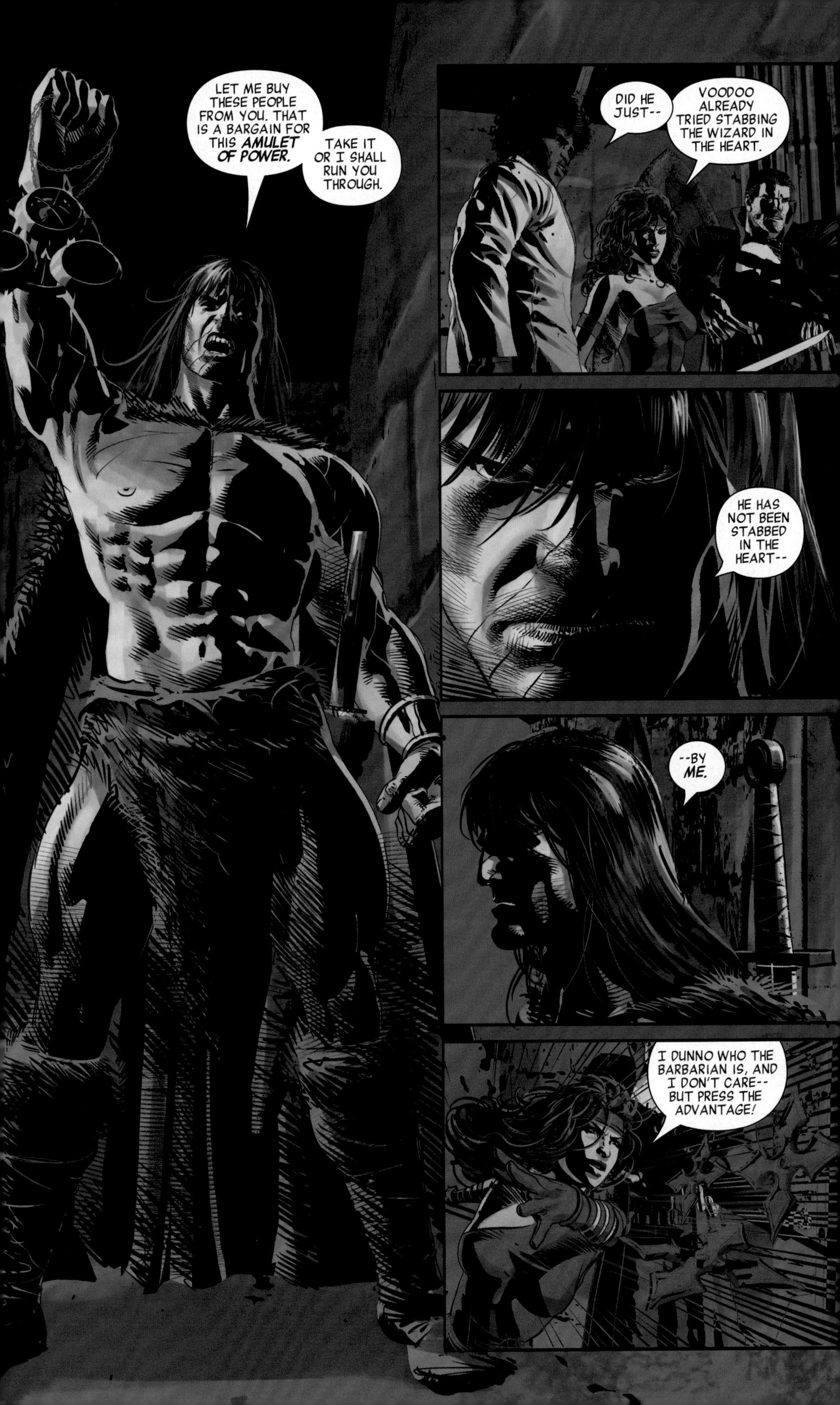

LET ME BUY THESE PEOPLE FROM YOU. THAT IS A BARGAIN FOR THIS AMULET OF POWER.
TAKE IT OR I SHALL RUN YOU THROUGH.
DID HE JUST--
VOODOO ALREADY TRIED STABBING THE WIZARD IN THE HEART.
HE HAS NOT BEEN STABBED IN THE HEART--
--BY ME.
I DUNNO WHO THE BARBARIAN IS, AND I DON'T CARE-- BUT PRESS THE ADVANTAGE!

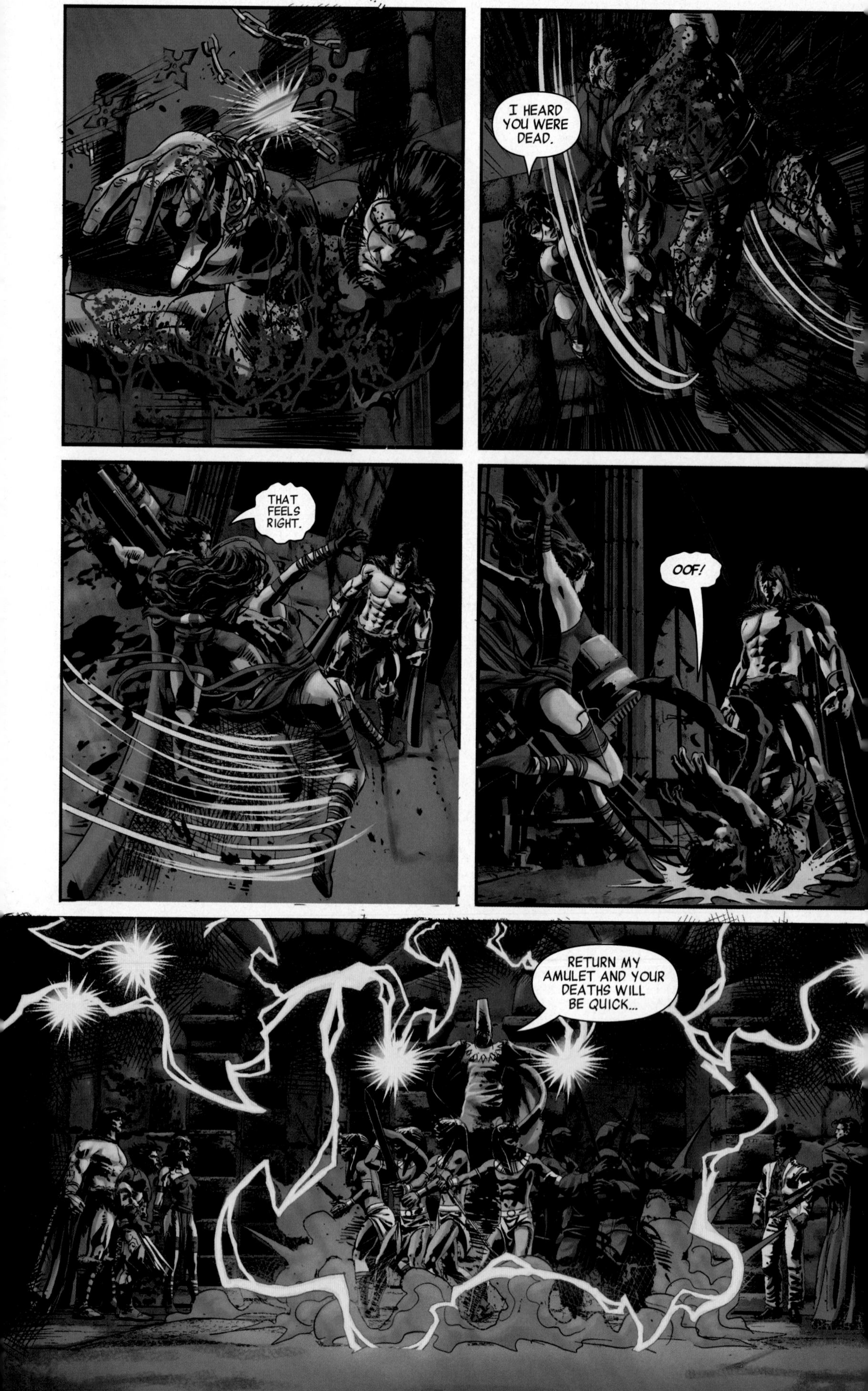
I HEARD YOU WERE DEAD.
THAT FEELS RIGHT.
OOF!
RETURN MY AMULET AND YOUR DEATHS WILL BE QUICK...

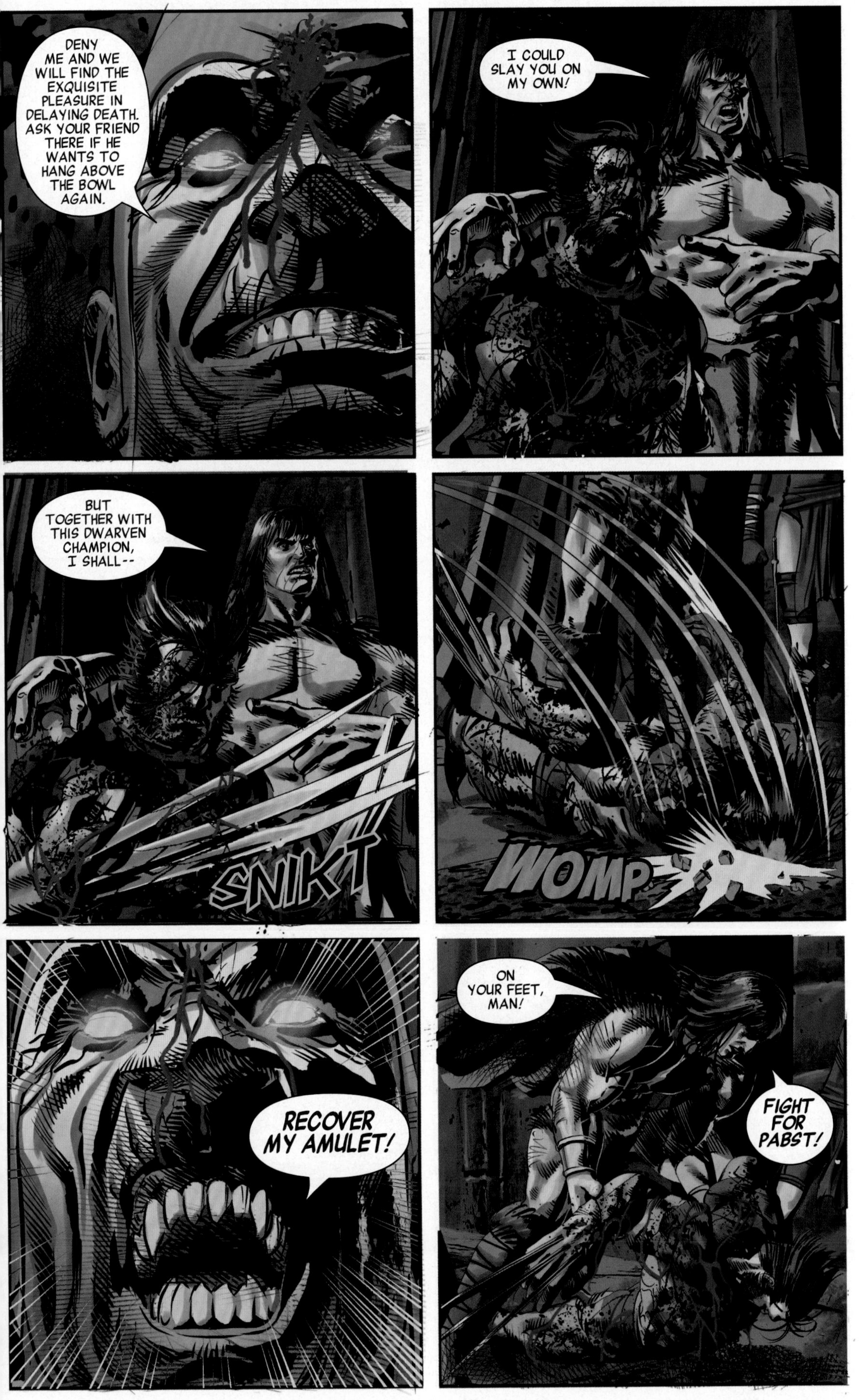
DENY ME AND WE WILL FIND THE EXQUISITE PLEASURE IN DELAYING DEATH. ASK YOUR FRIEND THERE IF HE WANTS TO HANG ABOVE THE BOWL AGAIN.
I COULD SLAY YOU ON MY OWN!
BUT TOGETHER WITH THIS DWARVEN CHAMPION, I SHALL--
SNIKT
WOMP
RECOVER MY AMULET!
ON YOUR FEET, MAN!
FIGHT FOR PABST!

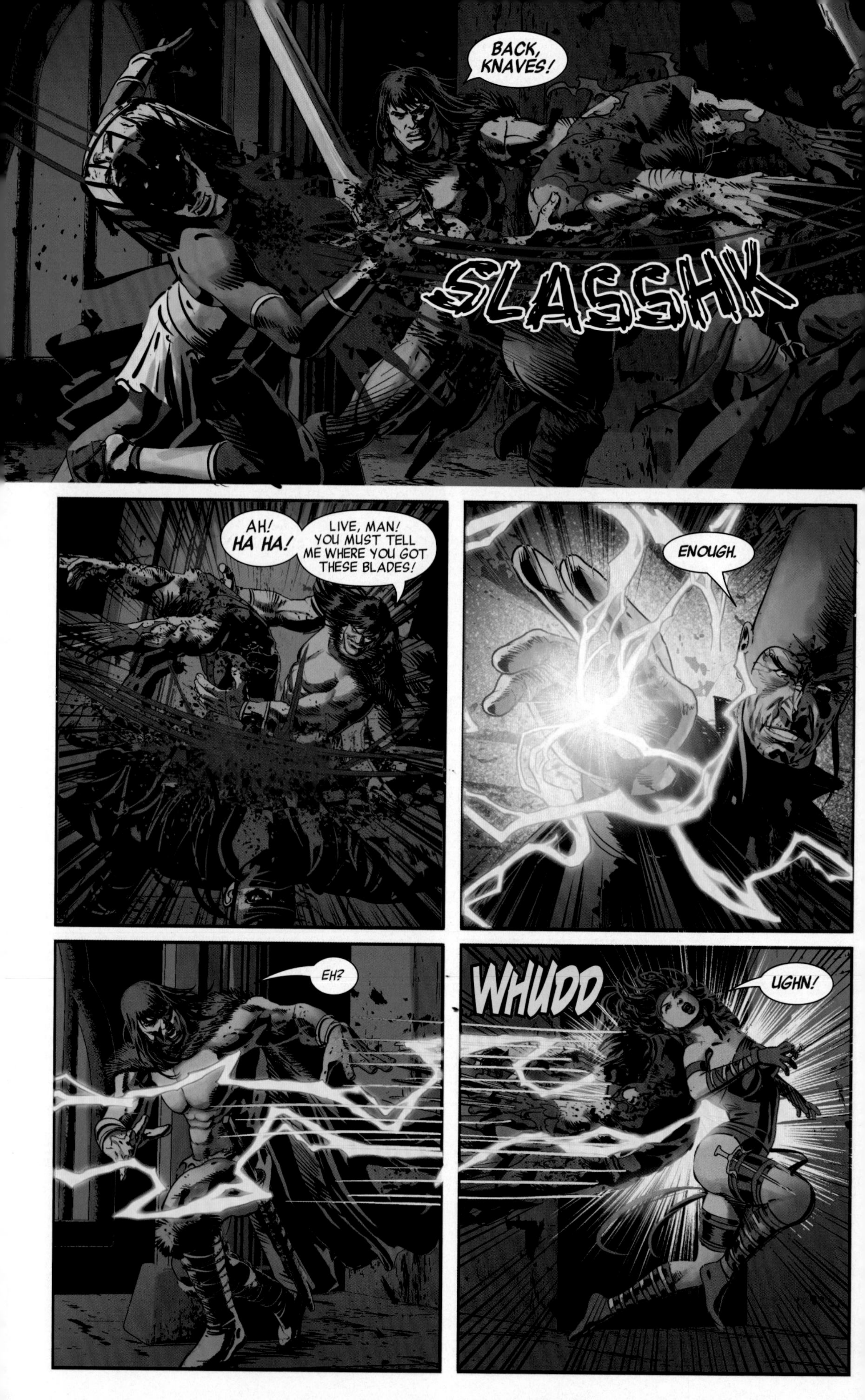
BACK, KNAVES!
SLASSHK
AH! HA HA!
LIVE, MAN! YOU MUST TELL ME WHERE YOU GOT THESE BLADES!
ENOUGH.
EH?
WHUDD
UGHN!

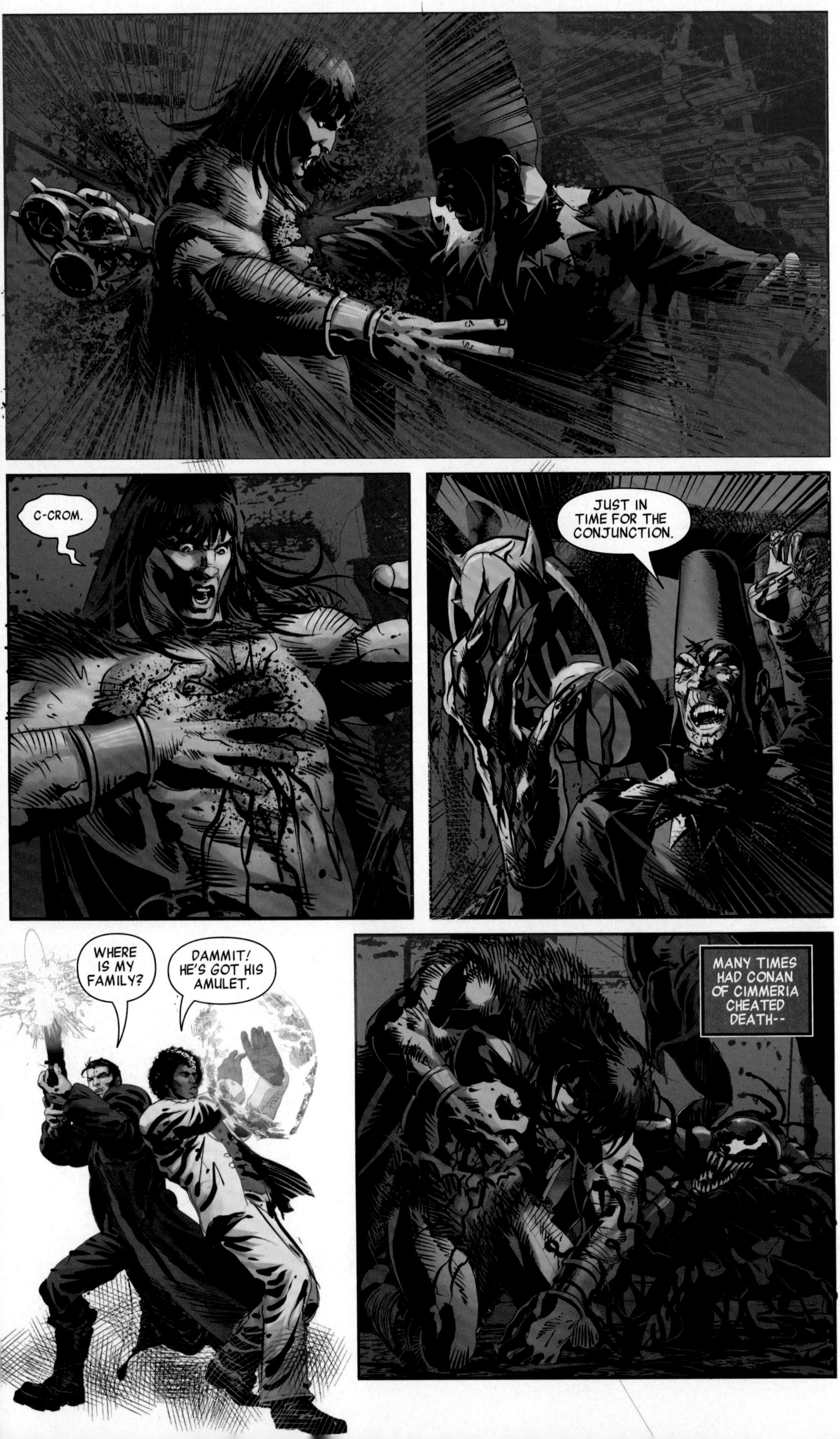
C-CROM.
JUST IN TIME FOR THE CONJUNCTION.
WHERE IS MY FAMILY?
DAMMIT! HE'S GOT HIS AMULET.
MANY TIMES HAD CONAN OF CIMMERIA CHEATED DEATH--

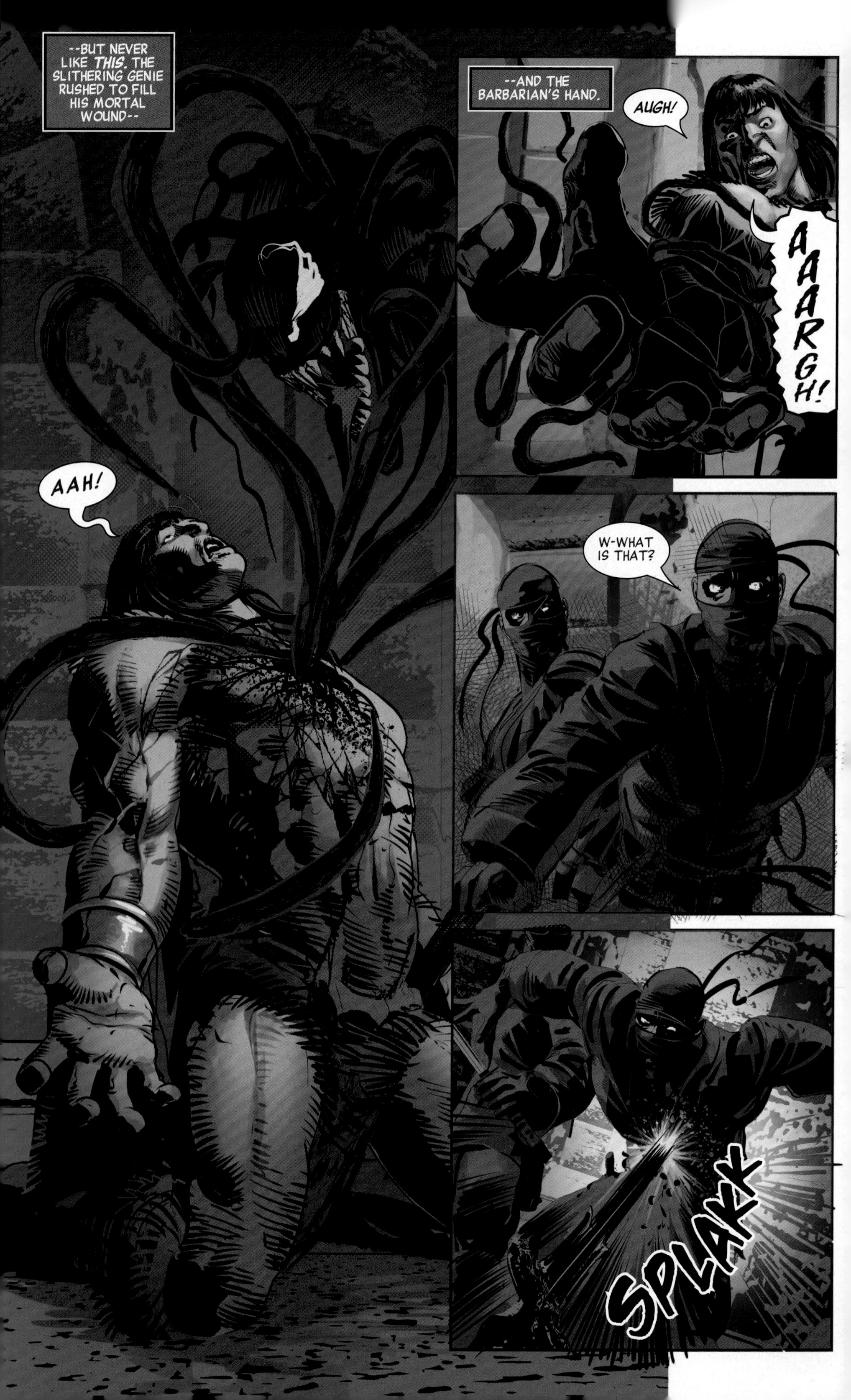
--BUT NEVER LIKE THIS. THE SLITHERING GENIE RUSHED TO FILL HIS MORTAL WOUND--
AAH!
--AND THE BARBARIAN'S HAND.
AUGH!
AAAARGH!
W-WHAT IS THAT?
SPLAKK

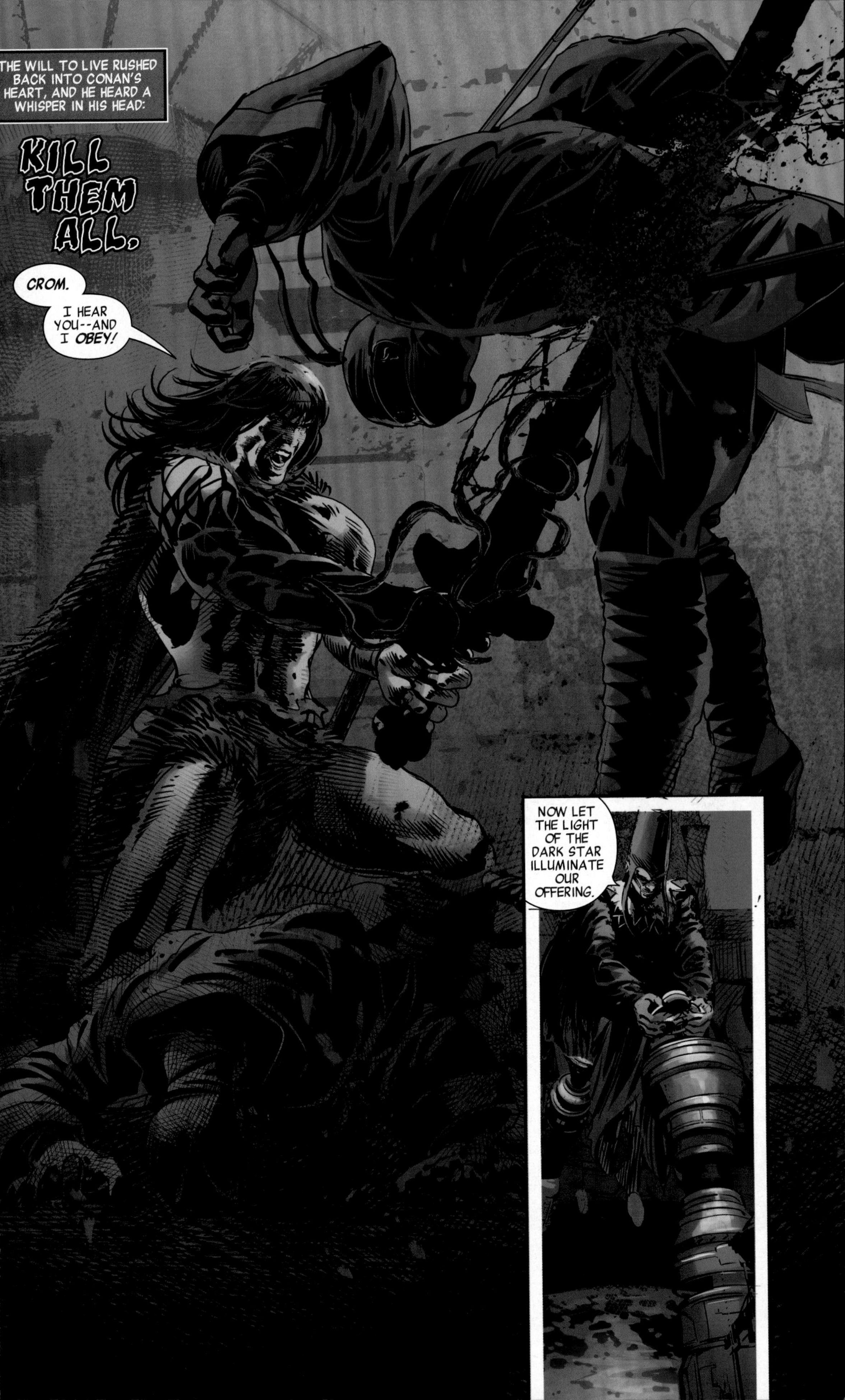
THE WILL TO LIVE RUSHED BACK INTO CONAN'S HEART, AND HE HEARD A WHISPER IN HIS HEAD:
KILL THEM ALL.
CROM.
I HEAR YOU--AND I OBEY!
NOW LET THE LIGHT OF THE DARK STAR ILLUMINATE OUR OFFERING.

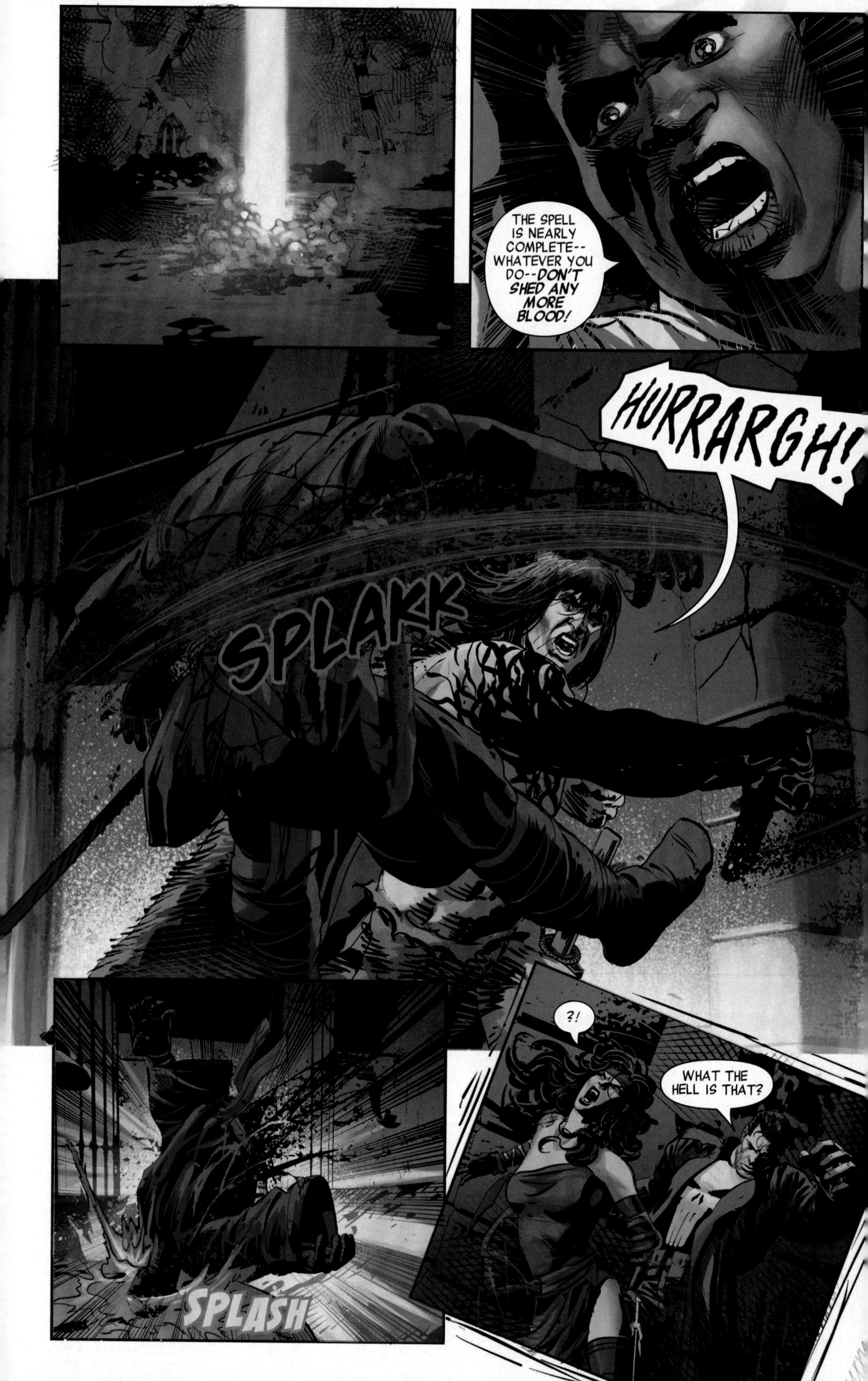

THE SPELL IS NEARLY COMPLETE--WHATEVER YOU DO--DON'T SHED ANY MORE BLOOD!
HURRARGH!
SPLAKK
SPLASH
?!
WHAT THE HELL IS THAT?

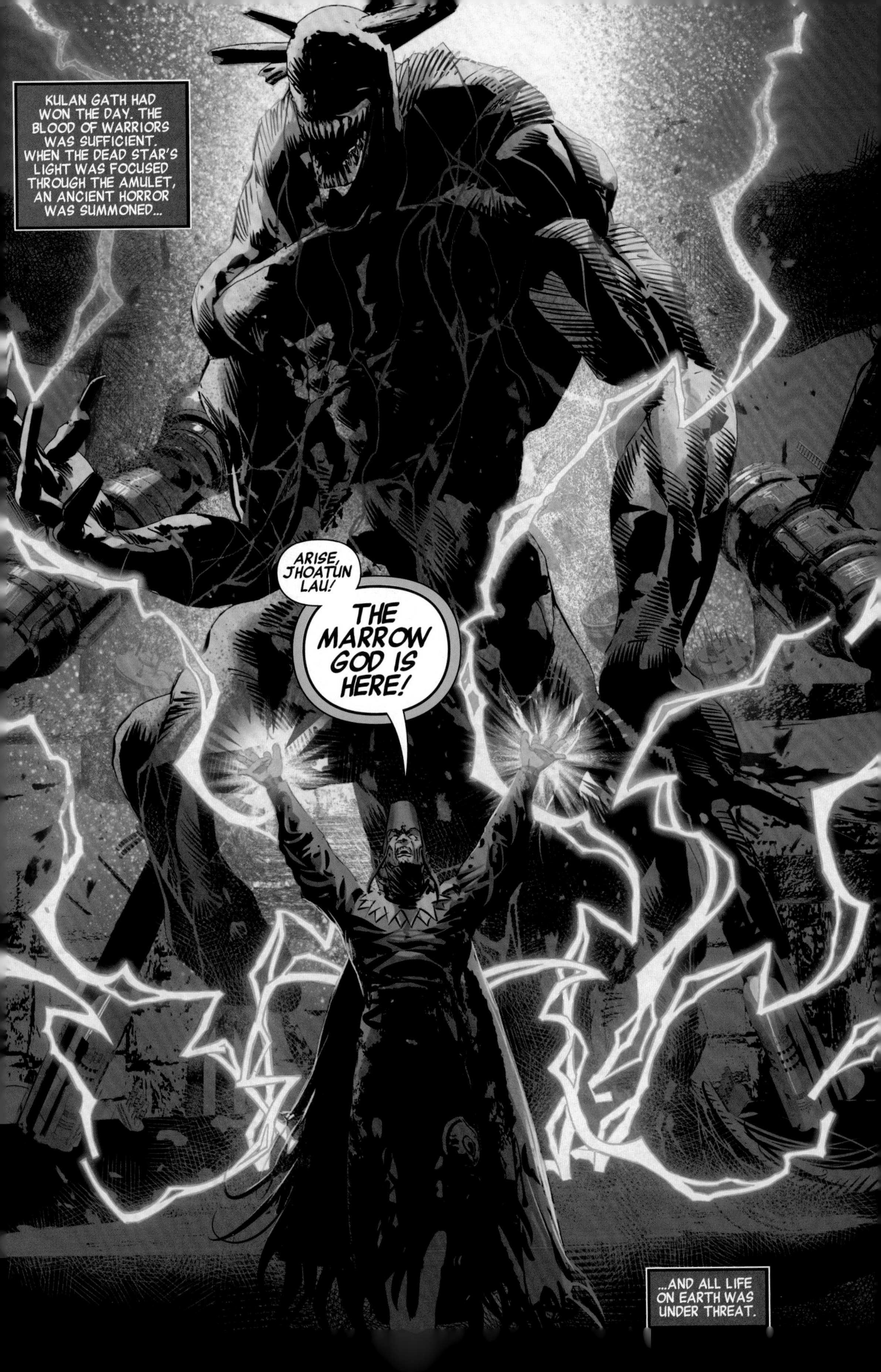
KULAN GATH HAD WON THE DAY. THE BLOOD OF WARRIORS WAS SUFFICIENT. WHEN THE DEAD STAR'S LIGHT WAS FOCUSED THROUGH THE AMULET, AN ANCIENT HORROR WAS SUMMONED...
ARISE, JHOATUN LAU!
THE MARROW GOD IS HERE!
...AND ALL LIFE ON EARTH WAS UNDER THREAT.

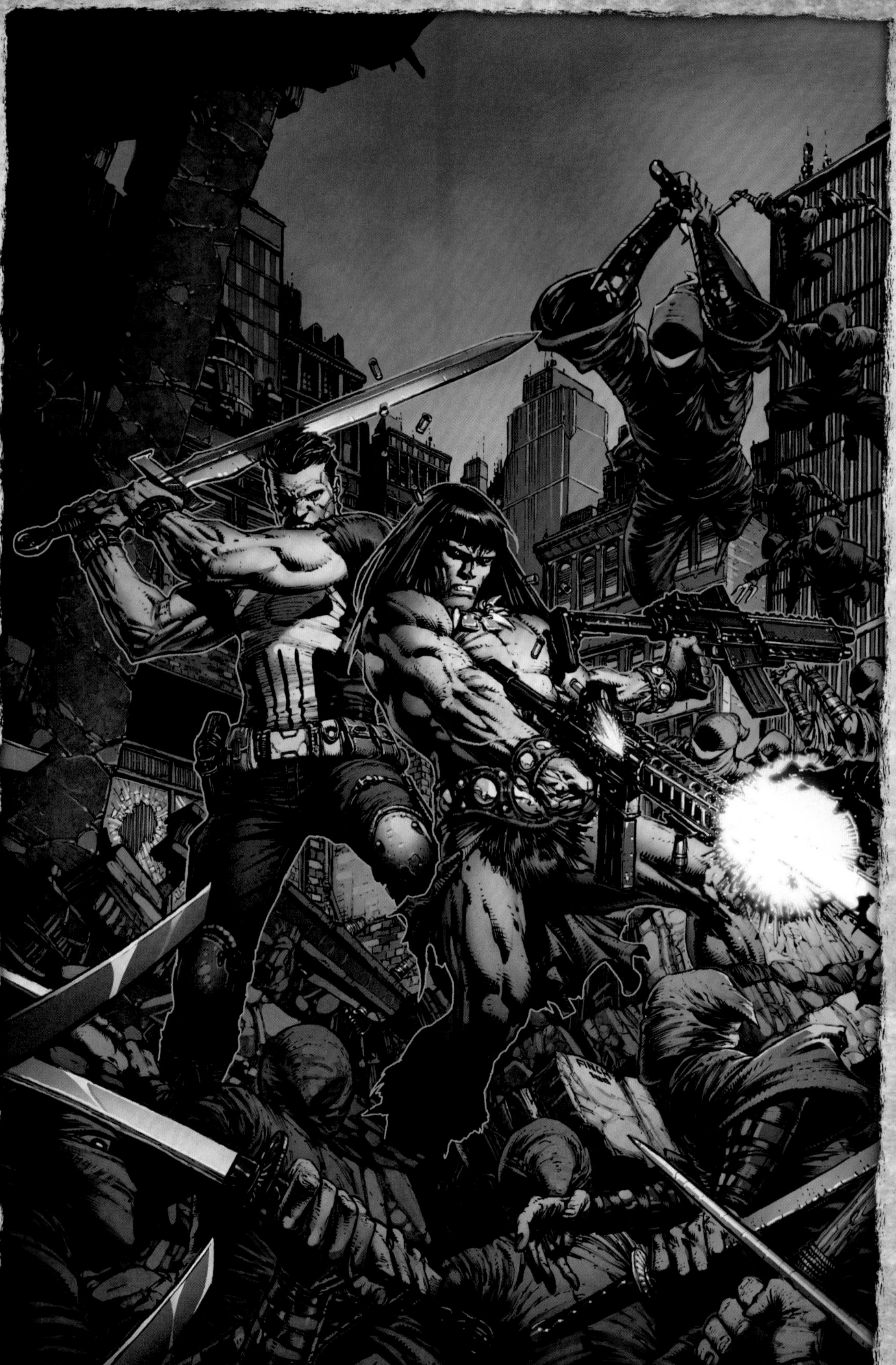

4: STRESS TEST

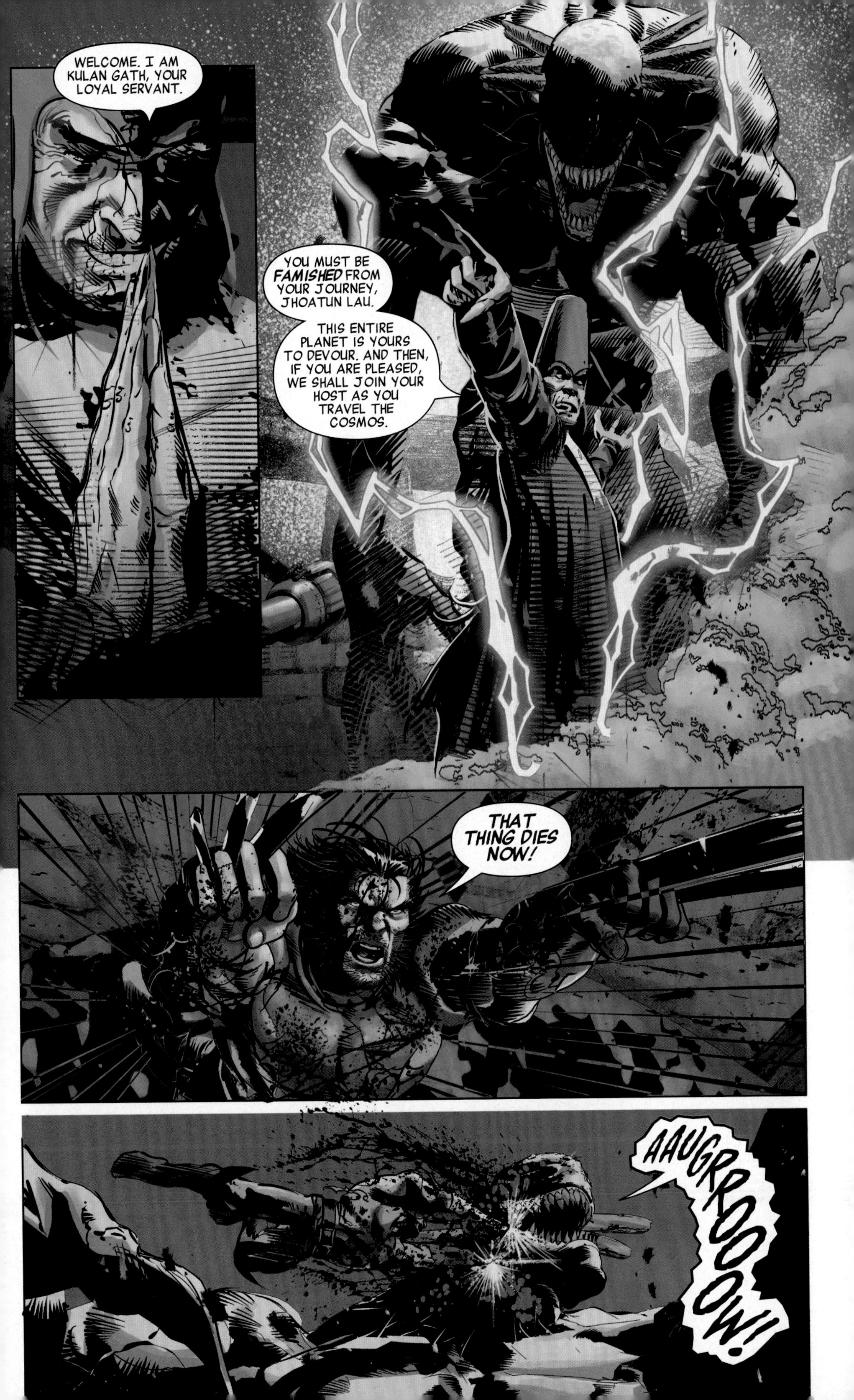
WELCOME. I AM KULAN GATH, YOUR LOYAL SERVANT.
YOU MUST BE FAMISHED FROM YOUR JOURNEY, JHOATUN LAU.
THIS ENTIRE PLANET IS YOURS TO DEVOUR. AND THEN, IF YOU ARE PLEASED, WE SHALL JOIN YOUR HOST AS YOU TRAVEL THE COSMOS.
THAT THING DIES NOW!
AAUGRROOOW!

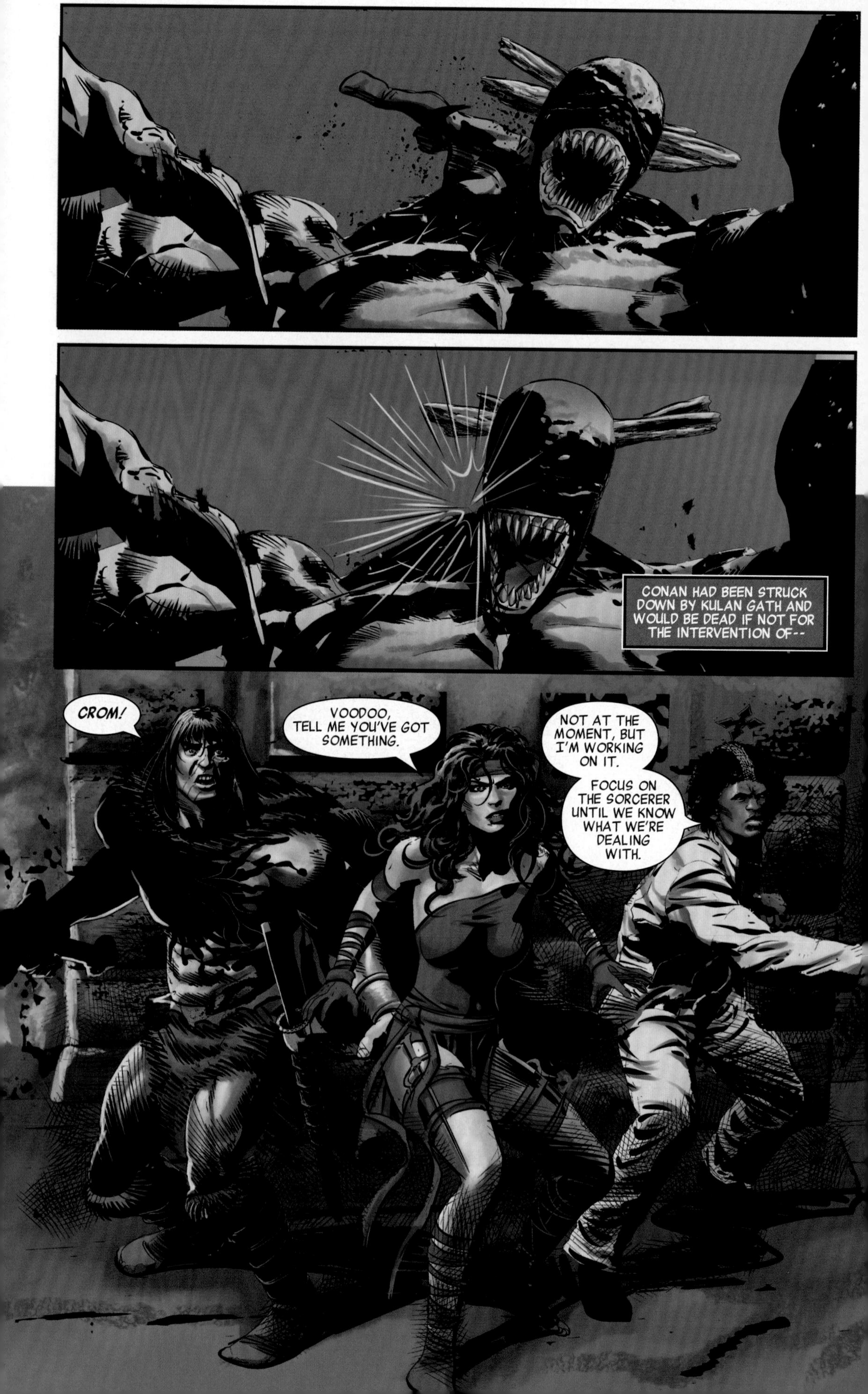

CONAN HAD BEEN STRUCK DOWN BY KULAN GATH AND WOULD BE DEAD IF NOT FOR THE INTERVENTION OF--
CROM!
VOODOO, TELL ME YOU'VE GOT SOMETHING.
NOT AT THE MOMENT, BUT I'M WORKING ON IT.
FOCUS ON THE SORCERER UNTIL WE KNOW WHAT WE'RE DEALING WITH.

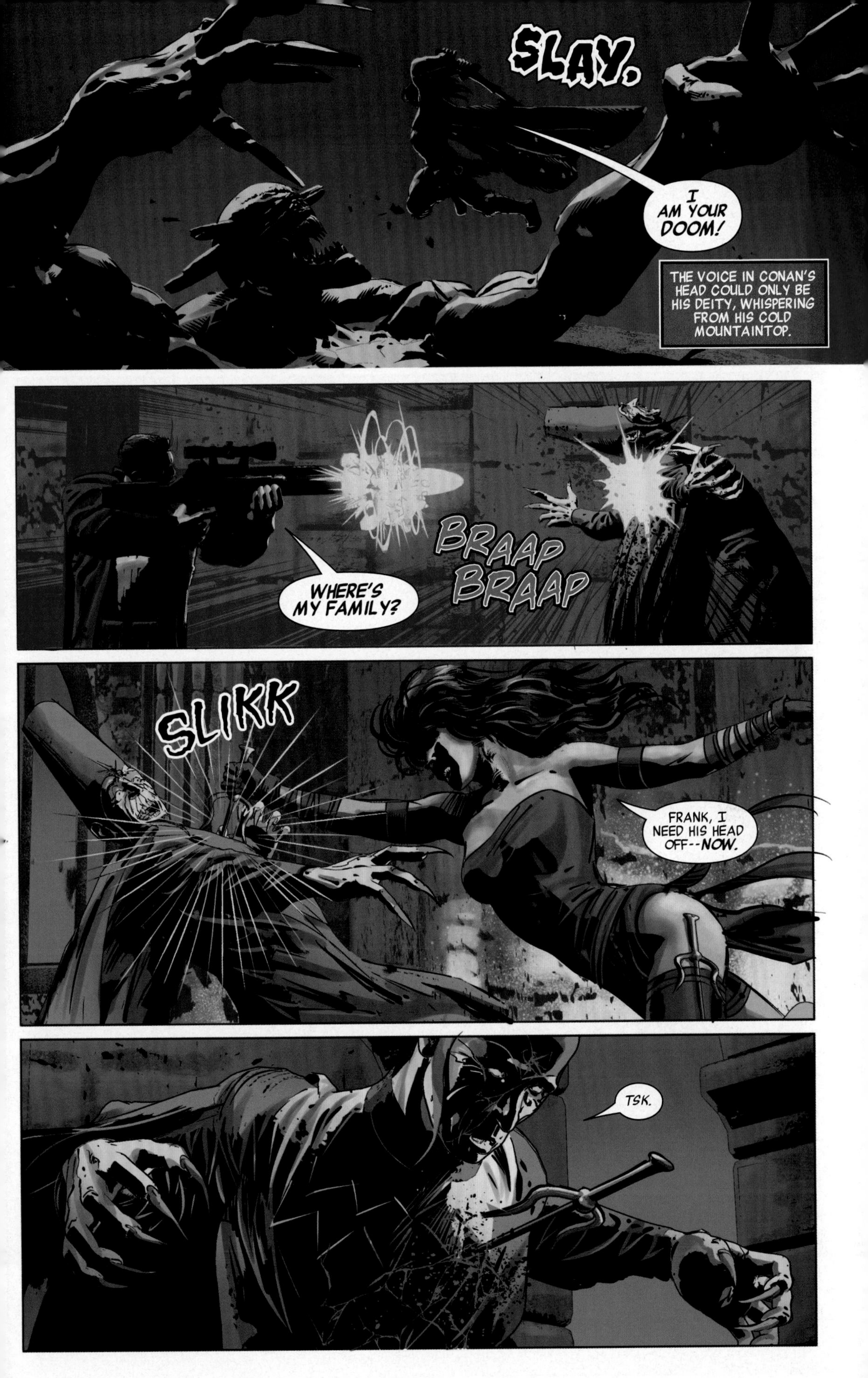
SLAY.
I AM YOUR DOOM!
THE VOICE IN CONAN'S HEAD COULD ONLY BE HIS DEITY, WHISPERING FROM HIS COLD MOUNTAINTOP.
WHERE'S MY FAMILY?
BRAAP BRAAP
SLIKK
FRANK, I NEED HIS HEAD OFF--NOW.
TSK.

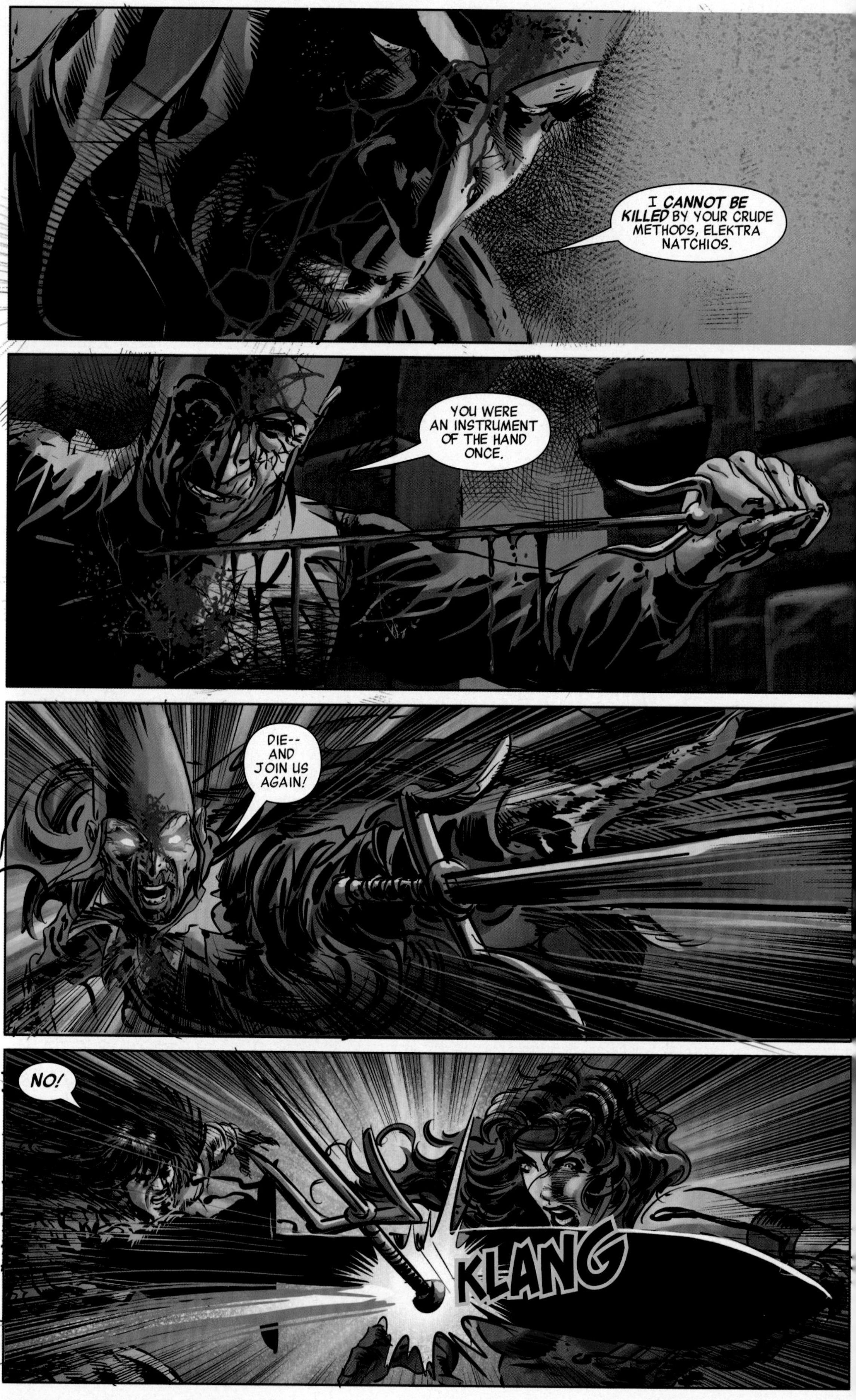
I CANNOT BE KILLED BY YOUR CRUDE METHODS, ELEKTRA NATCHIOS.
YOU WERE AN INSTRUMENT OF THE HAND ONCE.
DIE--AND JOIN US AGAIN!
NO!
KLANG

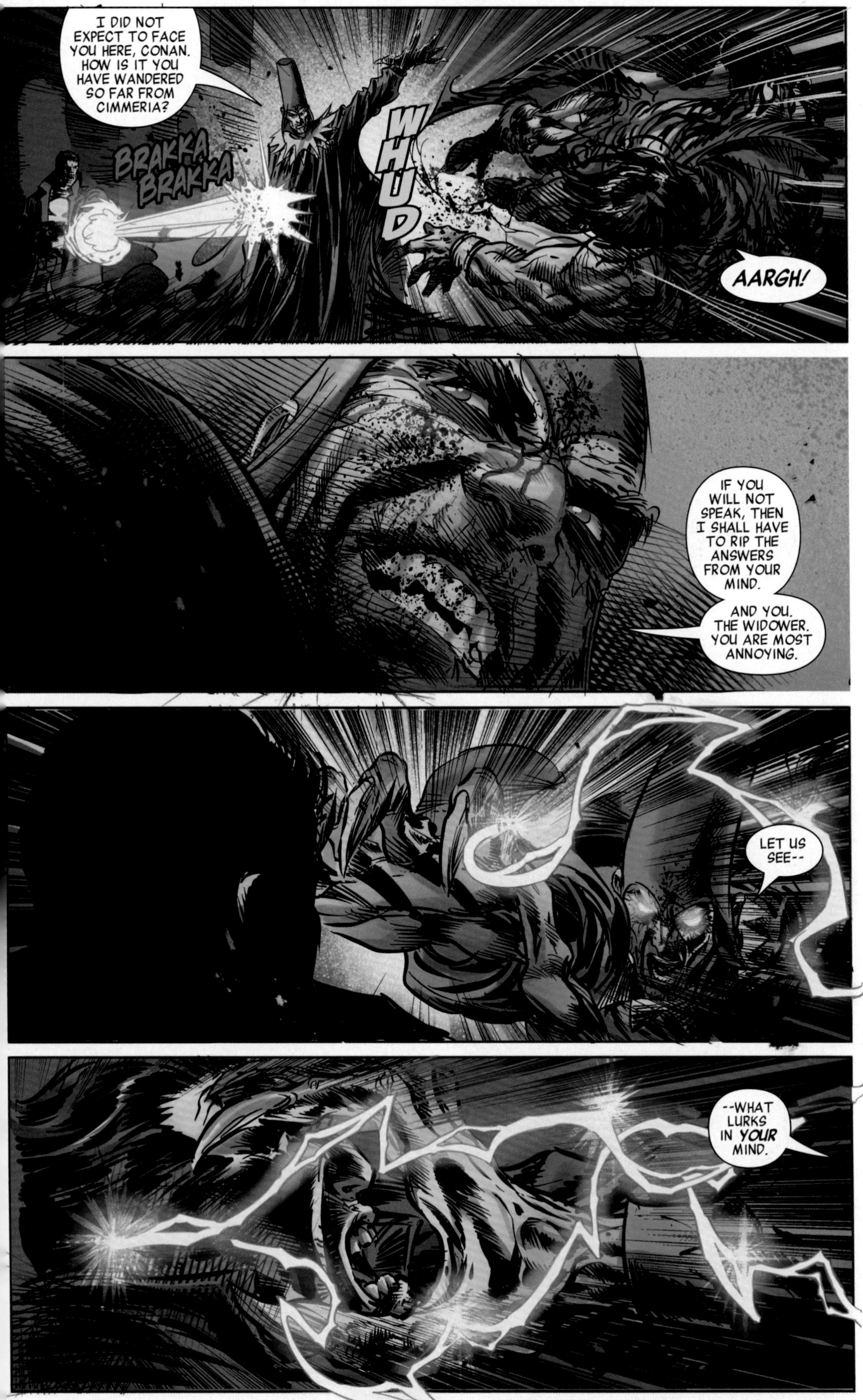

I DID NOT EXPECT TO FACE YOU HERE, CONAN. HOW IS IT YOU HAVE WANDERED SO FAR FROM CIMMERIA?
BRAKKA BRAKKA
WHUD
AARGH!
IF YOU WILL NOT SPEAK, THEN I SHALL HAVE TO RIP THE ANSWERS FROM YOUR MIND.
AND YOU, THE WIDOWER. YOU ARE MOST ANNOYING.
LET US SEE--
--WHAT LURKS IN YOUR MIND.

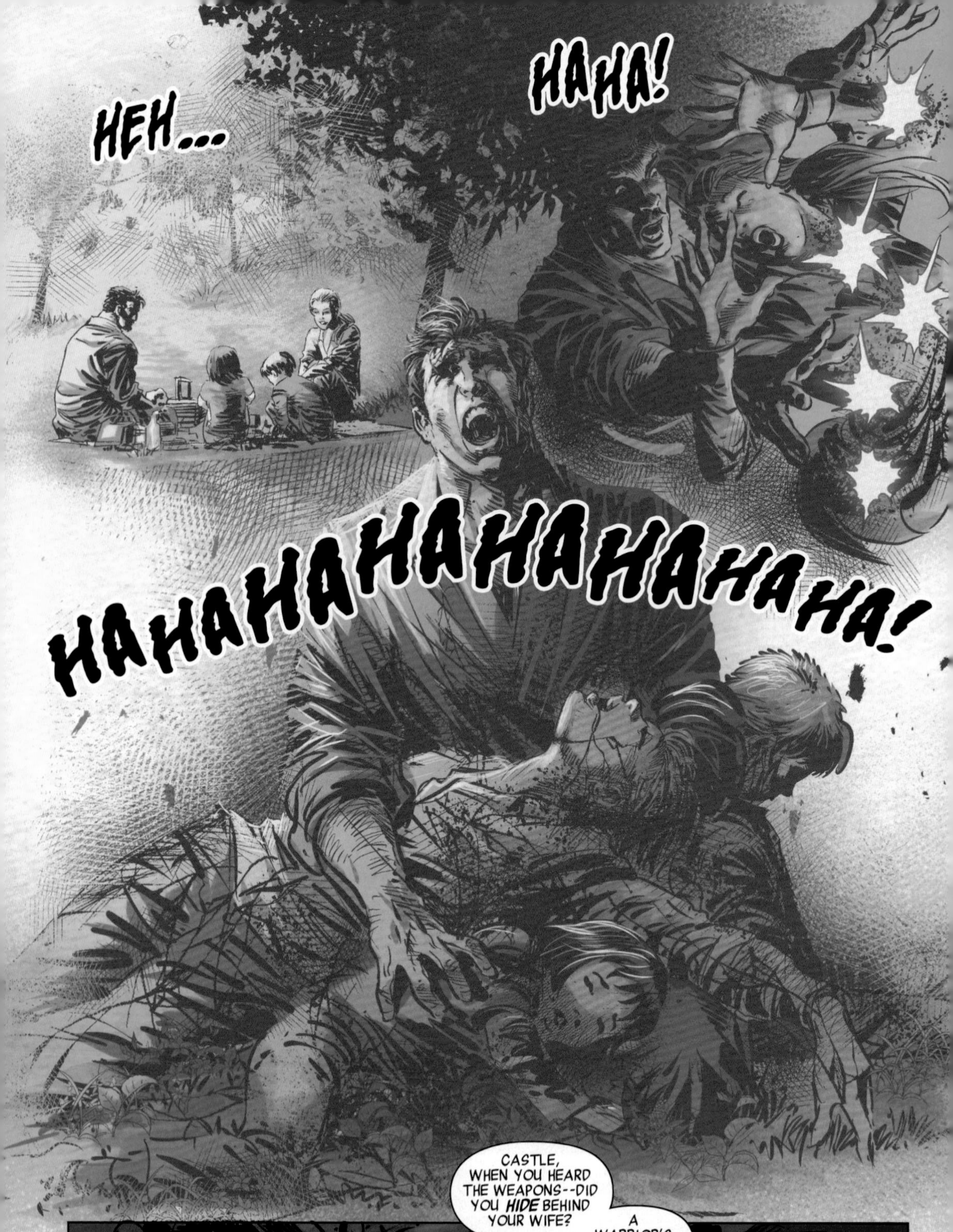
HEH...
HAHA!
HAHAHAHAHAHAHAHAHAHAHA!

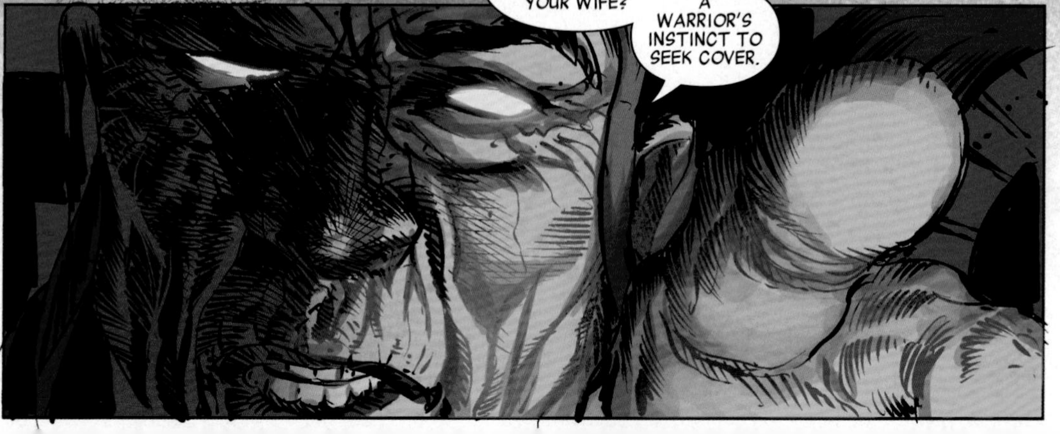
CASTLE, WHEN YOU HEARD THE WEAPONS--DID YOU *HIDE* BEHIND YOUR WIFE?
A WARRIOR'S INSTINCT TO SEEK COVER.

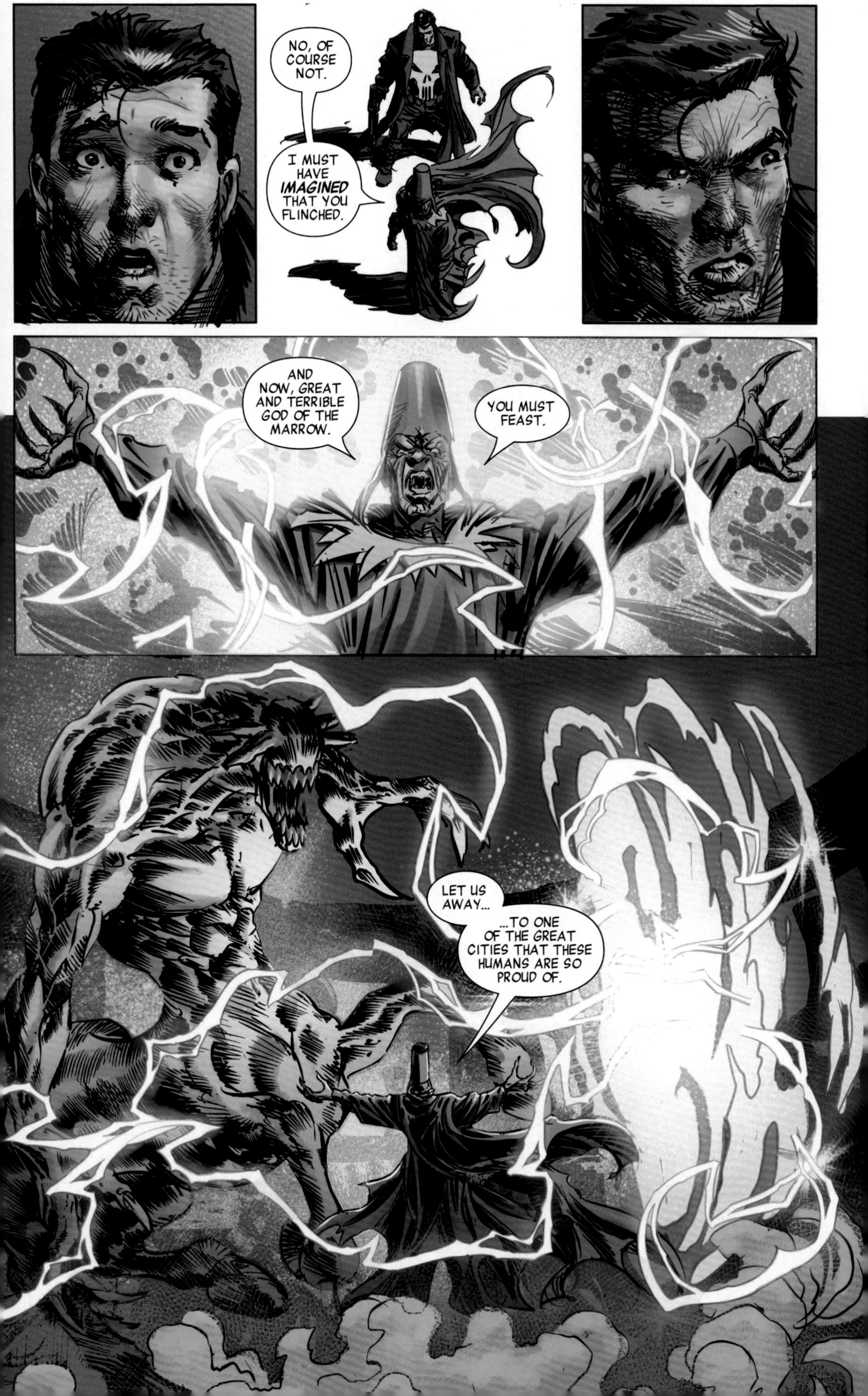
NO, OF COURSE NOT.
I MUST HAVE IMAGINED THAT YOU FLINCHED.
AND NOW, GREAT AND TERRIBLE GOD OF THE MARROW.
YOU MUST FEAST.
LET US AWAY...
...TO ONE OF THE GREAT CITIES THAT THESE HUMANS ARE SO PROUD OF.

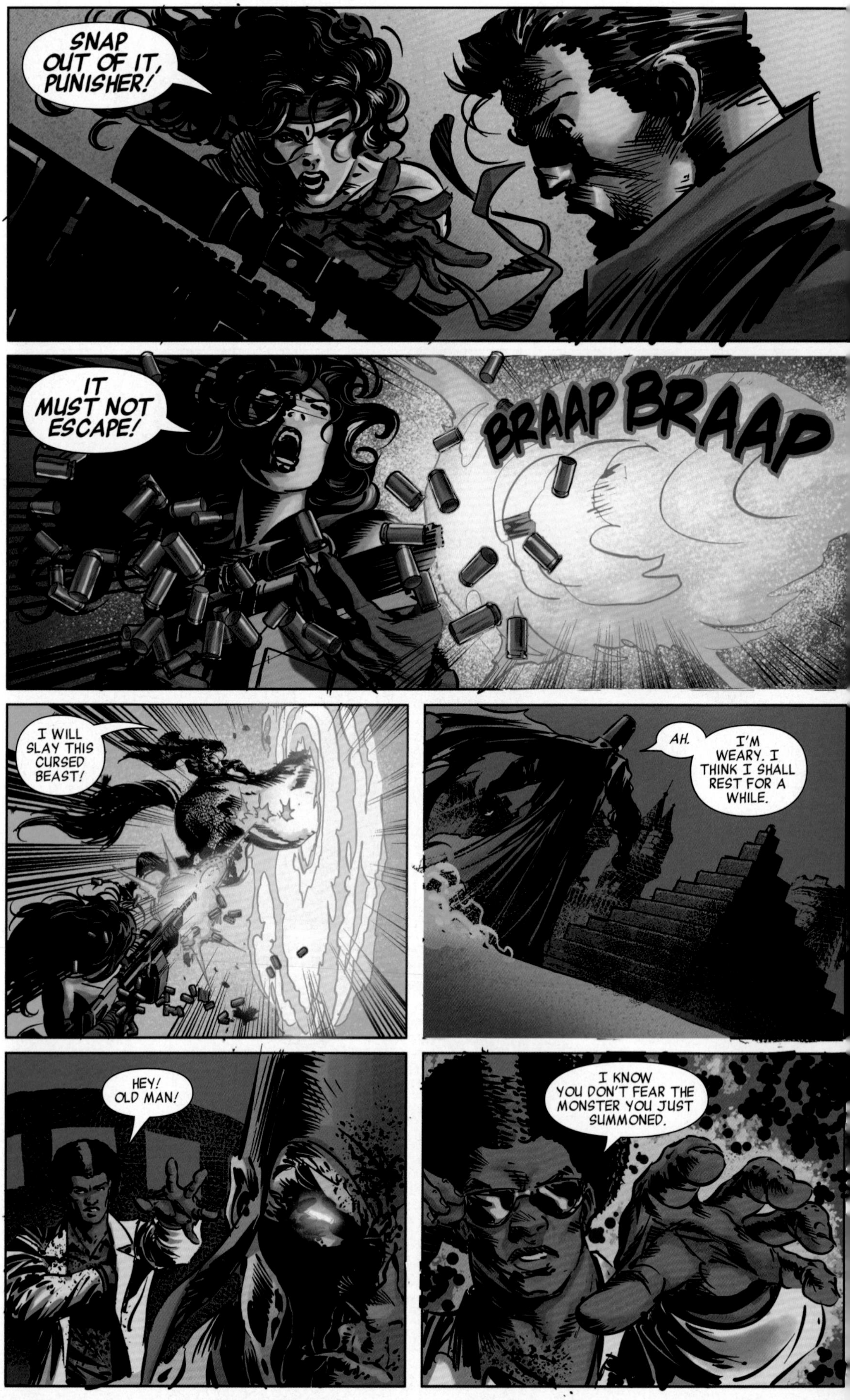
SNAP OUT OF IT, PUNISHER!
IT MUST NOT ESCAPE!
BRAAP BRAAP
I WILL SLAY THIS CURSED BEAST!
AH.
I'M WEARY. I THINK I SHALL REST FOR A WHILE.
HEY! OLD MAN!
I KNOW YOU DON'T FEAR THE MONSTER YOU JUST SUMMONED.

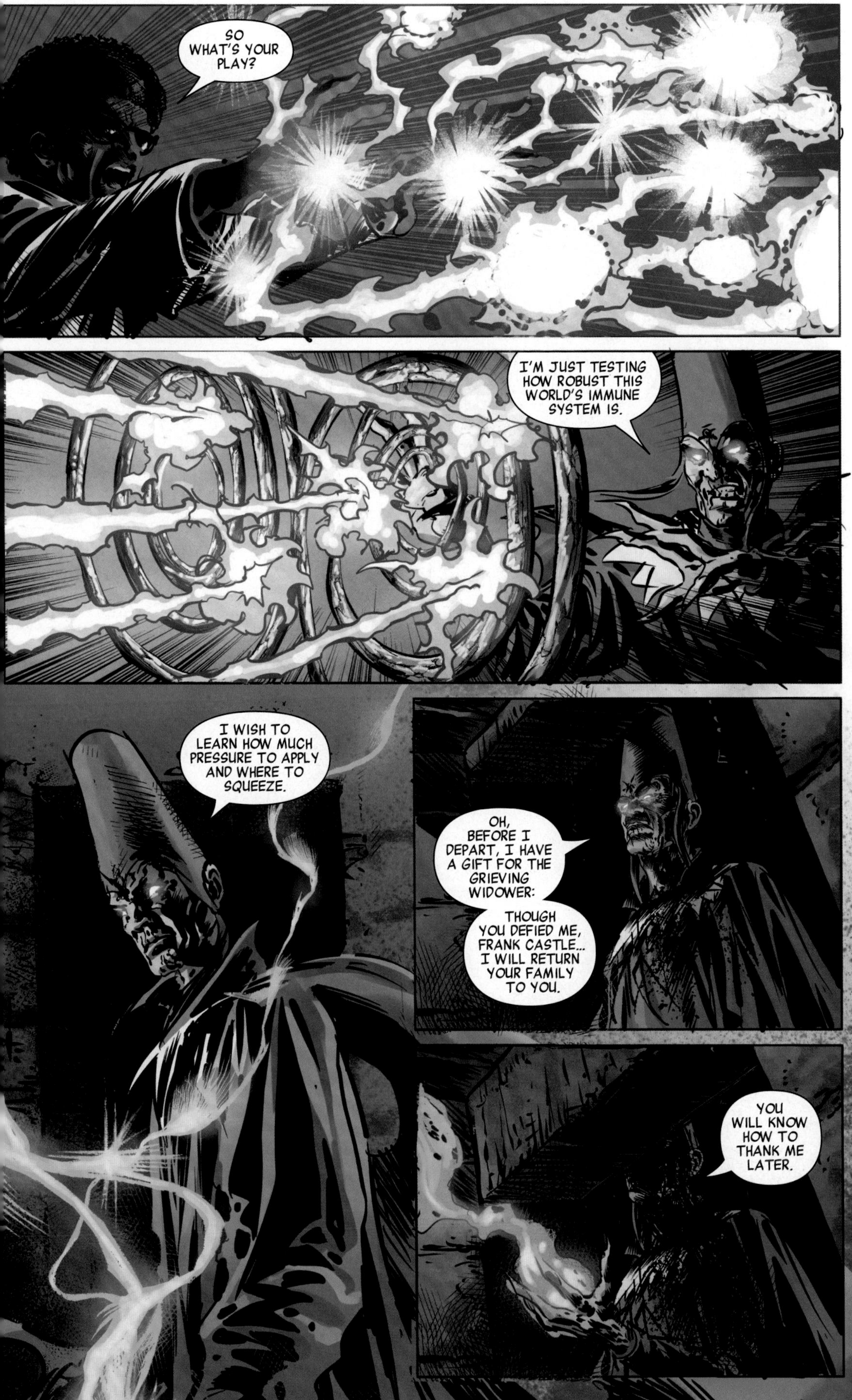
SO WHAT'S YOUR PLAY?
I'M JUST TESTING HOW ROBUST THIS WORLD'S IMMUNE SYSTEM IS.
I WISH TO LEARN HOW MUCH PRESSURE TO APPLY AND WHERE TO SQUEEZE.
OH, BEFORE I DEPART, I HAVE A GIFT FOR THE GRIEVING WIDOWER:
THOUGH YOU DEFIED ME, FRANK CASTLE... I WILL RETURN YOUR FAMILY TO YOU.
YOU WILL KNOW HOW TO THANK ME LATER.

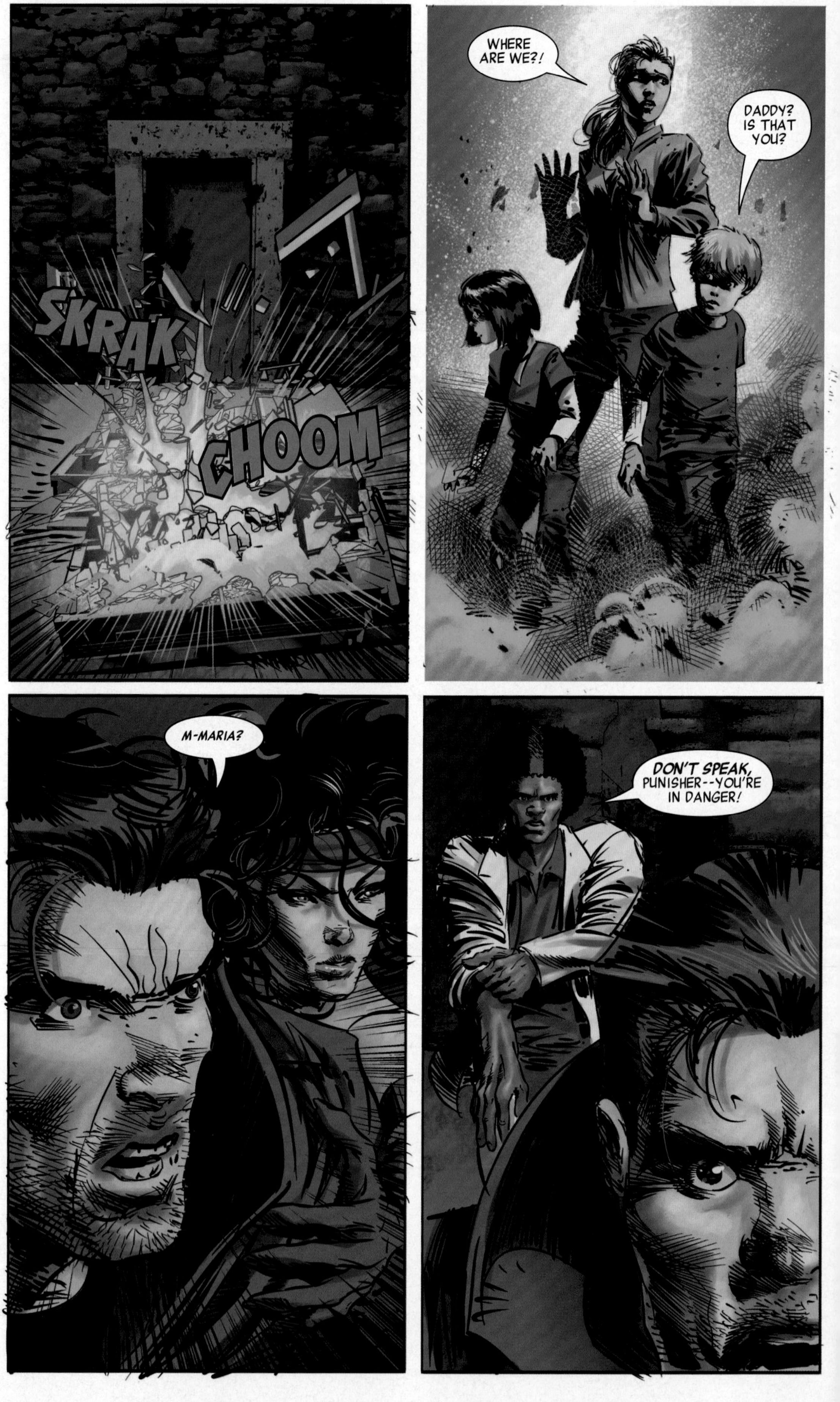
SKRAK
CHOOM
WHERE ARE WE?!
DADDY? IS THAT YOU?
M-MARIA?
DON'T SPEAK, PUNISHER--YOU'RE IN DANGER!

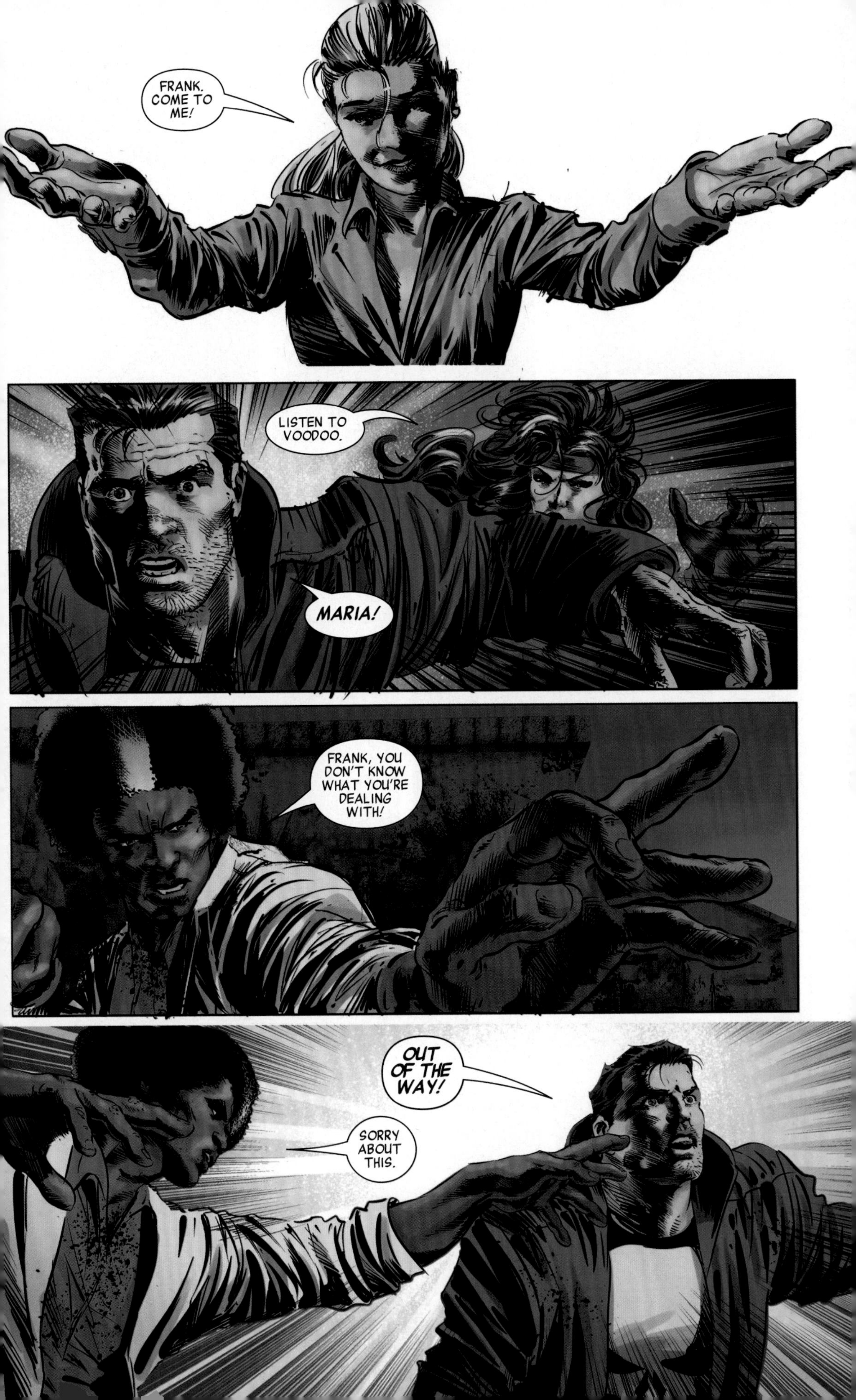
FRANK. COME TO ME!
LISTEN TO VOODOO.
MARIA!
FRANK, YOU DON'T KNOW WHAT YOU'RE DEALING WITH!
OUT OF THE WAY!
SORRY ABOUT THIS.

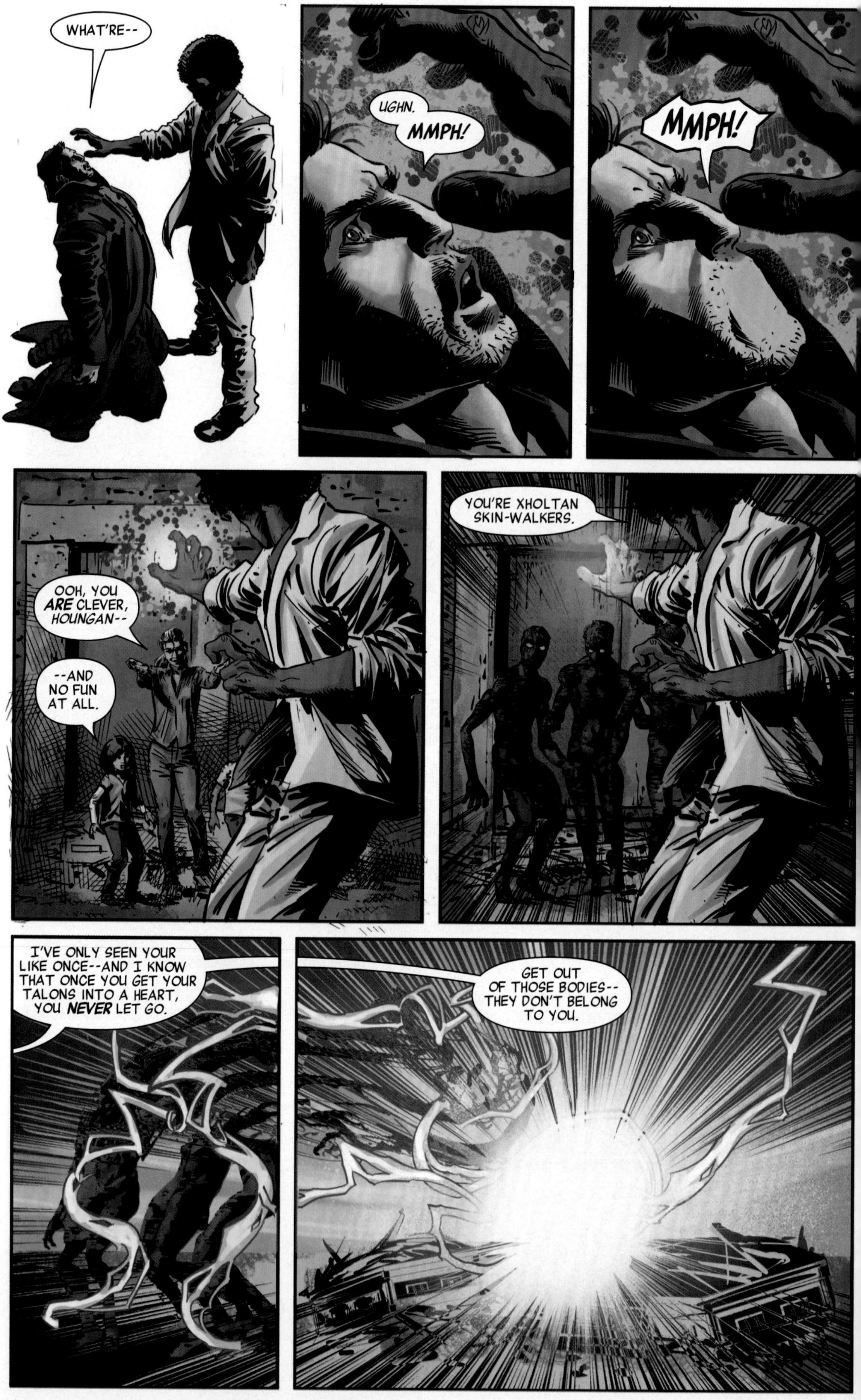
WHAT'RE--
UGHN.
MMPH!
MMPH!
OOH, YOU ARE CLEVER, HOUNGAN--
--AND NO FUN AT ALL.
YOU'RE XHOLTAN SKIN-WALKERS.
I'VE ONLY SEEN YOUR LIKE ONCE--AND I KNOW THAT ONCE YOU GET YOUR TALONS INTO A HEART, YOU NEVER LET GO.
GET OUT OF THOSE BODIES--THEY DON'T BELONG TO YOU.

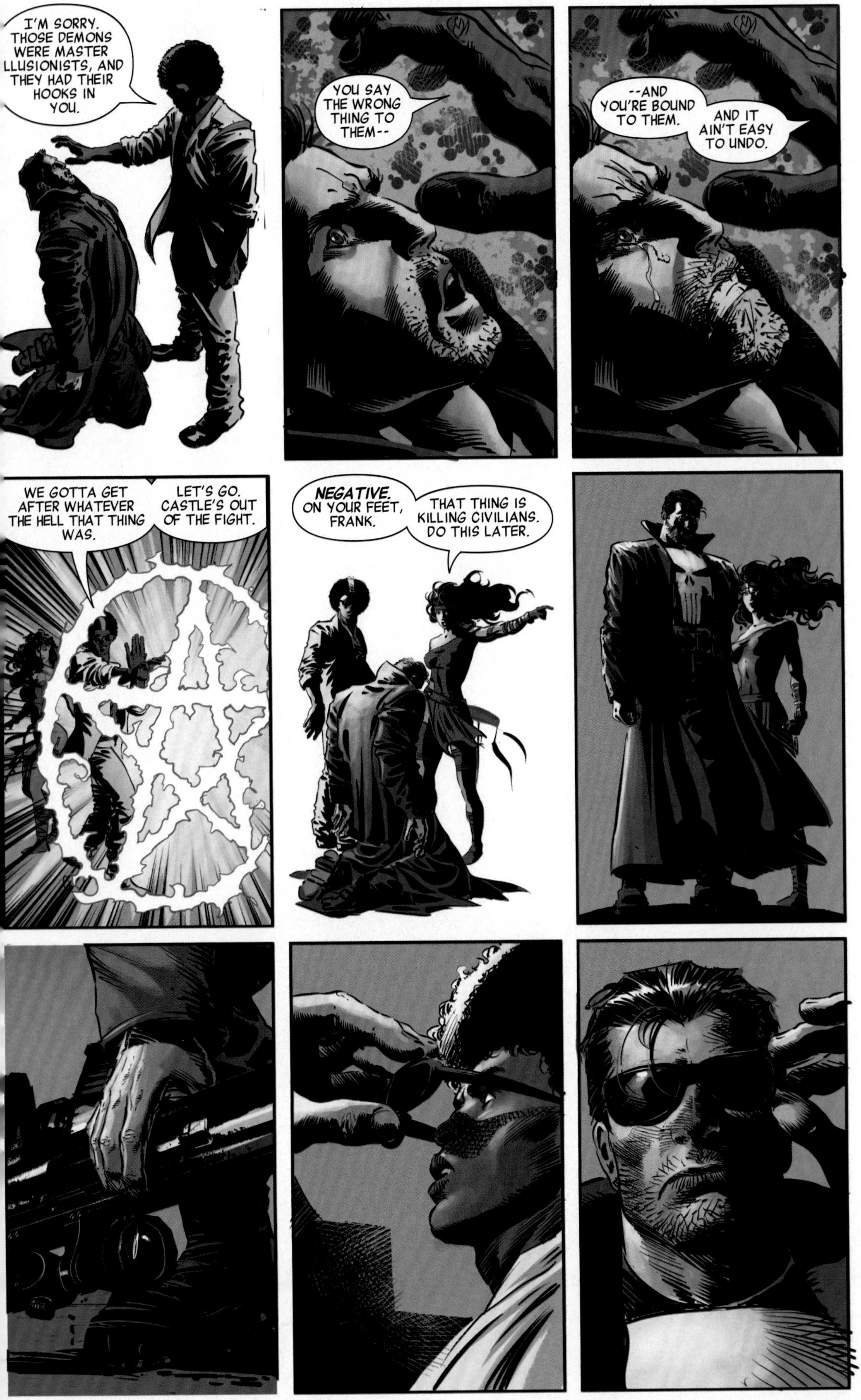
I'M SORRY. THOSE DEMONS WERE MASTER ILLUSIONISTS, AND THEY HAD THEIR HOOKS IN YOU.
YOU SAY THE WRONG THING TO THEM--
--AND YOU'RE BOUND TO THEM.
AND IT AIN'T EASY TO UNDO.
WE GOTTA GET AFTER WHATEVER THE HELL THAT THING WAS.
LET'S GO. CASTLE'S OUT OF THE FIGHT.
NEGATIVE. ON YOUR FEET, FRANK.
THAT THING IS KILLING CIVILIANS. DO THIS LATER.

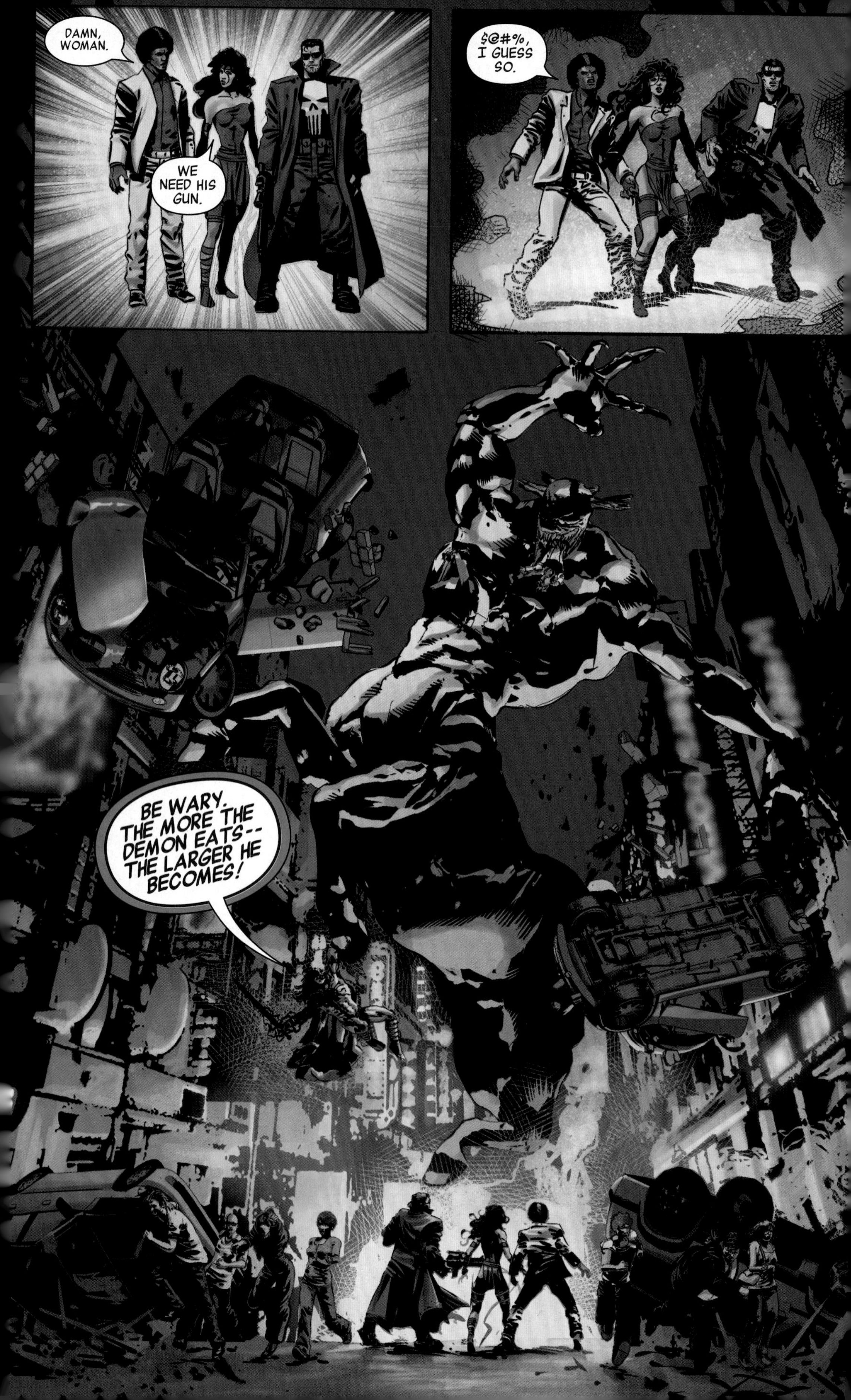
DAMN, WOMAN.
WE NEED HIS GUN.
$@#%, I GUESS SO.
BE WARY. THE MORE THE DEMON EATS-- THE LARGER HE BECOMES!

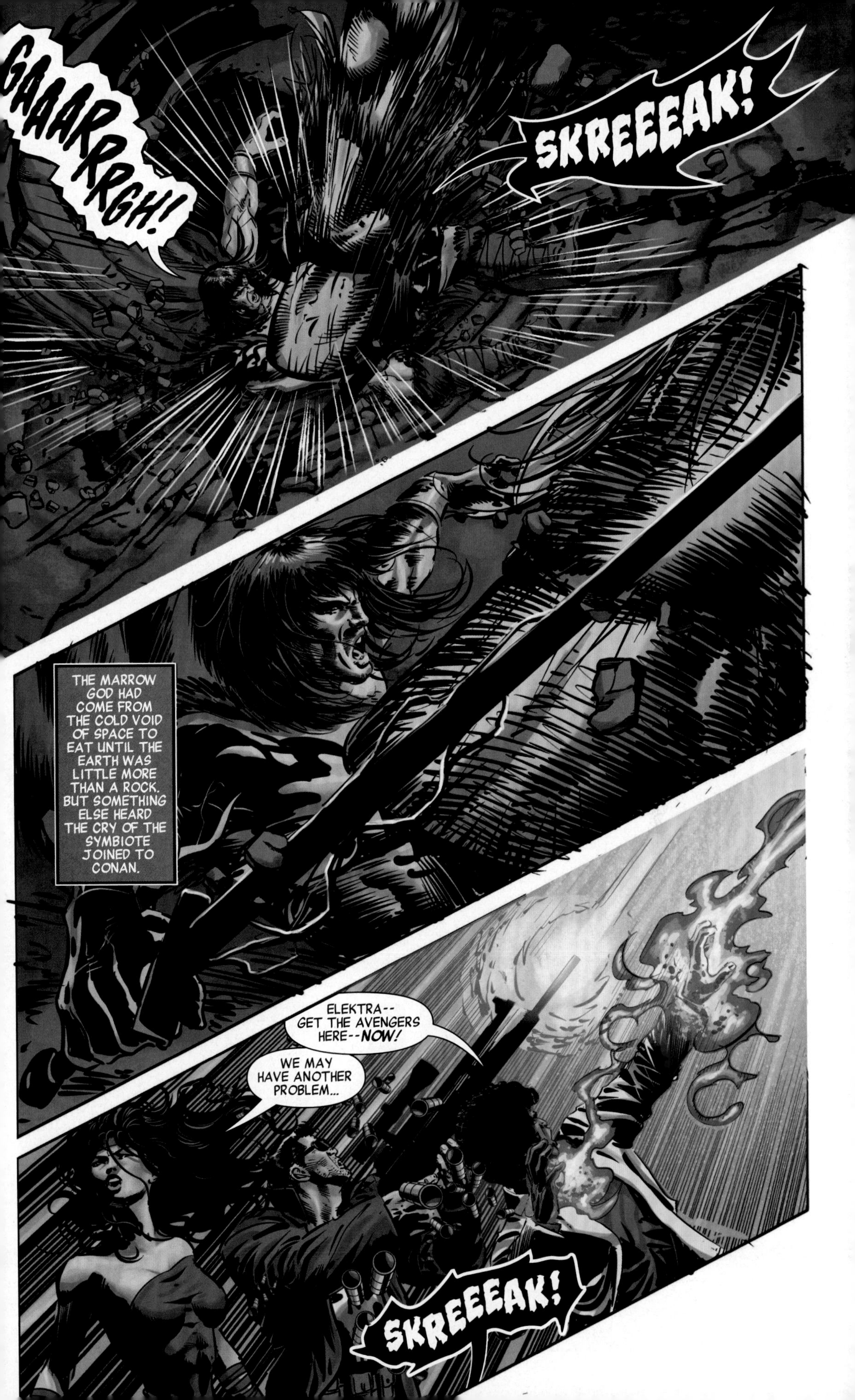
GAAARRRGH!
SKREEEAK!
THE MARROW GOD HAD COME FROM THE COLD VOID OF SPACE TO EAT UNTIL THE EARTH WAS LITTLE MORE THAN A ROCK. BUT SOMETHING ELSE HEARD THE CRY OF THE SYMBIOTE JOINED TO CONAN.
ELEKTRA-- GET THE AVENGERS HERE--NOW!
WE MAY HAVE ANOTHER PROBLEM...
SKREEEAK!

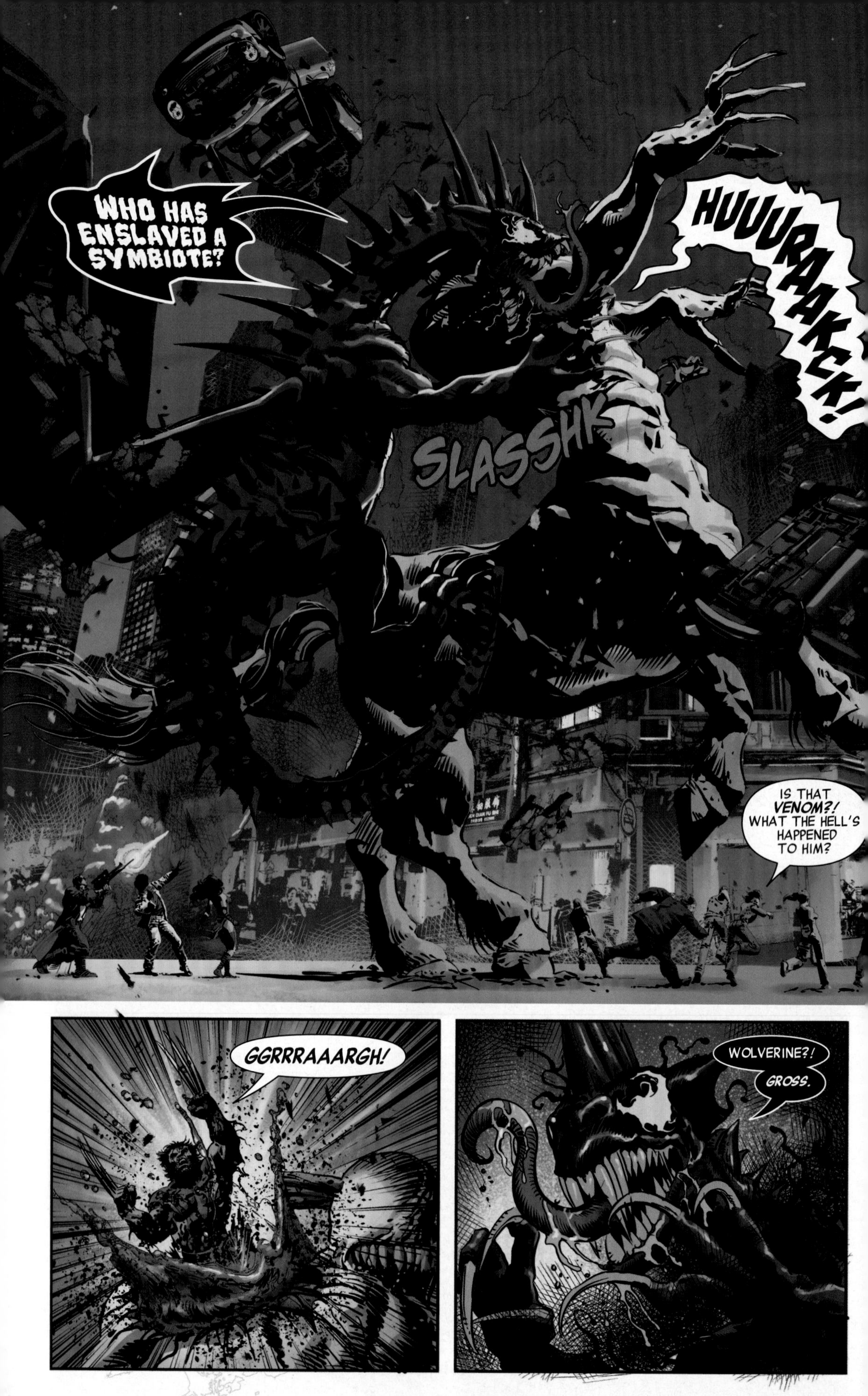
WHO HAS ENSLAVED A SYMBIOTE?
HUUURAAKK!
SLASSHK
IS THAT VENOM?! WHAT THE HELL'S HAPPENED TO HIM?
GGRRRAAARGH!
WOLVERINE?!
GROSS.

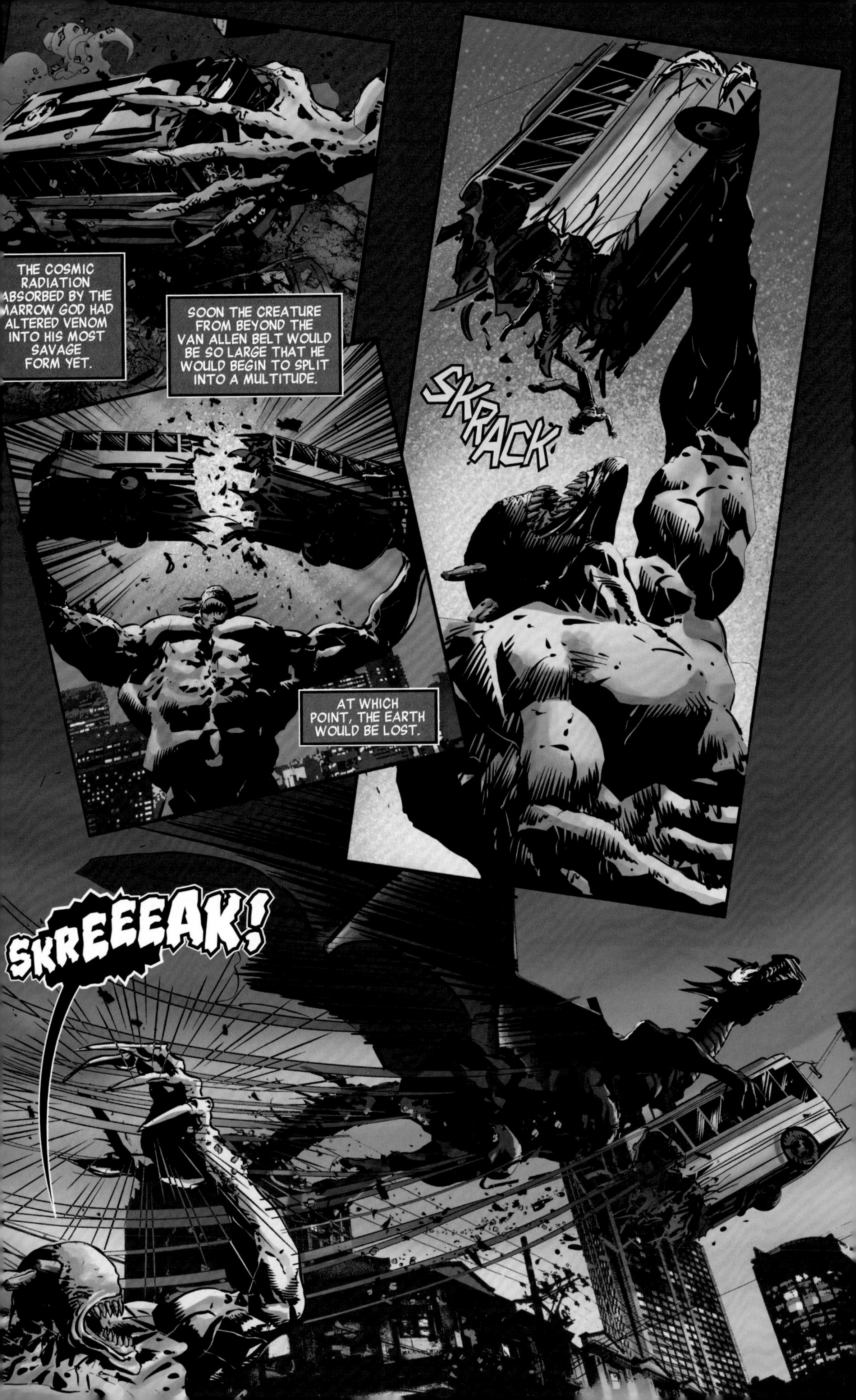
THE COSMIC RADIATION ABSORBED BY THE MARROW GOD HAD ALTERED VENOM INTO HIS MOST SAVAGE FORM YET.
SOON THE CREATURE FROM BEYOND THE VAN ALLEN BELT WOULD BE SO LARGE THAT HE WOULD BEGIN TO SPLIT INTO A MULTITUDE.
SKRACK
AT WHICH POINT, THE EARTH WOULD BE LOST.
SKREEEAK!

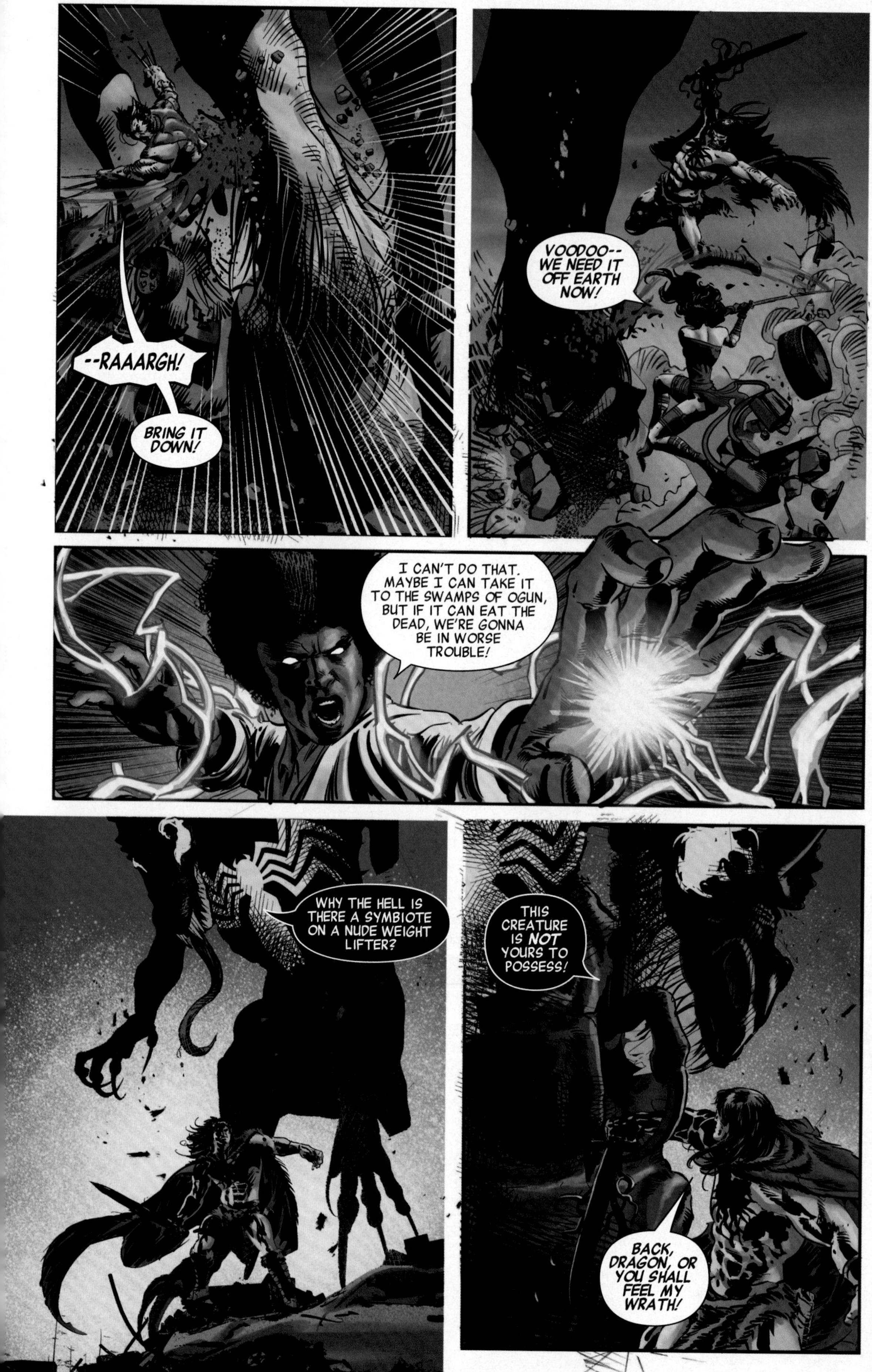
--RAAARGH!
BRING IT DOWN!
VOODOO--WE NEED IT OFF EARTH NOW!
I CAN'T DO THAT. MAYBE I CAN TAKE IT TO THE SWAMPS OF OGUN, BUT IF IT CAN EAT THE DEAD, WE'RE GONNA BE IN WORSE TROUBLE!
WHY THE HELL IS THERE A SYMBIOTE ON A NUDE WEIGHT LIFTER?
THIS CREATURE IS NOT YOURS TO POSSESS!
BACK, DRAGON, OR YOU SHALL FEEL MY WRATH!

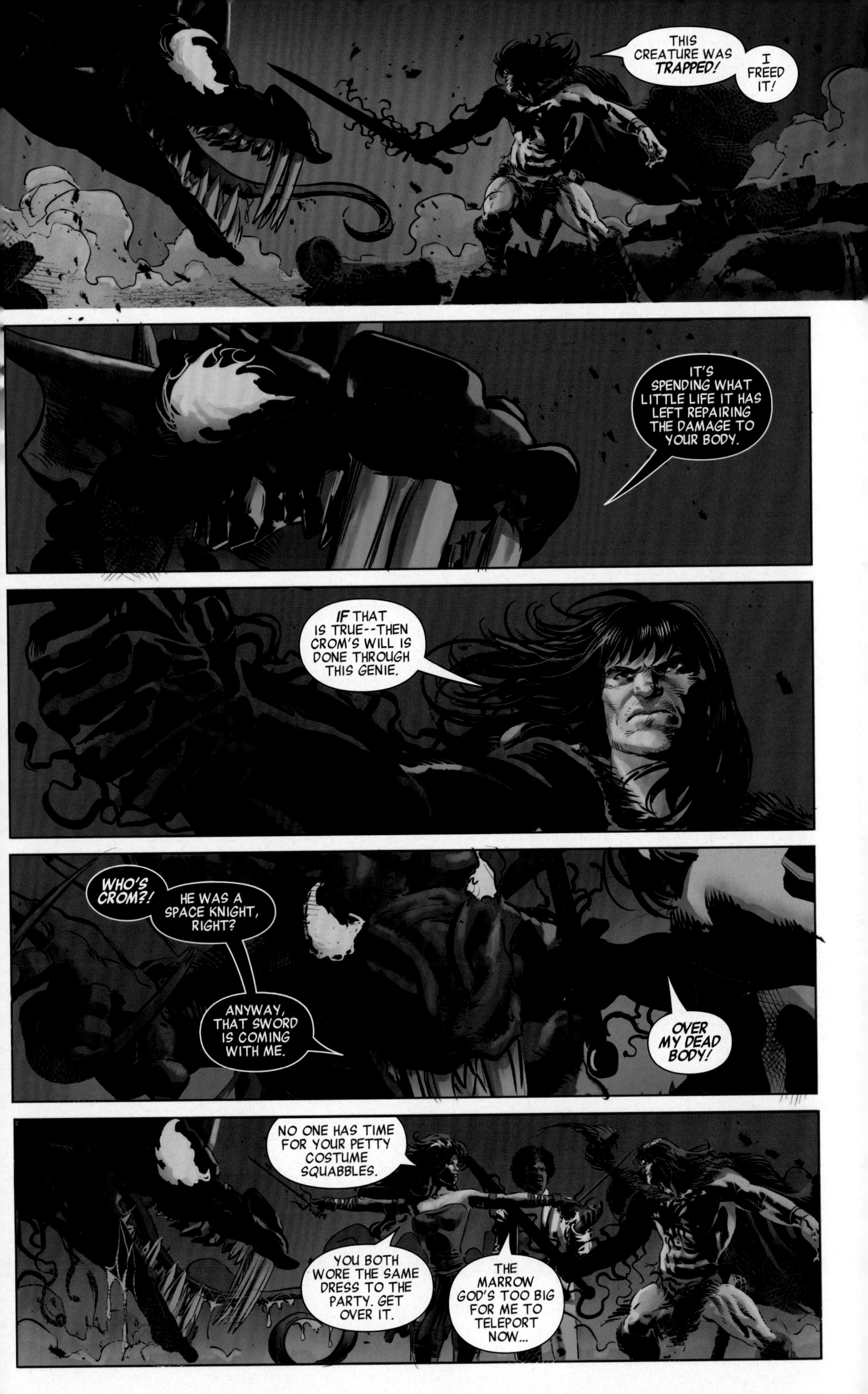
THIS CREATURE WAS TRAPPED!
I FREED IT!
IT'S SPENDING WHAT LITTLE LIFE IT HAS LEFT REPAIRING THE DAMAGE TO YOUR BODY.
IF THAT IS TRUE--THEN CROM'S WILL IS DONE THROUGH THIS GENIE.
WHO'S CROM?!
HE WAS A SPACE KNIGHT, RIGHT?
ANYWAY, THAT SWORD IS COMING WITH ME.
OVER MY DEAD BODY!
NO ONE HAS TIME FOR YOUR PETTY COSTUME SQUABBLES.
YOU BOTH WORE THE SAME DRESS TO THE PARTY. GET OVER IT.
THE MARROW GOD'S TOO BIG FOR ME TO TELEPORT NOW...

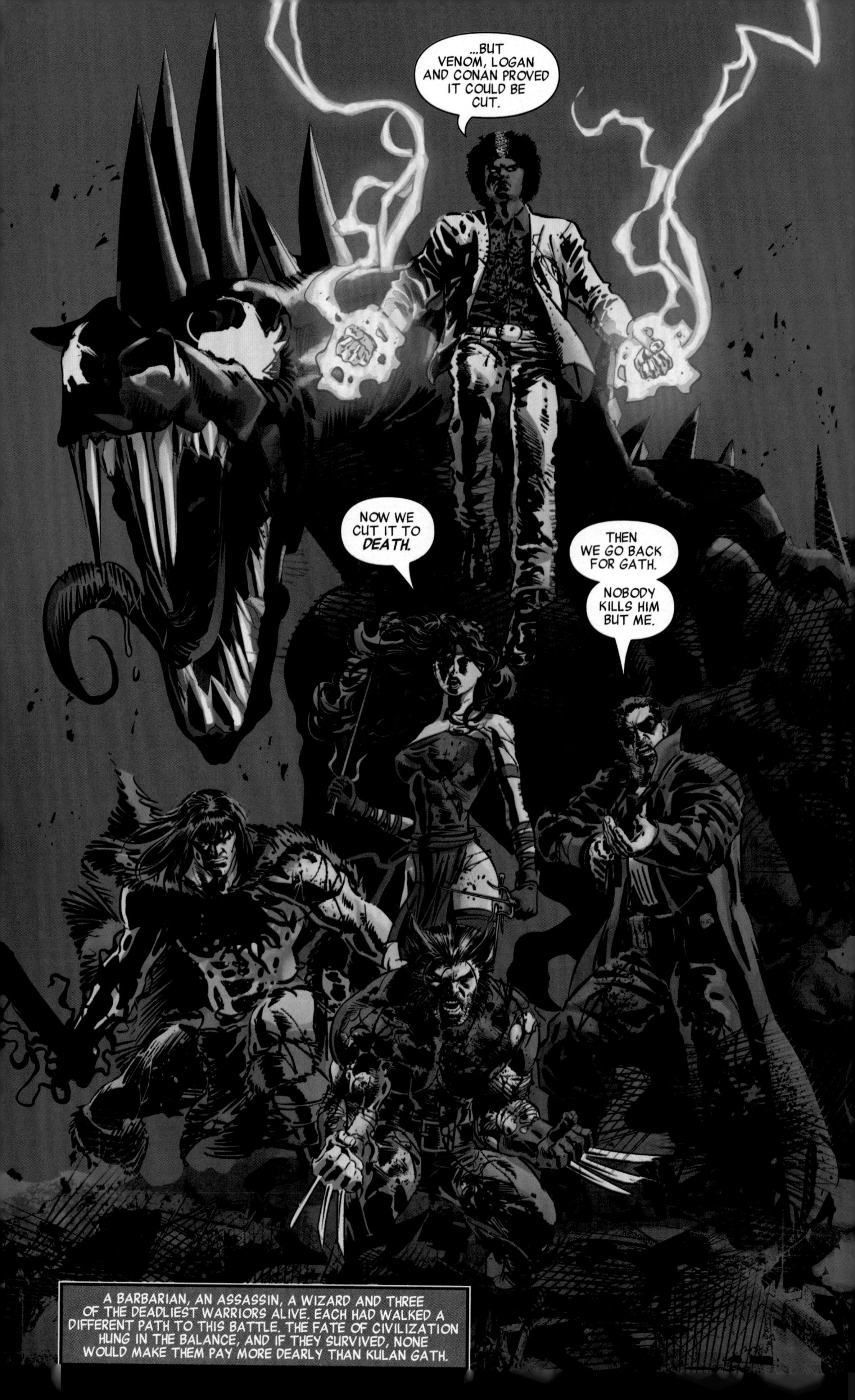
...BUT VENOM, LOGAN AND CONAN PROVED IT COULD BE CUT.
NOW WE CUT IT TO DEATH.
THEN WE GO BACK FOR GATH.
NOBODY KILLS HIM BUT ME.
A BARBARIAN, AN ASSASSIN, A WIZARD AND THREE OF THE DEADLIEST WARRIORS ALIVE. EACH HAD WALKED A DIFFERENT PATH TO THIS BATTLE. THE FATE OF CIVILIZATION HUNG IN THE BALANCE, AND IF THEY SURVIVED, NONE WOULD MAKE THEM PAY MORE DEARLY THAN KULAN GATH.

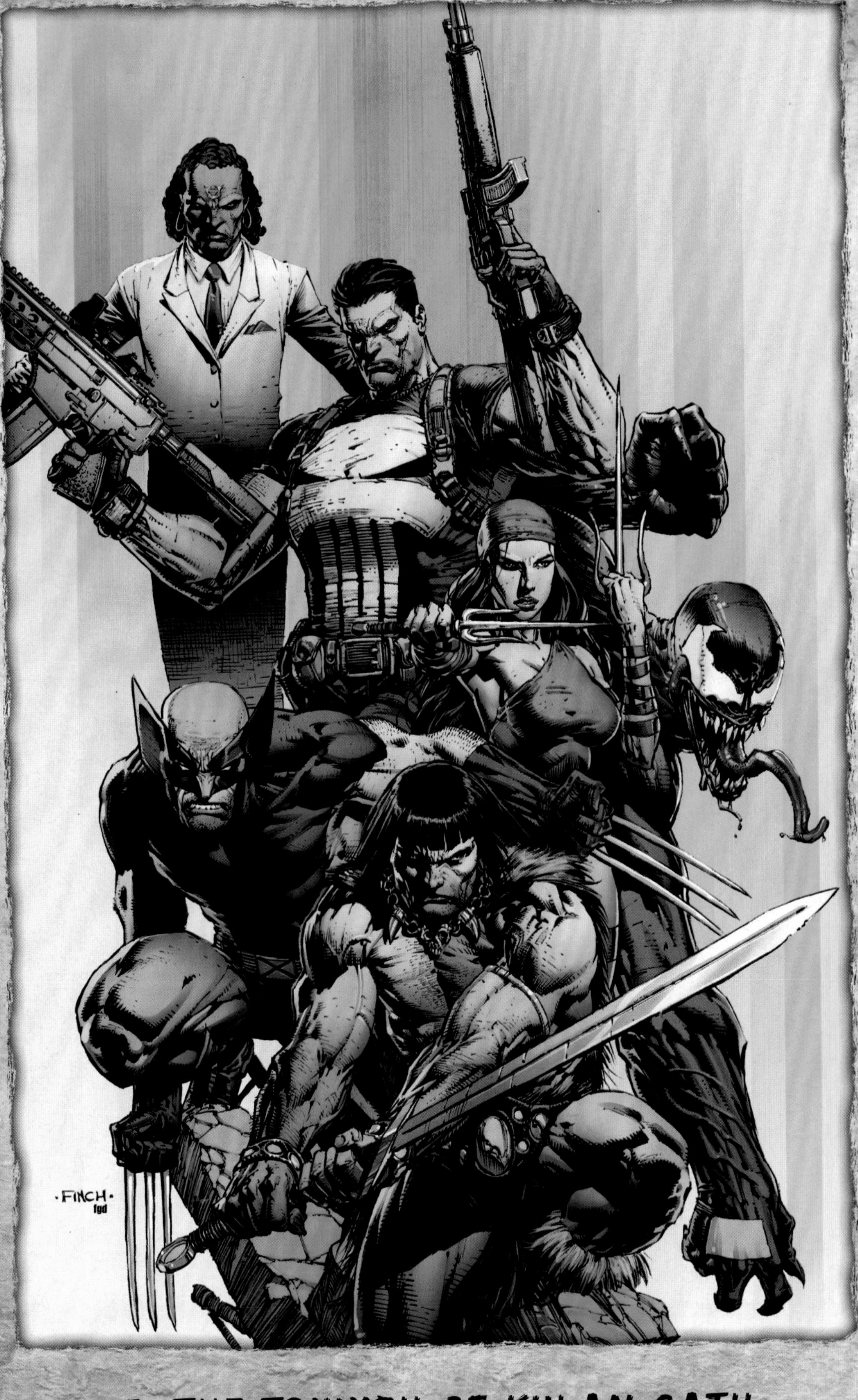

·FINCH·
fgd

5: THE TRIUMPH OF KULAN GATH

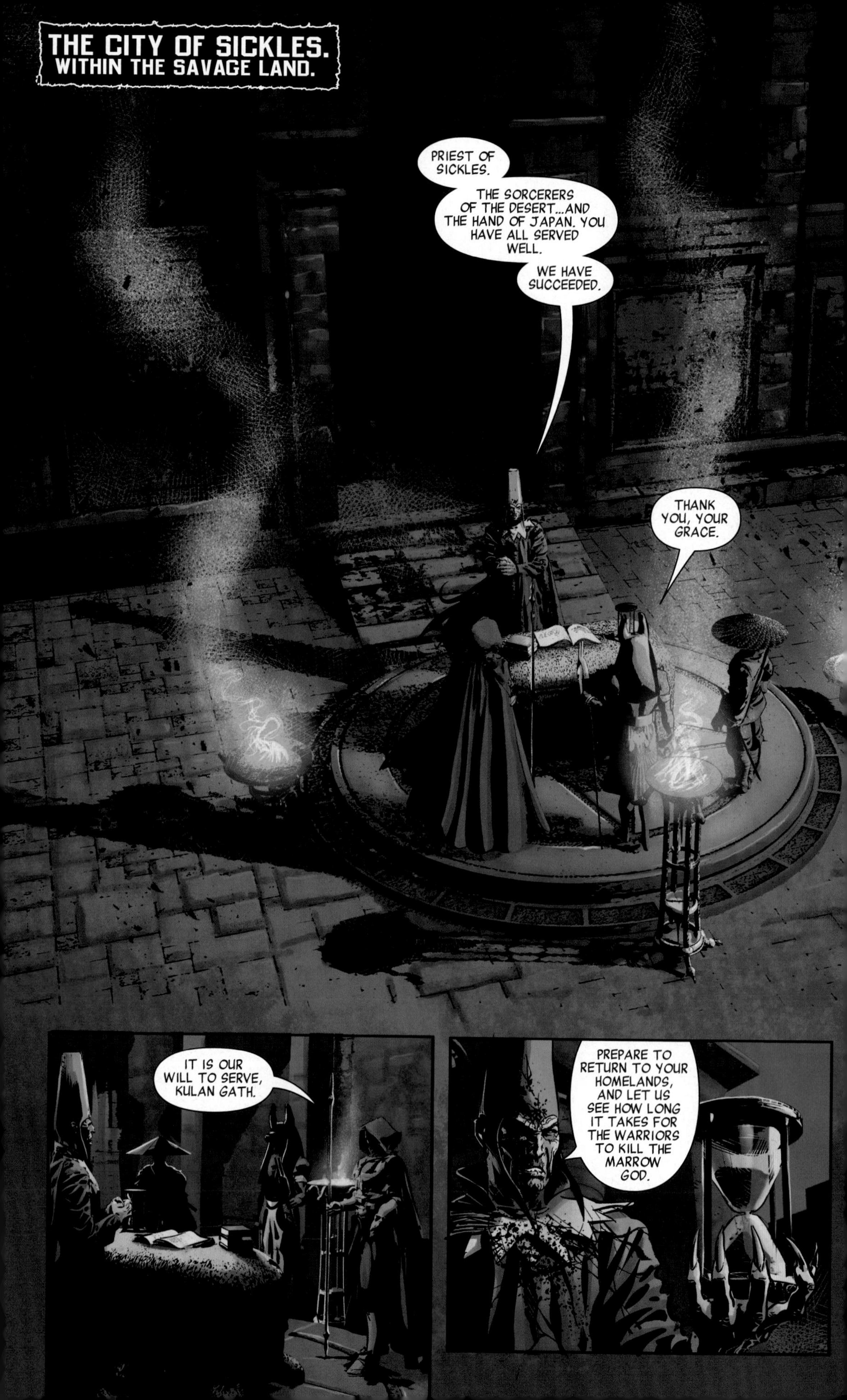
THE CITY OF SICKLES. WITHIN THE SAVAGE LAND.
PRIEST OF SICKLES.
THE SORCERERS OF THE DESERT...AND THE HAND OF JAPAN. YOU HAVE ALL SERVED WELL.
WE HAVE SUCCEEDED.
THANK YOU, YOUR GRACE.
IT IS OUR WILL TO SERVE, KULAN GATH.
PREPARE TO RETURN TO YOUR HOMELANDS, AND LET US SEE HOW LONG IT TAKES FOR THE WARRIORS TO KILL THE MARROW GOD.

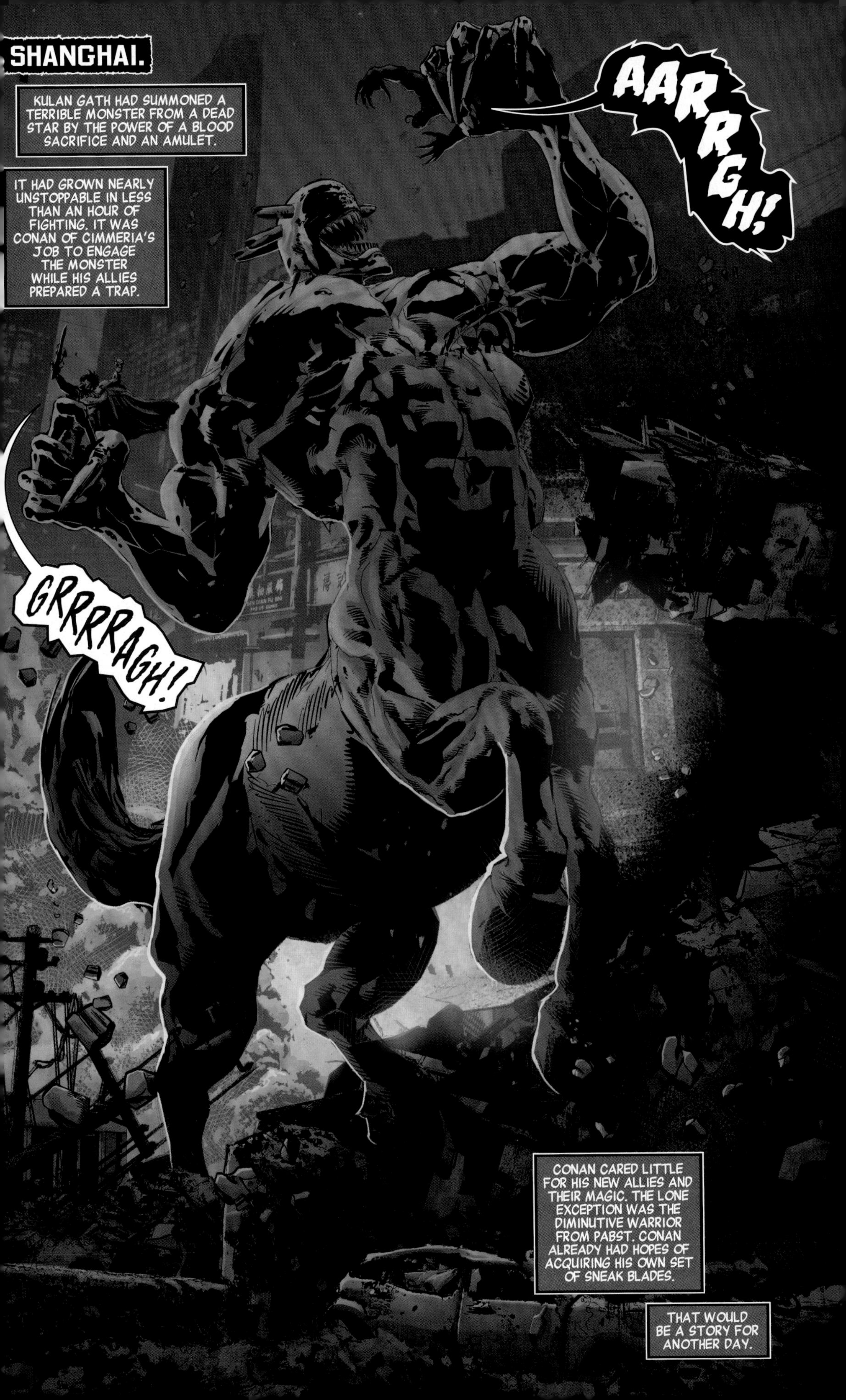
SHANGHAI.
KULAN GATH HAD SUMMONED A TERRIBLE MONSTER FROM A DEAD STAR BY THE POWER OF A BLOOD SACRIFICE AND AN AMULET.
IT HAD GROWN NEARLY UNSTOPPABLE IN LESS THAN AN HOUR OF FIGHTING. IT WAS CONAN OF CIMMERIA'S JOB TO ENGAGE THE MONSTER WHILE HIS ALLIES PREPARED A TRAP.
AARRGH!
GRRRRAGH!
CONAN CARED LITTLE FOR HIS NEW ALLIES AND THEIR MAGIC. THE LONE EXCEPTION WAS THE DIMINUTIVE WARRIOR FROM PABST. CONAN ALREADY HAD HOPES OF ACQUIRING HIS OWN SET OF SNEAK BLADES.
THAT WOULD BE A STORY FOR ANOTHER DAY.

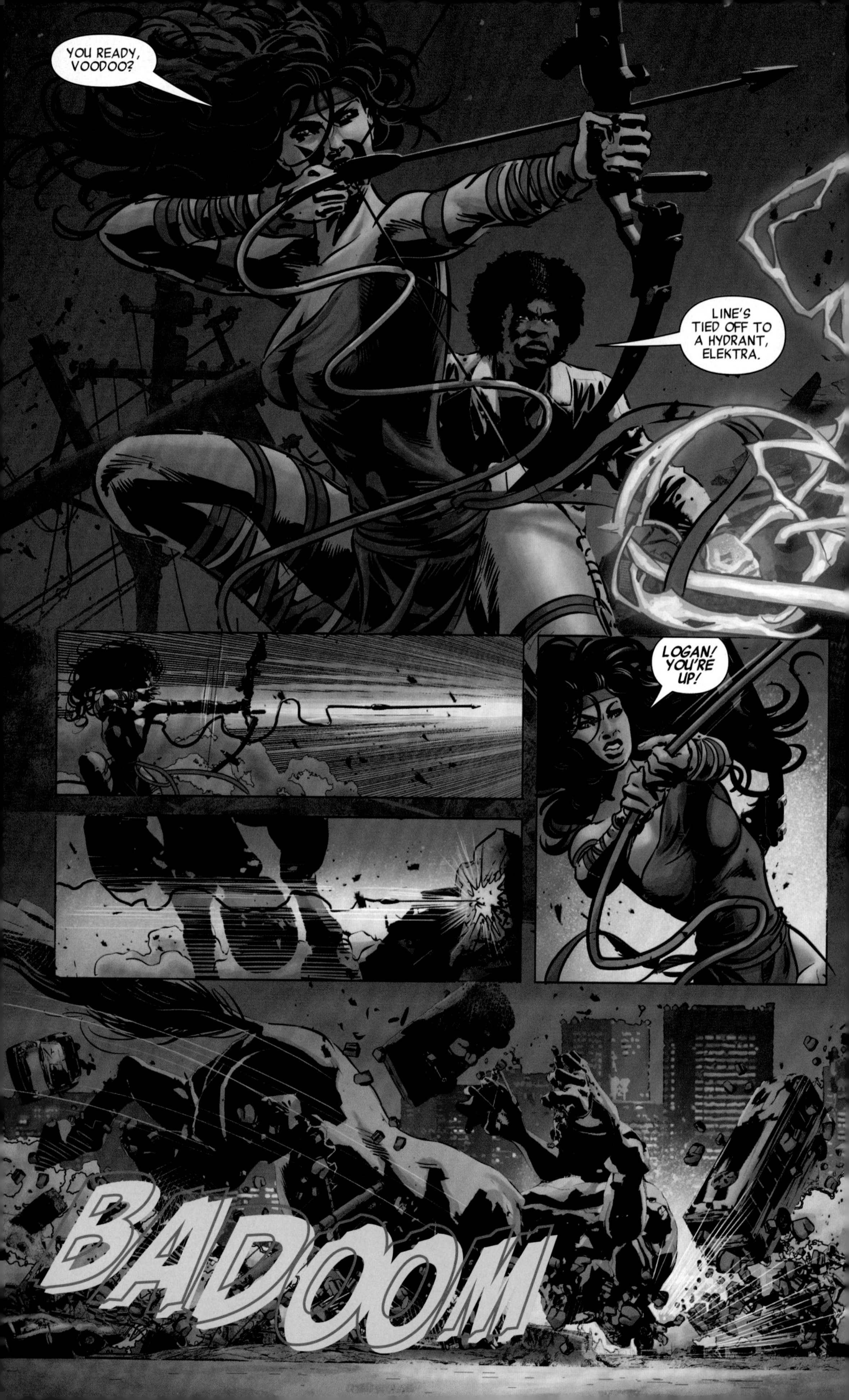
YOU READY, VOODOO?
LINE'S TIED OFF TO A HYDRANT, ELEKTRA.
LOGAN! YOU'RE UP!
BADOOM

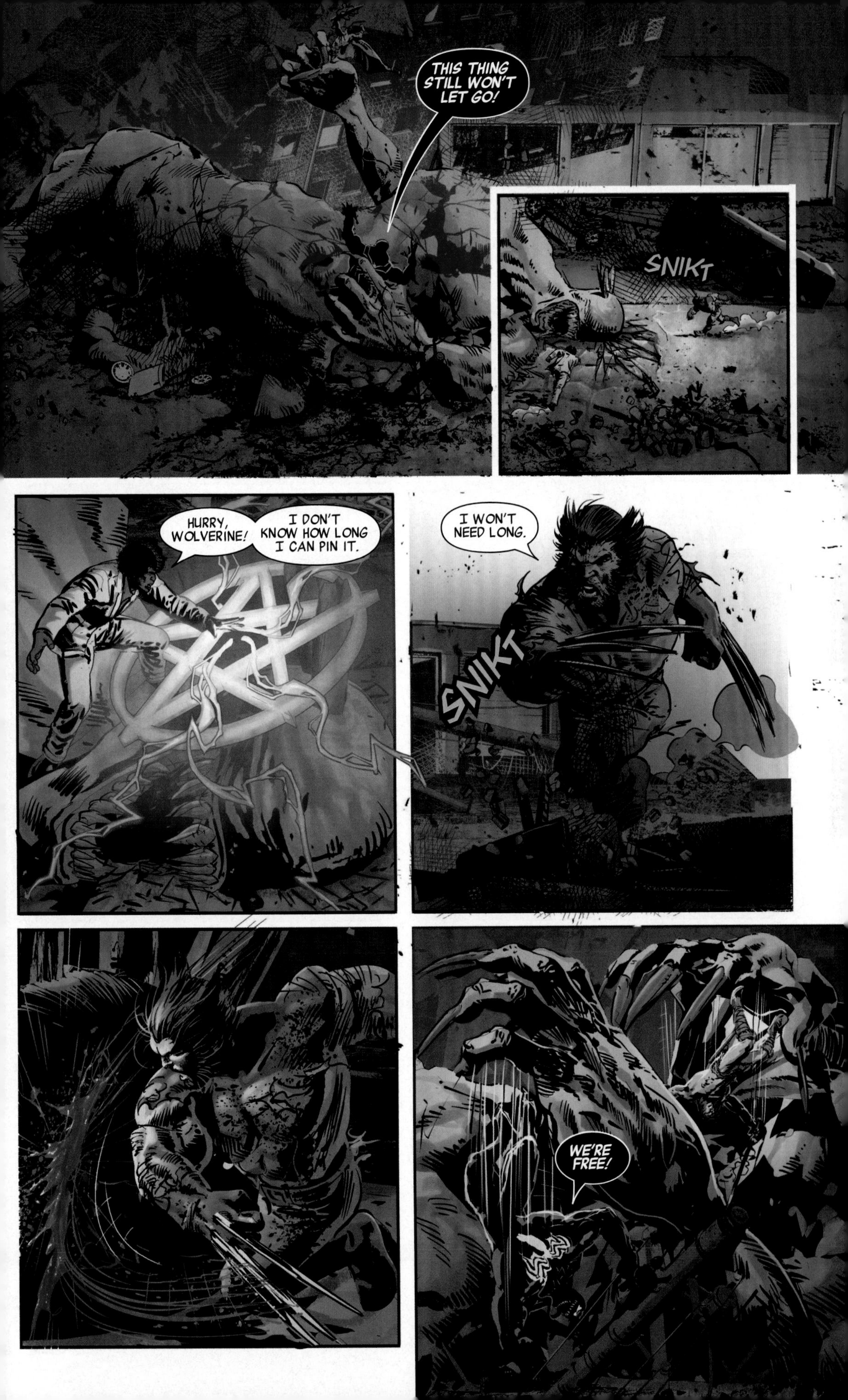
THIS THING STILL WON'T LET GO!
SNIKT
HURRY, WOLVERINE!
I DON'T KNOW HOW LONG I CAN PIN IT.
I WON'T NEED LONG.
SNIKT
WE'RE FREE!

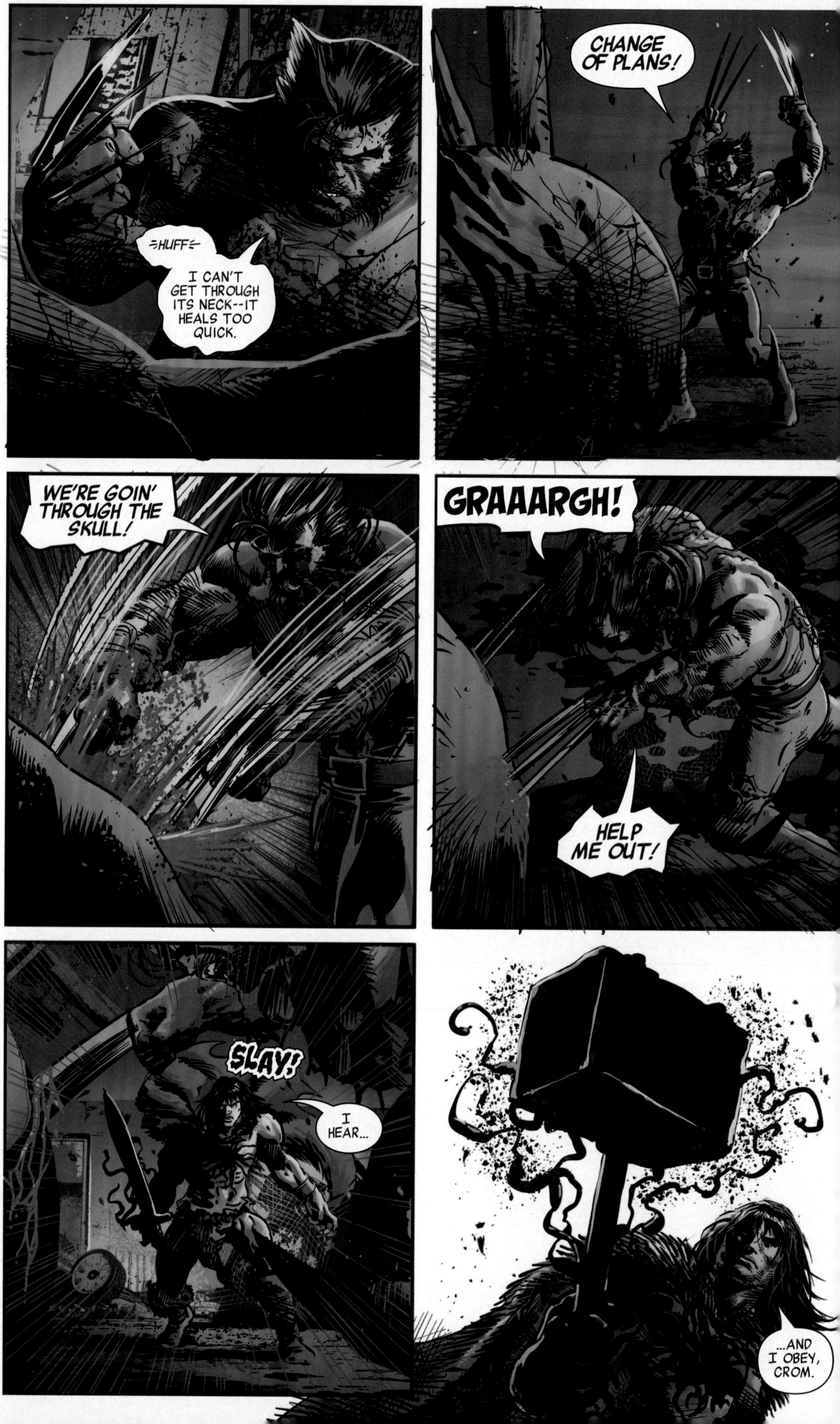
=HUFF=
I CAN'T GET THROUGH ITS NECK--IT HEALS TOO QUICK.
CHANGE OF PLANS!
WE'RE GOIN' THROUGH THE SKULL!
GRAAARGH!
HELP ME OUT!
SLAY!
I HEAR...
...AND I OBEY, CROM.

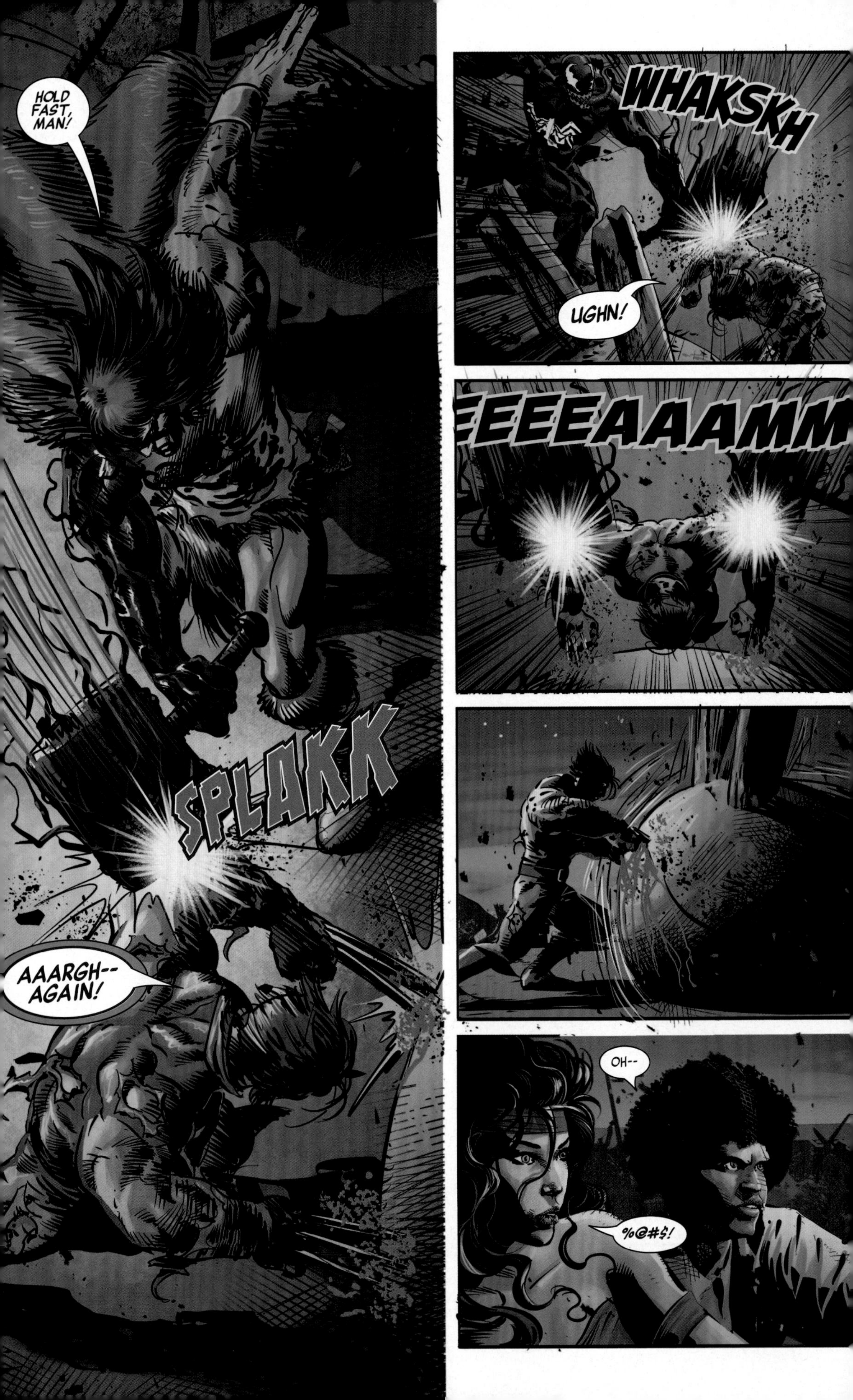
HOLD FAST, MAN!
SPLAKK
AAARGH-- AGAIN!
WHAKSKH
UGHN!
EEEEAAAMM
OH--
%@#$!

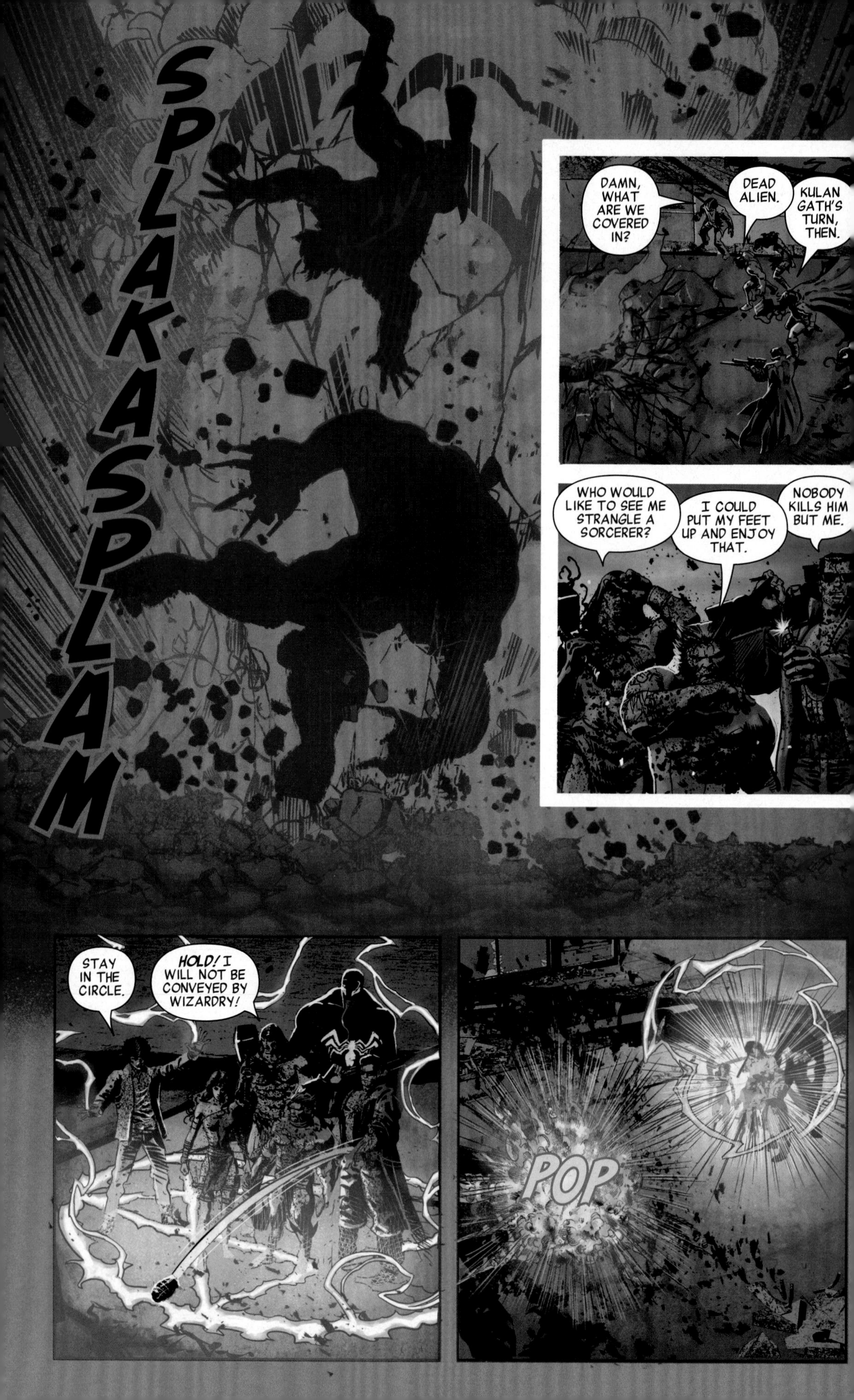
SPLAKASPLAM
DAMN, WHAT ARE WE COVERED IN?
DEAD ALIEN.
KULAN GATH'S TURN, THEN.
WHO WOULD LIKE TO SEE ME STRANGLE A SORCERER?
I COULD PUT MY FEET UP AND ENJOY THAT.
NOBODY KILLS HIM BUT ME.
STAY IN THE CIRCLE.
HOLD! I WILL NOT BE CONVEYED BY WIZARDRY!
POP

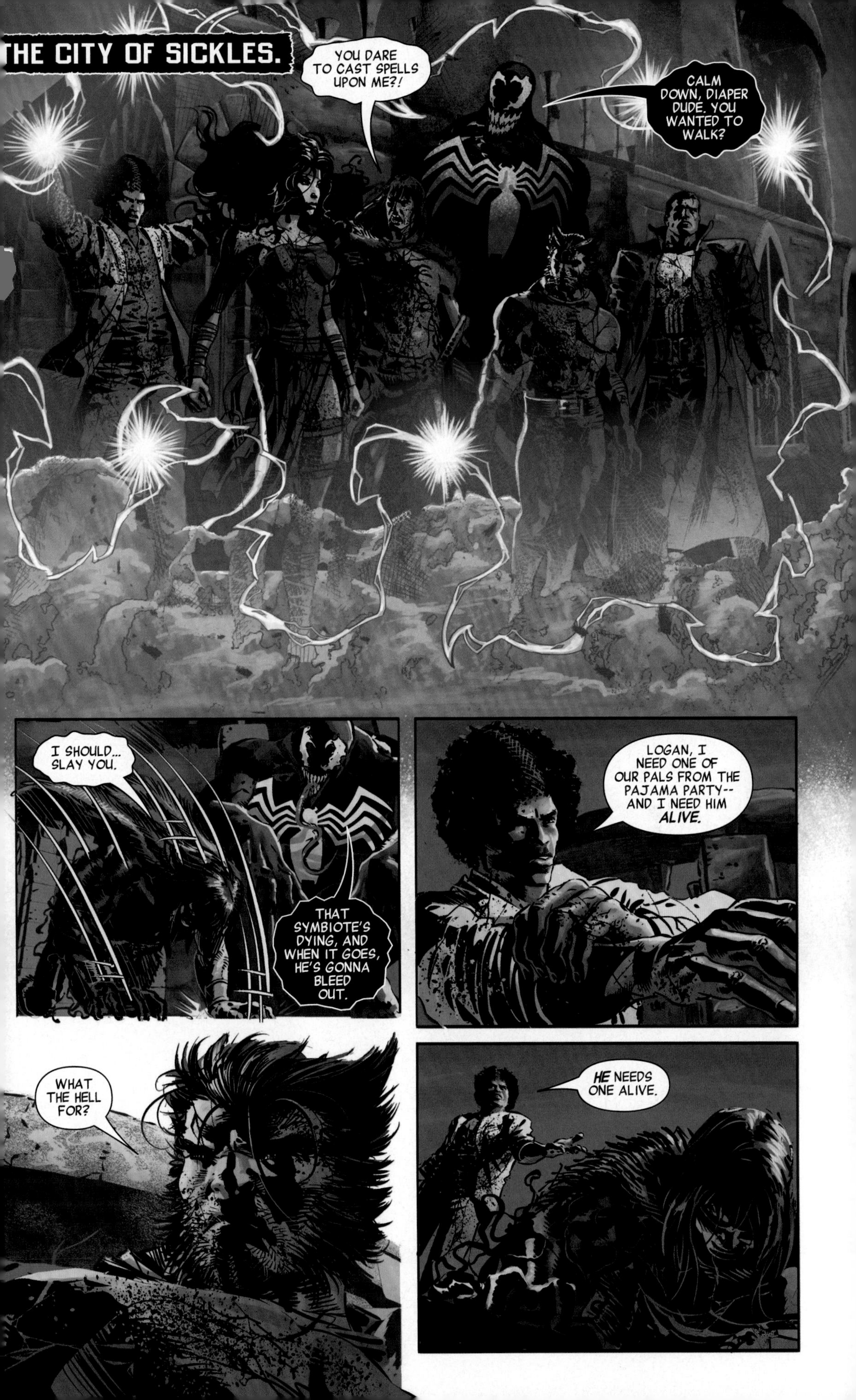
THE CITY OF SICKLES.
YOU DARE TO CAST SPELLS UPON ME?!
CALM DOWN, DIAPER DUDE. YOU WANTED TO WALK?
I SHOULD... SLAY YOU.
THAT SYMBIOTE'S DYING, AND WHEN IT GOES, HE'S GONNA BLEED OUT.
LOGAN, I NEED ONE OF OUR PALS FROM THE PAJAMA PARTY-- AND I NEED HIM *ALIVE*.
WHAT THE HELL FOR?
HE NEEDS ONE ALIVE.

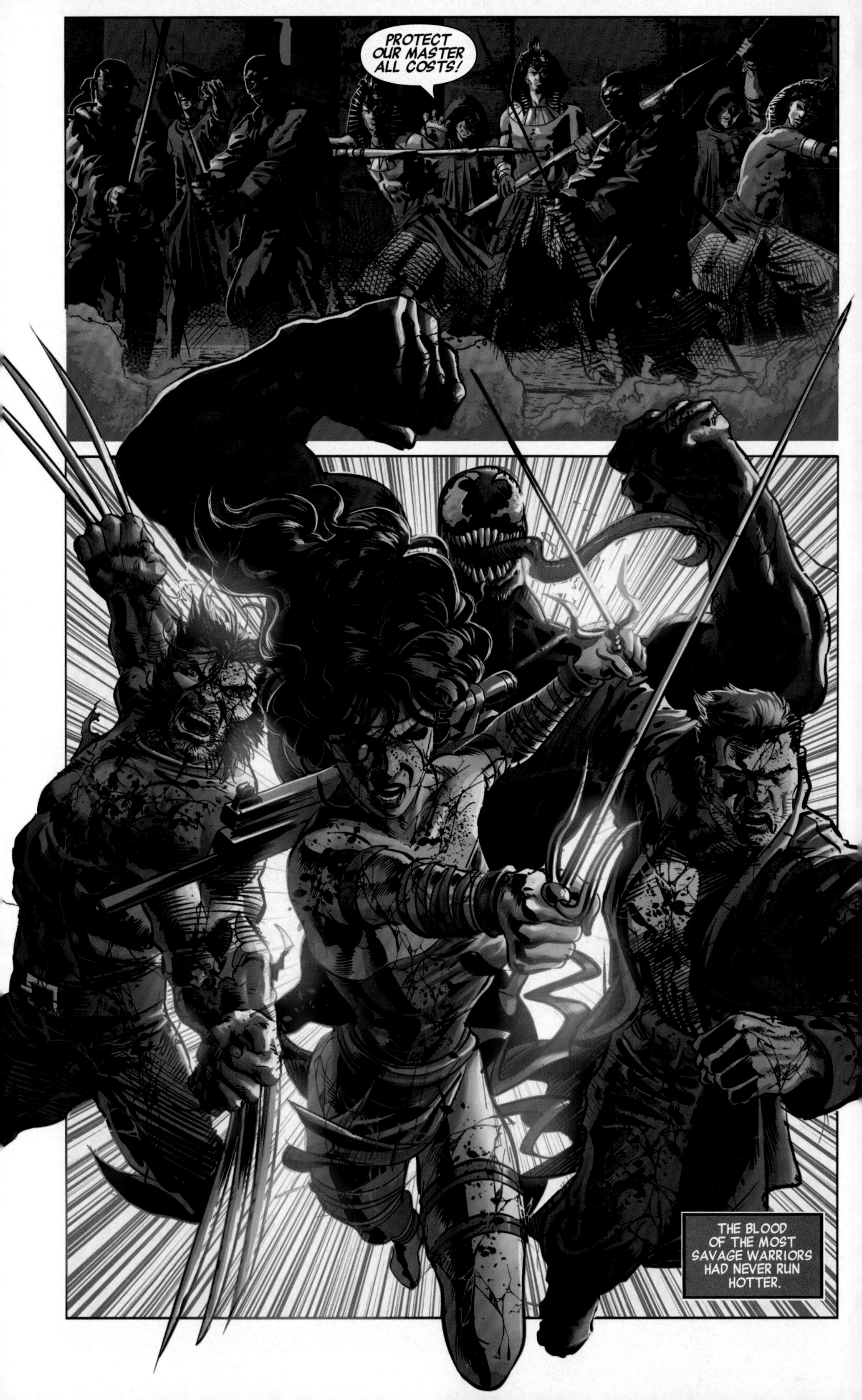
PROTECT OUR MASTER ALL COSTS!
THE BLOOD OF THE MOST SAVAGE WARRIORS HAD NEVER RUN HOTTER.

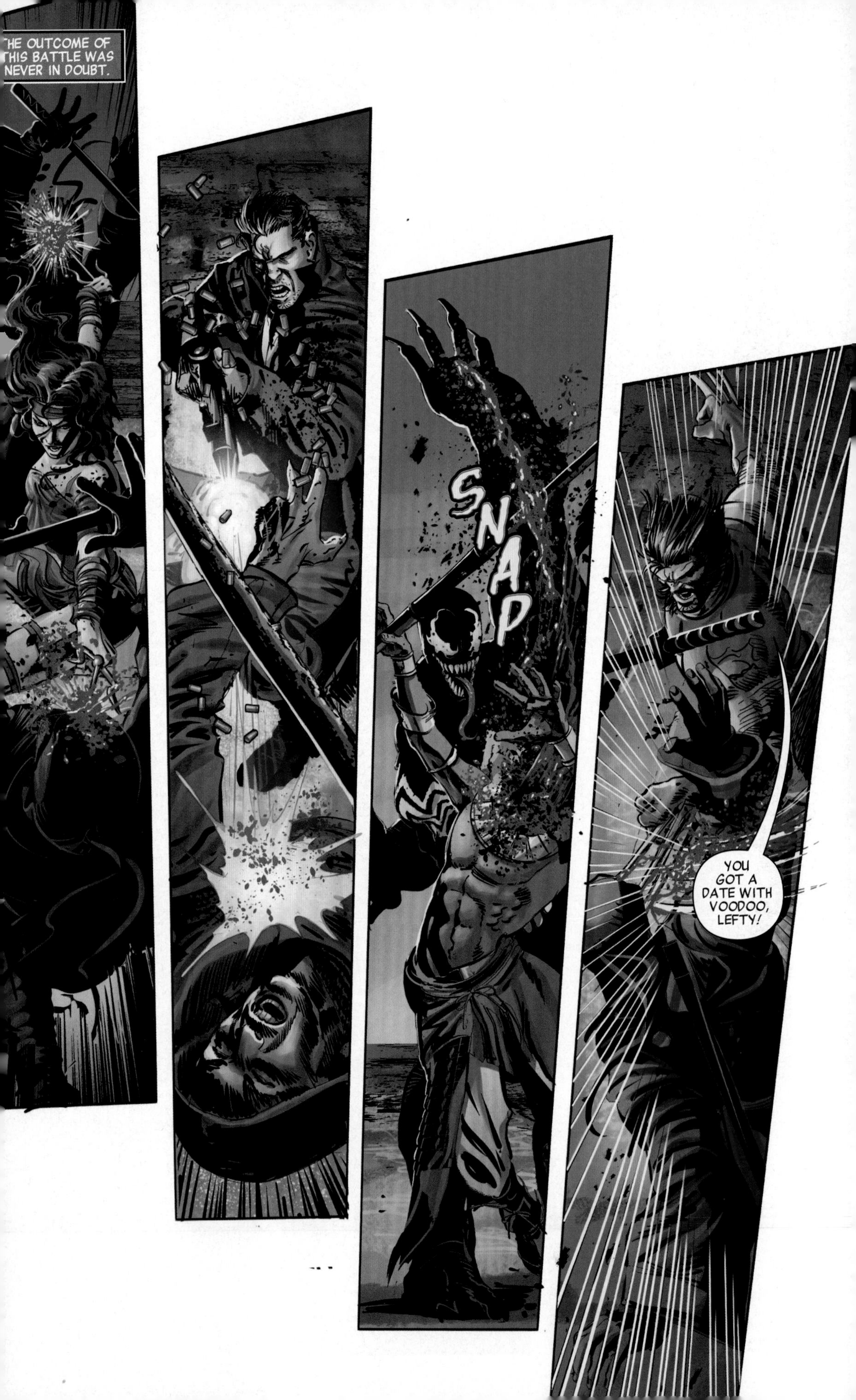
THE OUTCOME OF THIS BATTLE WAS NEVER IN DOUBT.
SNAP
YOU GOT A DATE WITH VOODOO, LEFTY!

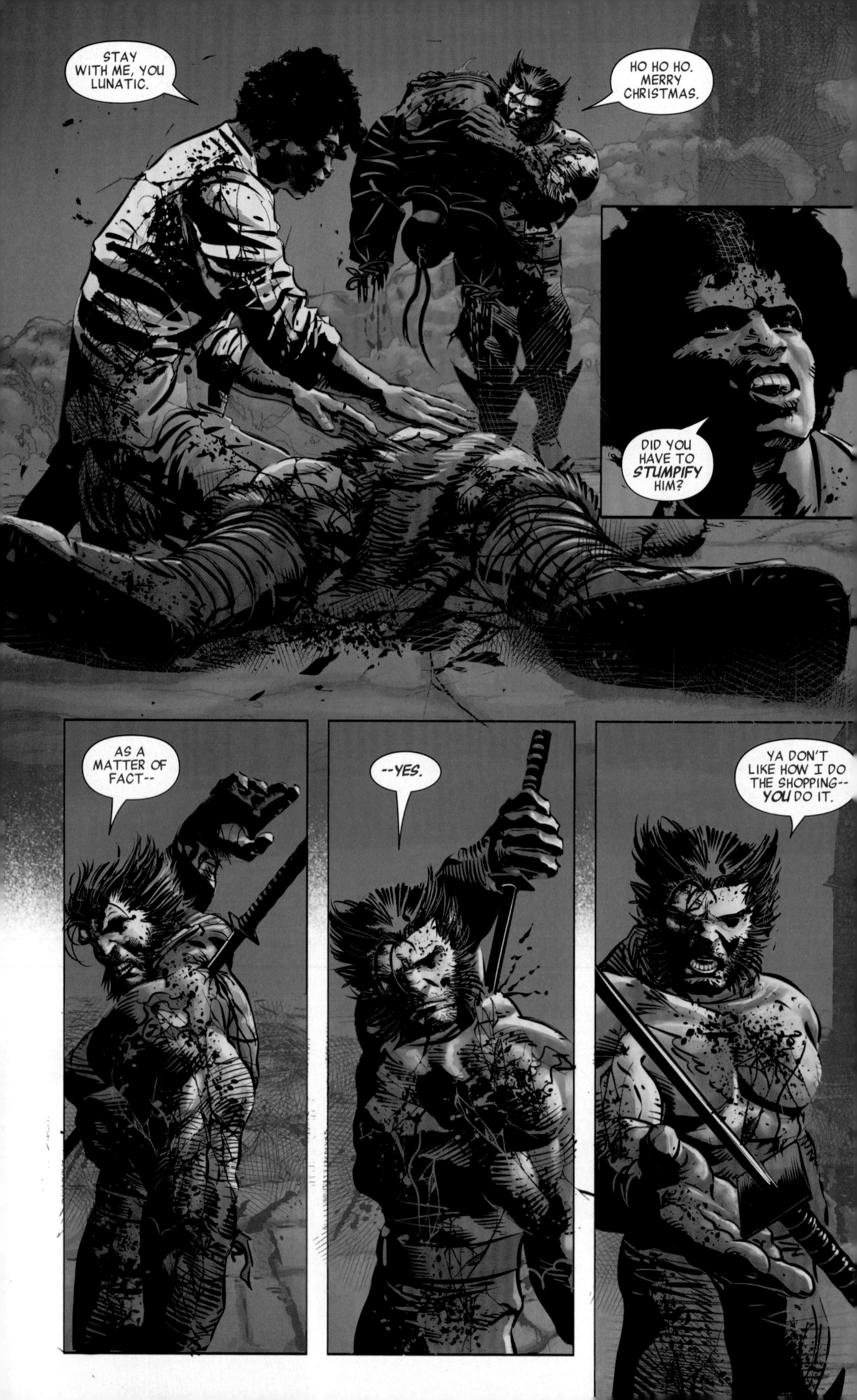
STAY WITH ME, YOU LUNATIC.
HO HO HO. MERRY CHRISTMAS.
DID YOU HAVE TO STUMPIFY HIM?
AS A MATTER OF FACT--
--YES.
YA DON'T LIKE HOW I DO THE SHOPPING-- YOU DO IT.

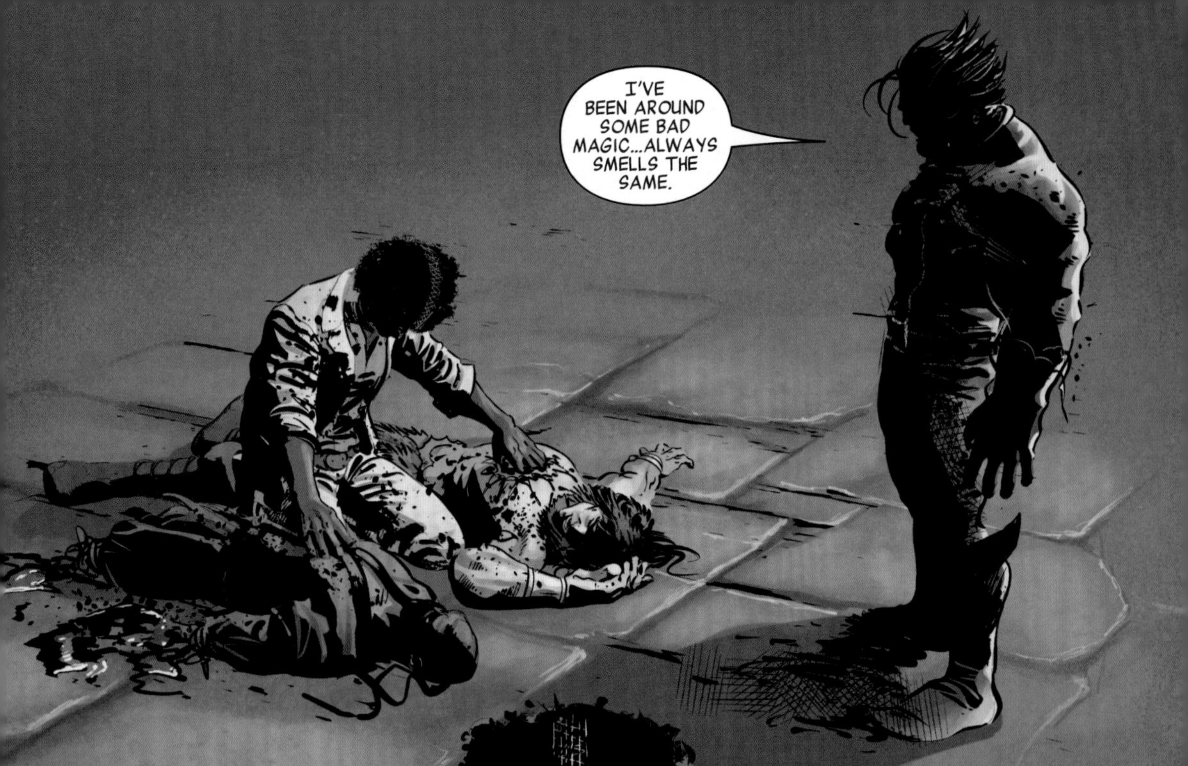
I'VE BEEN AROUND SOME BAD MAGIC...ALWAYS SMELLS THE SAME.

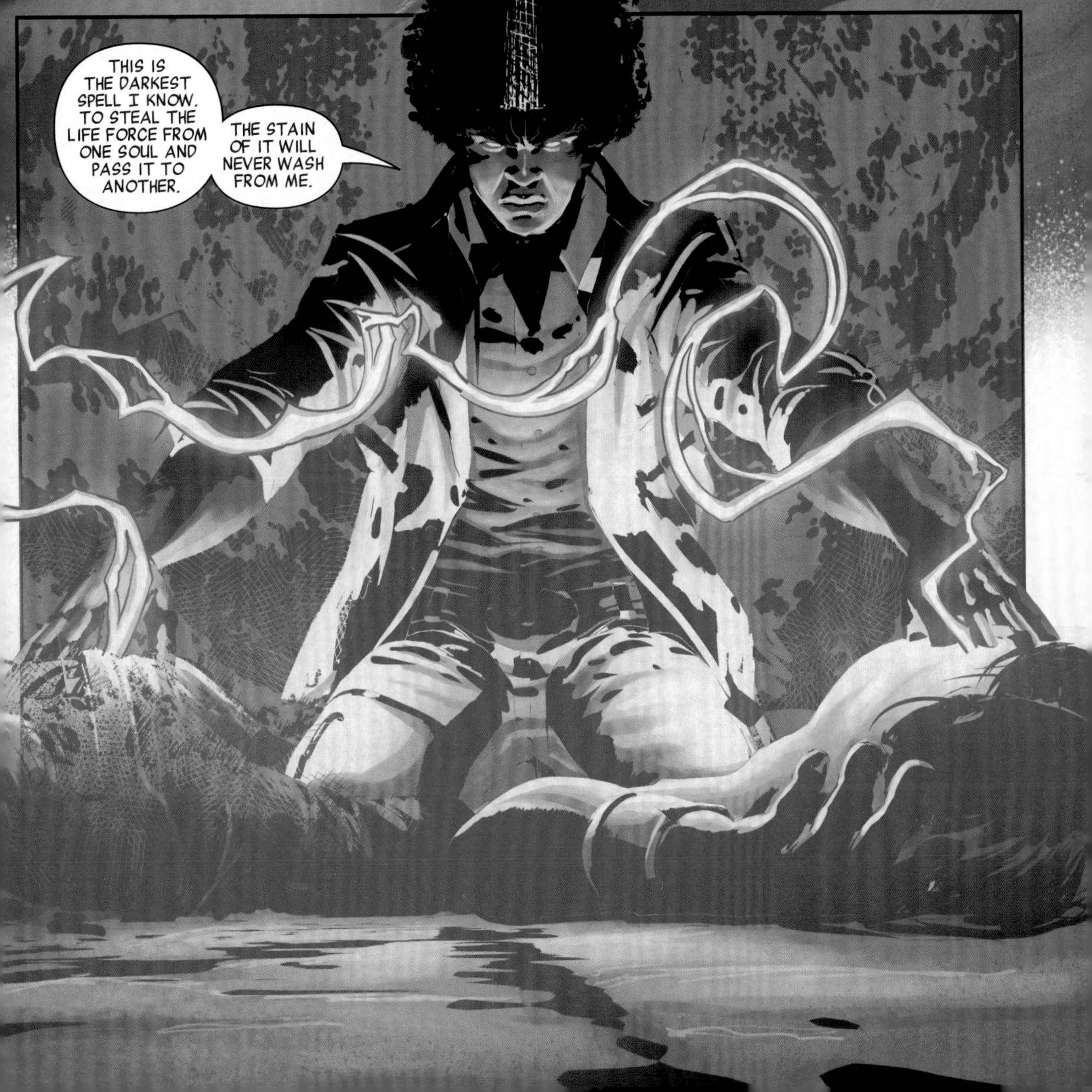
THIS IS THE DARKEST SPELL I KNOW. TO STEAL THE LIFE FORCE FROM ONE SOUL AND PASS IT TO ANOTHER.
THE STAIN OF IT WILL NEVER WASH FROM ME.

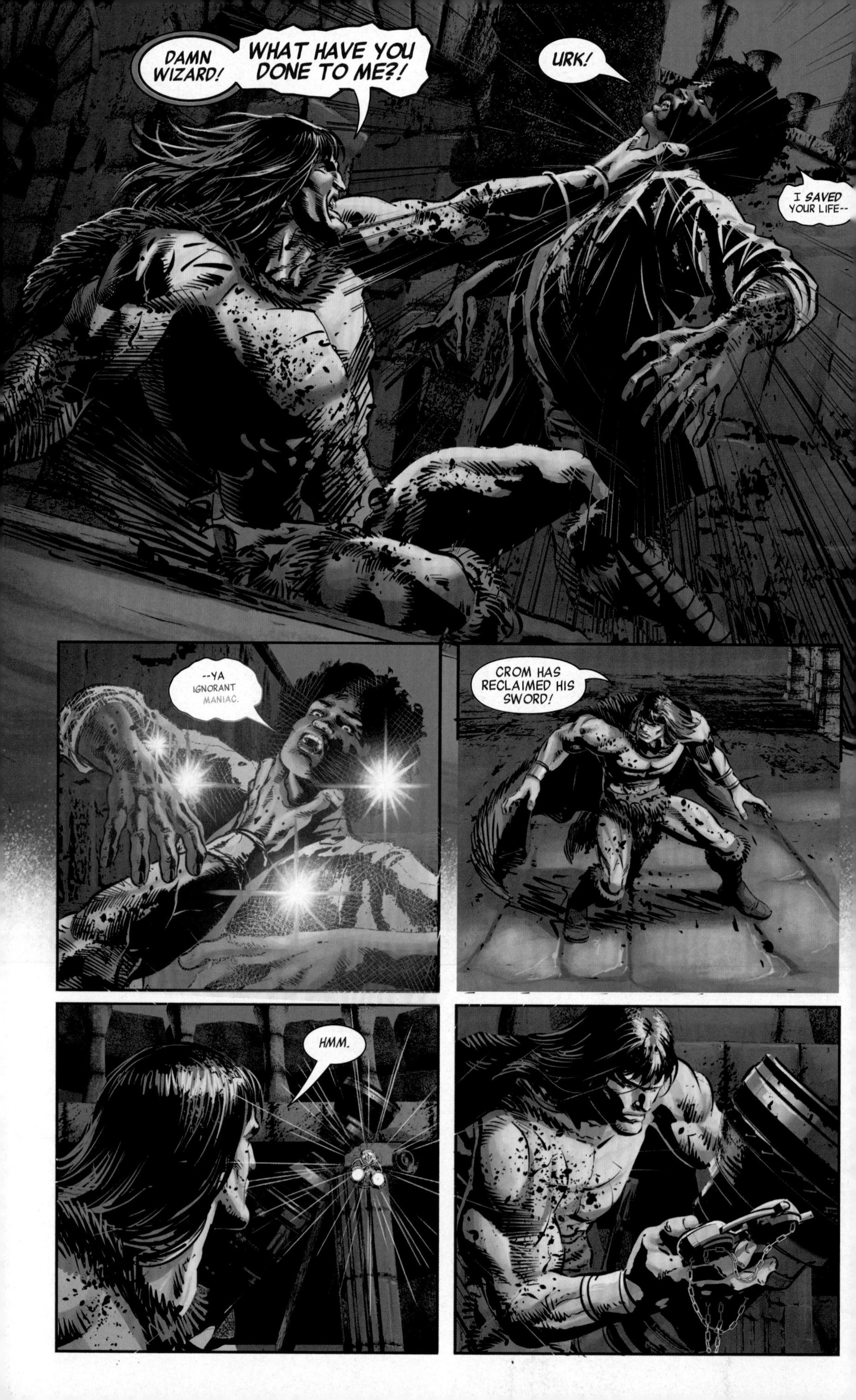
DAMN WIZARD!
WHAT HAVE YOU DONE TO ME?!
URK!
I SAVED YOUR LIFE--
--YA IGNORANT MANIAC.
CROM HAS RECLAIMED HIS SWORD!
HMM.

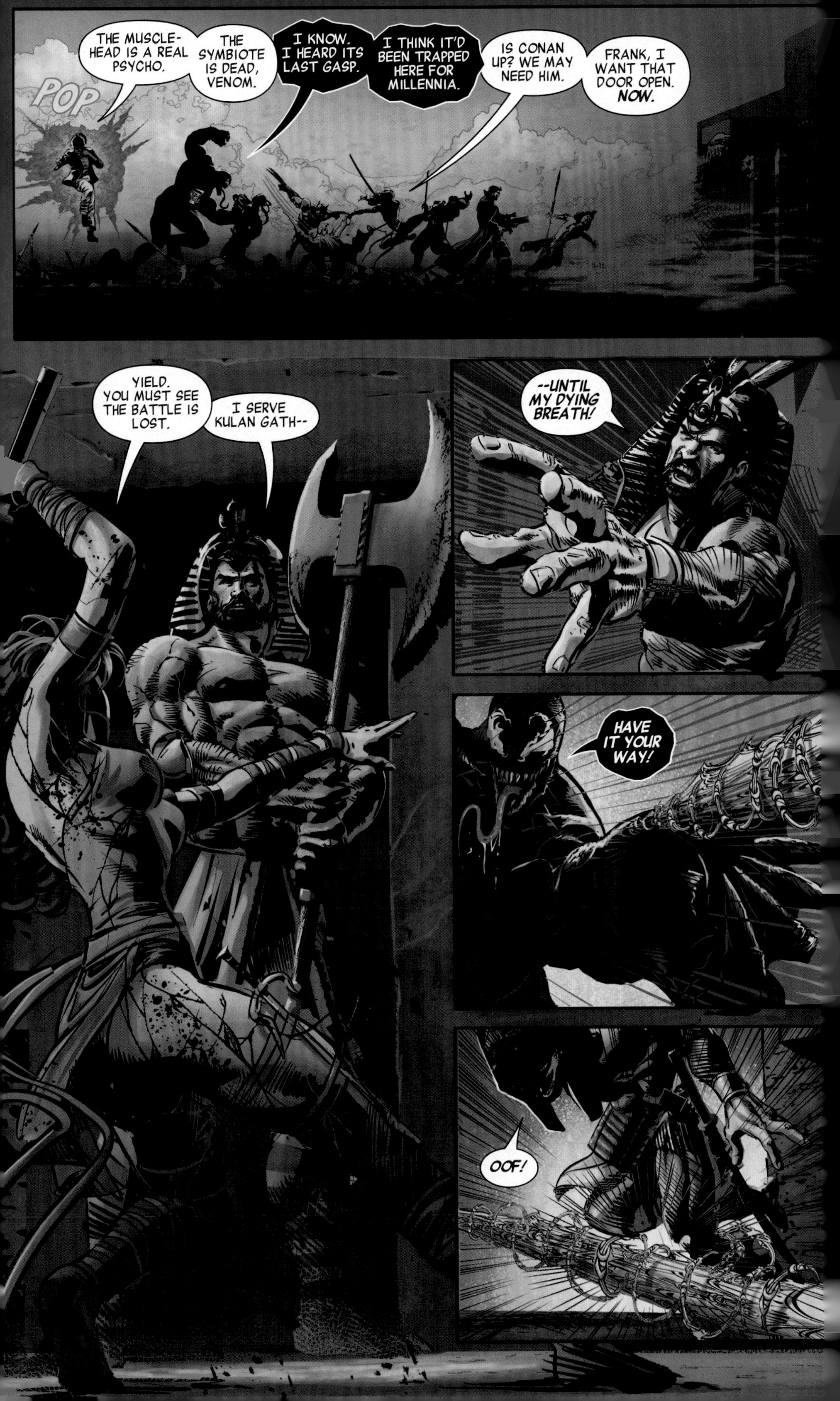
POP
THE MUSCLE-HEAD IS A REAL PSYCHO.
THE SYMBIOTE IS DEAD, VENOM.
I KNOW. I HEARD ITS LAST GASP.
I THINK IT'D BEEN TRAPPED HERE FOR MILLENNIA.
IS CONAN UP? WE MAY NEED HIM.
FRANK, I WANT THAT DOOR OPEN. NOW.
YIELD. YOU MUST SEE THE BATTLE IS LOST.
I SERVE KULAN GATH--
--UNTIL MY DYING BREATH!
HAVE IT YOUR WAY!
OOF!

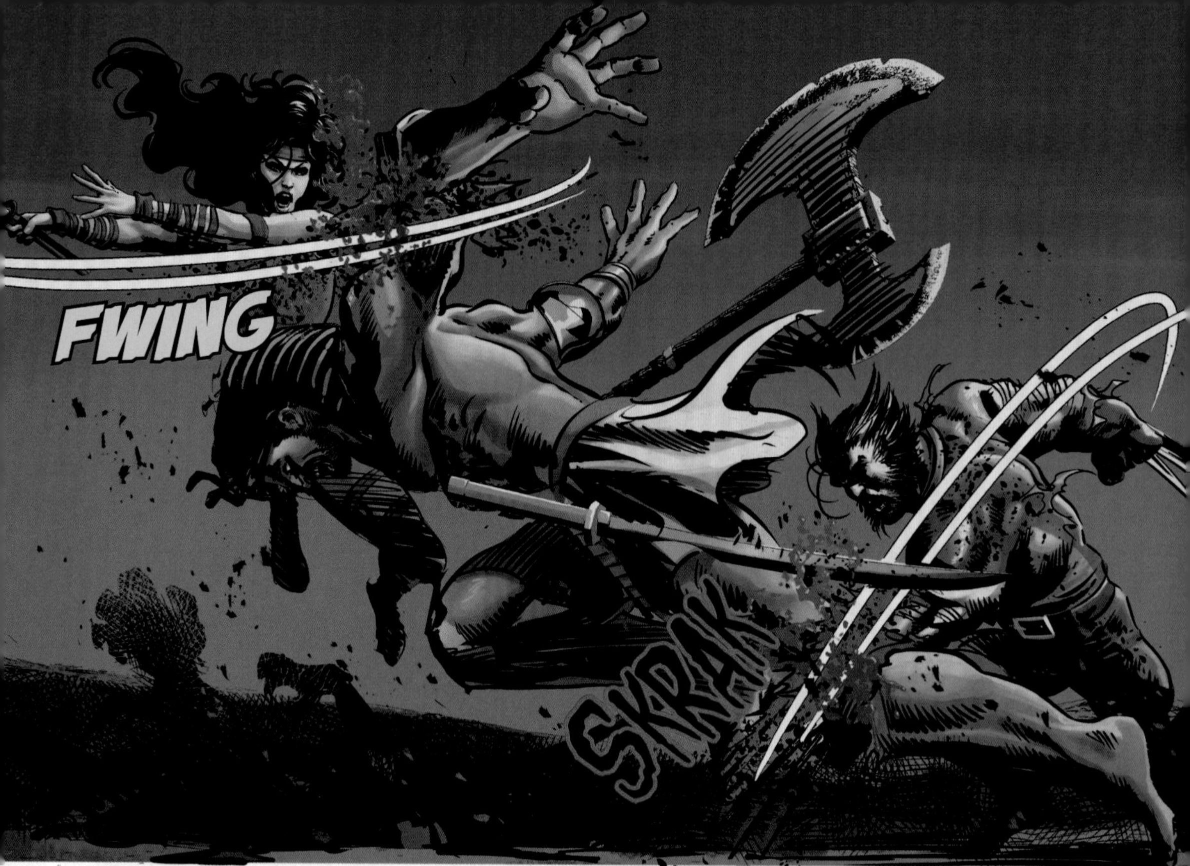
FWING
SKRAK

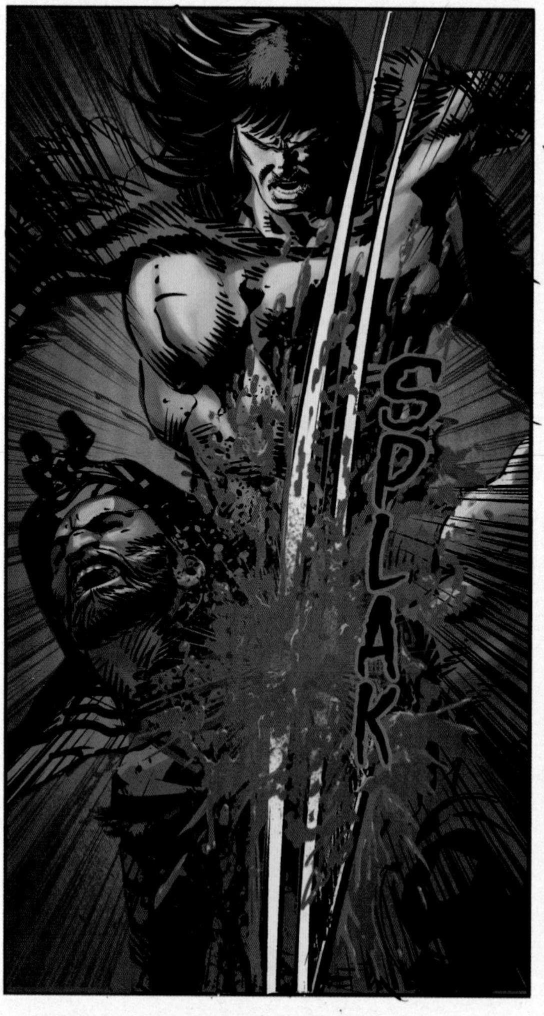
SPLLAK

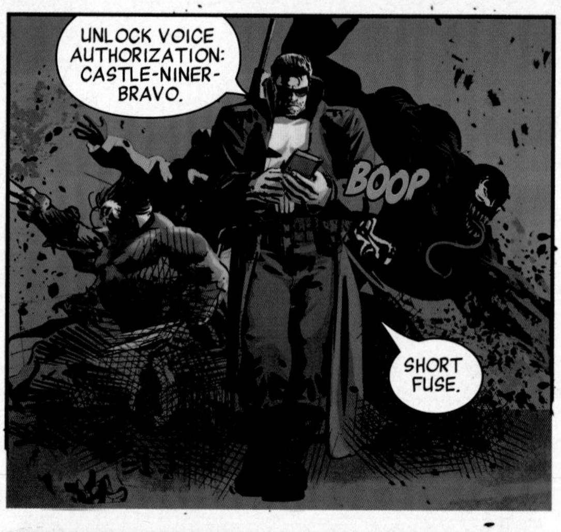
UNLOCK VOICE AUTHORIZATION: CASTLE-NINER-BRAVO.
BOOP
SHORT FUSE.

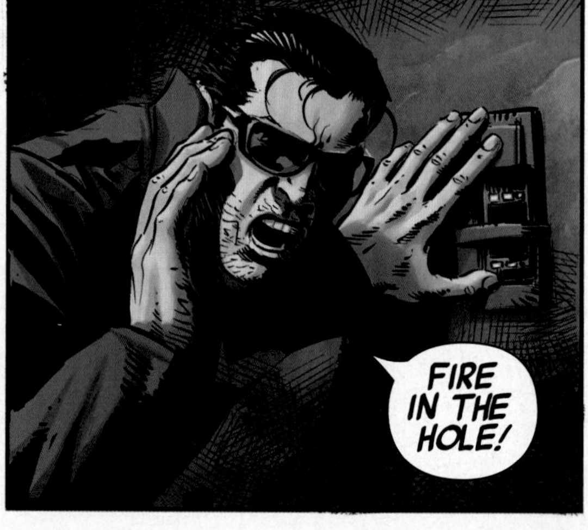
FIRE IN THE HOLE!

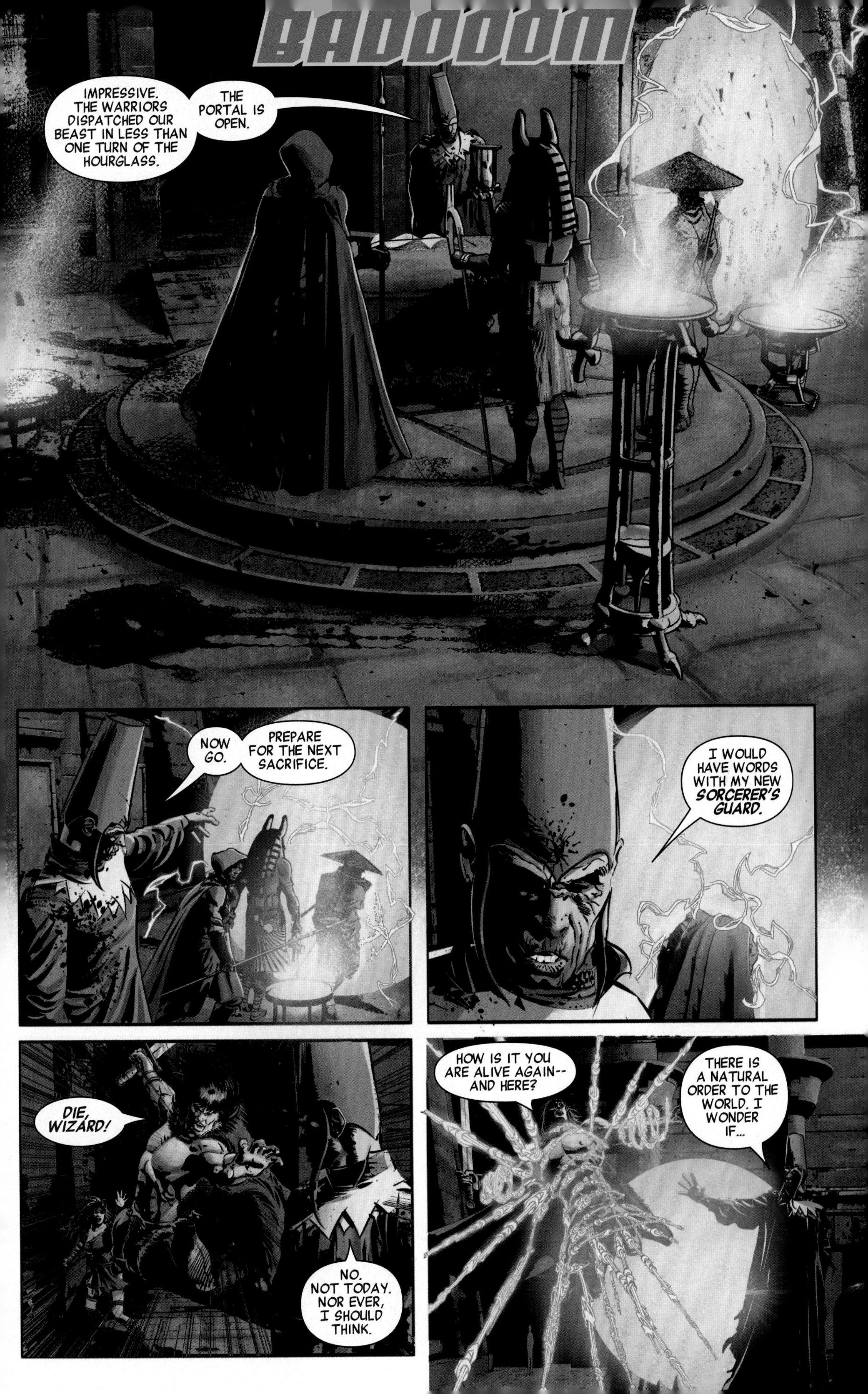
BADOOOM
IMPRESSIVE. THE WARRIORS DISPATCHED OUR BEAST IN LESS THAN ONE TURN OF THE HOURGLASS.
THE PORTAL IS OPEN.
NOW GO.
PREPARE FOR THE NEXT SACRIFICE.
I WOULD HAVE WORDS WITH MY NEW SORCERER'S GUARD.
DIE, WIZARD!
NO. NOT TODAY. NOR EVER, I SHOULD THINK.
HOW IS IT YOU ARE ALIVE AGAIN-- AND HERE?
THERE IS A NATURAL ORDER TO THE WORLD. I WONDER IF...

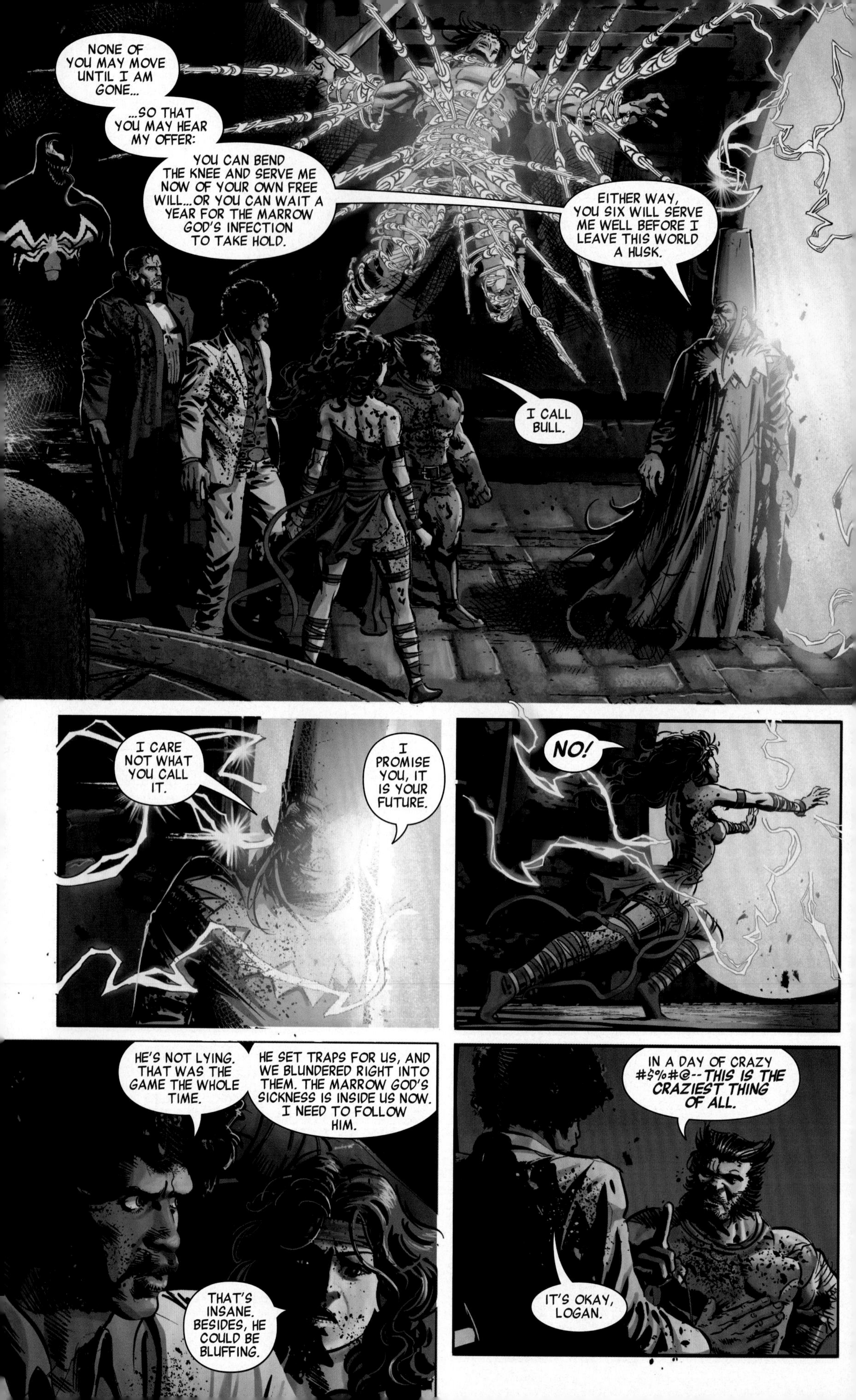
NONE OF YOU MAY MOVE UNTIL I AM GONE...
...SO THAT YOU MAY HEAR MY OFFER:
YOU CAN BEND THE KNEE AND SERVE ME NOW OF YOUR OWN FREE WILL...OR YOU CAN WAIT A YEAR FOR THE MARROW GOD'S INFECTION TO TAKE HOLD.
EITHER WAY, YOU SIX WILL SERVE ME WELL BEFORE I LEAVE THIS WORLD A HUSK.
I CALL BULL.
I CARE NOT WHAT YOU CALL IT.
I PROMISE YOU, IT IS YOUR FUTURE.
NO!
HE'S NOT LYING. THAT WAS THE GAME THE WHOLE TIME.
HE SET TRAPS FOR US, AND WE BLUNDERED RIGHT INTO THEM. THE MARROW GOD'S SICKNESS IS INSIDE US NOW. I NEED TO FOLLOW HIM.
THAT'S INSANE. BESIDES, HE COULD BE BLUFFING.
IN A DAY OF CRAZY #$%#@--THIS IS THE CRAZIEST THING OF ALL.
IT'S OKAY, LOGAN.

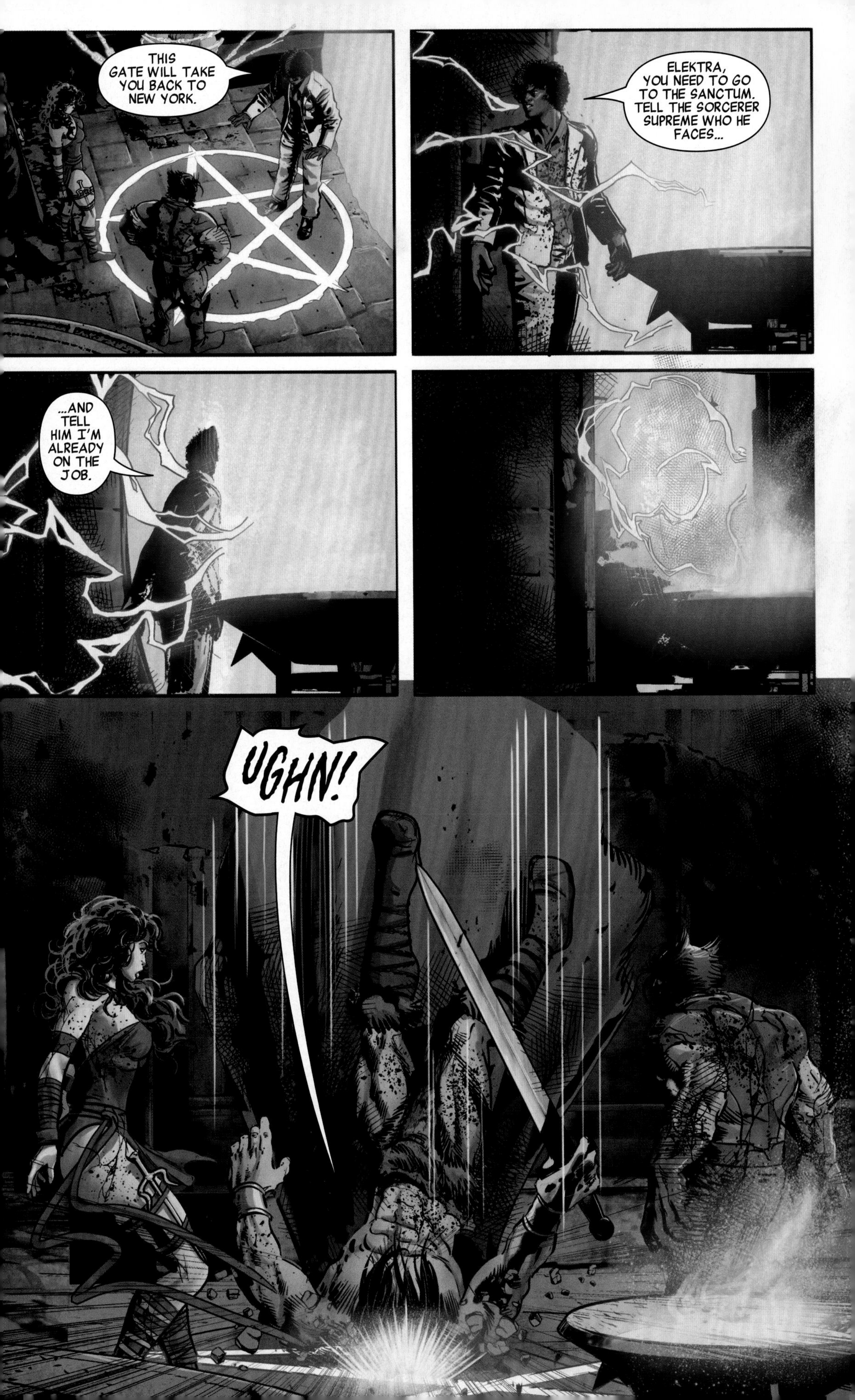
THIS GATE WILL TAKE YOU BACK TO NEW YORK.
ELEKTRA, YOU NEED TO GO TO THE SANCTUM. TELL THE SORCERER SUPREME WHO HE FACES...
...AND TELL HIM I'M ALREADY ON THE JOB.
UGHN!

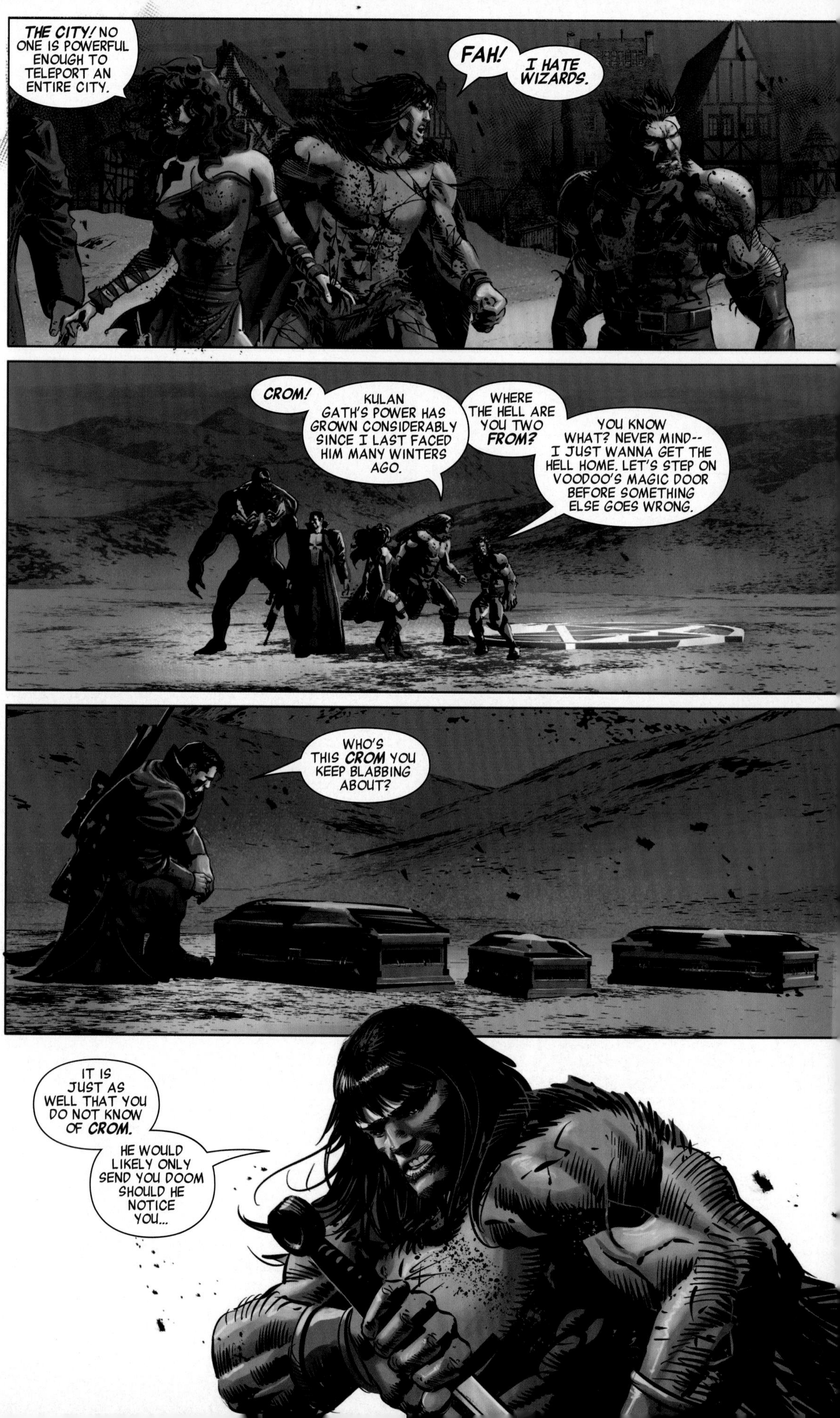
THE CITY! NO ONE IS POWERFUL ENOUGH TO TELEPORT AN ENTIRE CITY.
FAH!
I HATE WIZARDS.
CROM!
KULAN GATH'S POWER HAS GROWN CONSIDERABLY SINCE I LAST FACED HIM MANY WINTERS AGO.
WHERE THE HELL ARE YOU TWO FROM?
YOU KNOW WHAT? NEVER MIND-- I JUST WANNA GET THE HELL HOME. LET'S STEP ON VOODOO'S MAGIC DOOR BEFORE SOMETHING ELSE GOES WRONG.
WHO'S THIS CROM YOU KEEP BLABBING ABOUT?
IT IS JUST AS WELL THAT YOU DO NOT KNOW OF CROM.
HE WOULD LIKELY ONLY SEND YOU DOOM SHOULD HE NOTICE YOU...

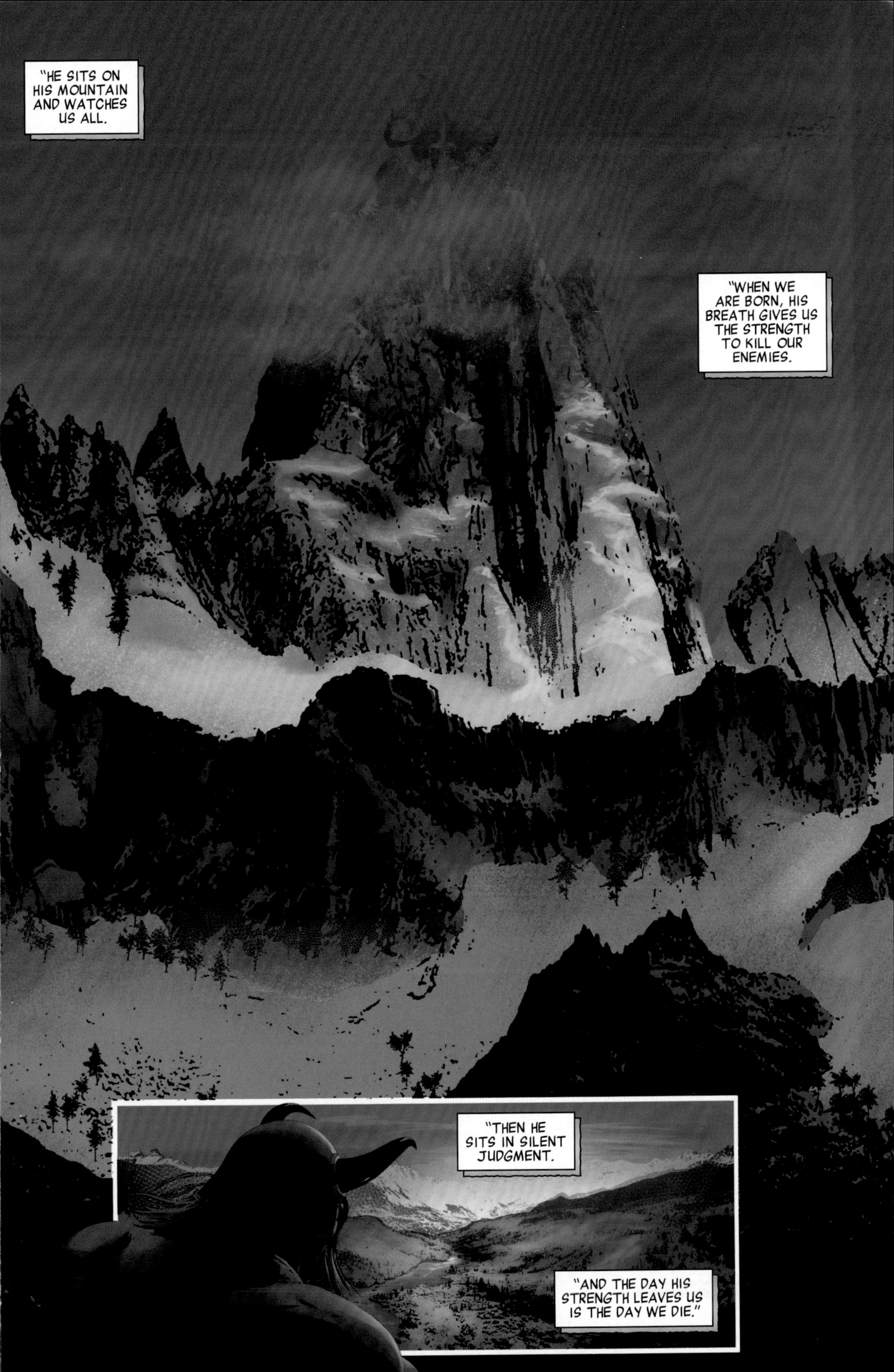
"HE SITS ON HIS MOUNTAIN AND WATCHES US ALL.
"WHEN WE ARE BORN, HIS BREATH GIVES US THE STRENGTH TO KILL OUR ENEMIES.
"THEN HE SITS IN SILENT JUDGMENT.
"AND THE DAY HIS STRENGTH LEAVES US IS THE DAY WE DIE."

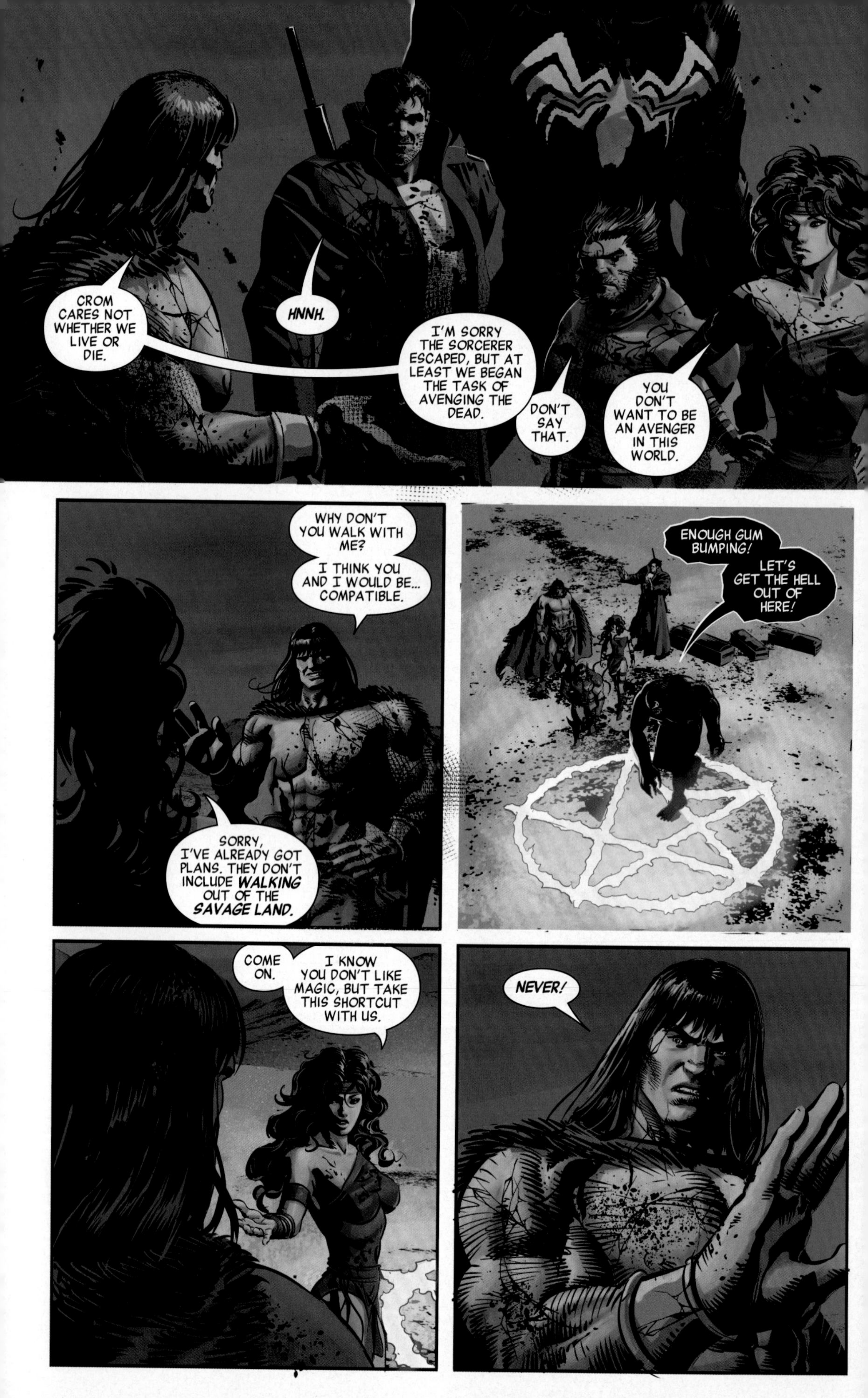
CROM CARES NOT WHETHER WE LIVE OR DIE.
HNNH.
I'M SORRY THE SORCERER ESCAPED, BUT AT LEAST WE BEGAN THE TASK OF AVENGING THE DEAD.
DON'T SAY THAT.
YOU DON'T WANT TO BE AN AVENGER IN THIS WORLD.
WHY DON'T YOU WALK WITH ME?
I THINK YOU AND I WOULD BE... COMPATIBLE.
SORRY, I'VE ALREADY GOT PLANS. THEY DON'T INCLUDE WALKING OUT OF THE SAVAGE LAND.
ENOUGH GUM BUMPING!
LET'S GET THE HELL OUT OF HERE!
COME ON.
I KNOW YOU DON'T LIKE MAGIC, BUT TAKE THIS SHORTCUT WITH US.
NEVER!

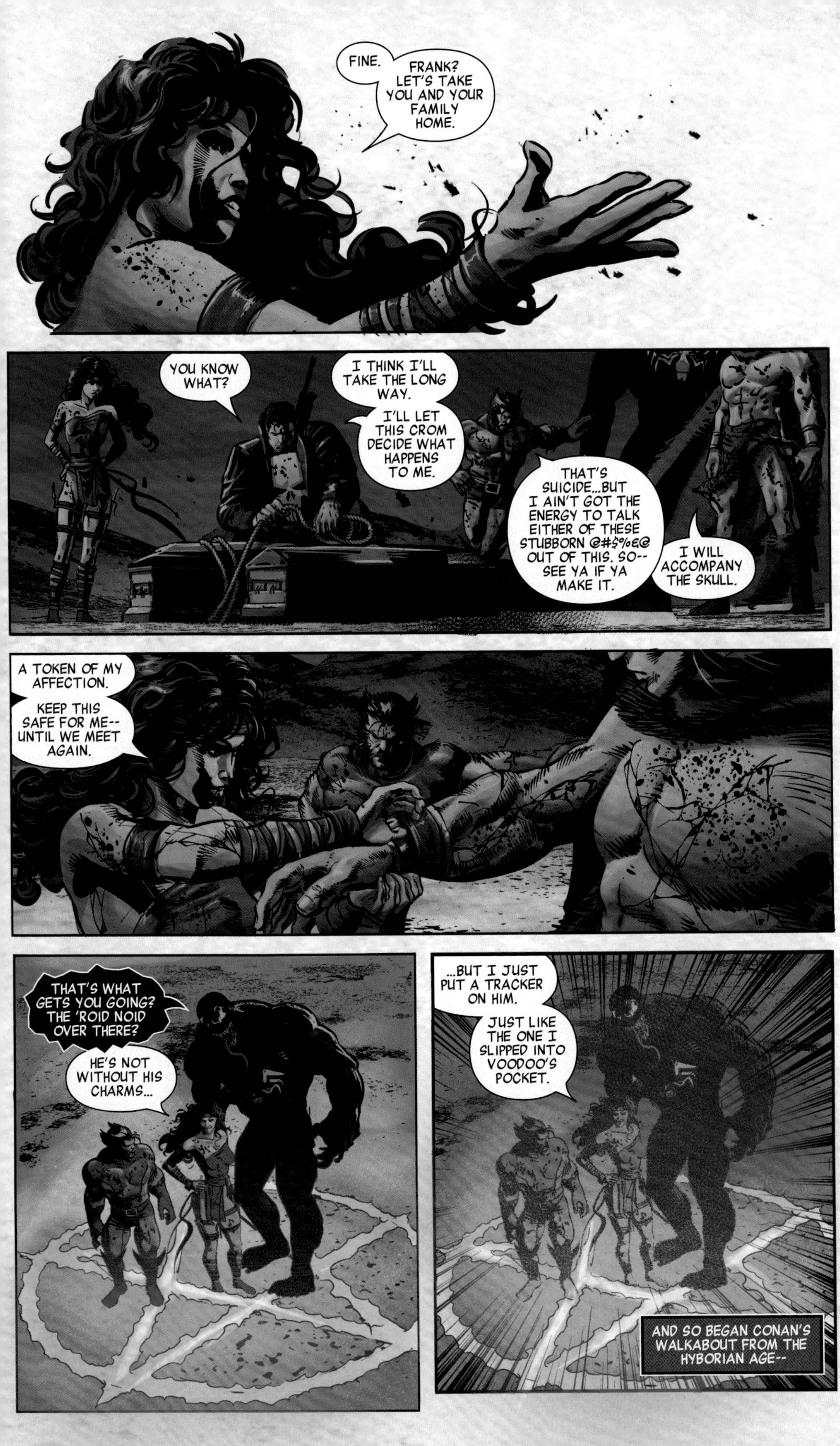
FINE.
FRANK? LET'S TAKE YOU AND YOUR FAMILY HOME.
YOU KNOW WHAT?
I THINK I'LL TAKE THE LONG WAY.
I'LL LET THIS CROM DECIDE WHAT HAPPENS TO ME.
THAT'S SUICIDE...BUT I AIN'T GOT THE ENERGY TO TALK EITHER OF THESE STUBBORN @#$%&@ OUT OF THIS. SO-- SEE YA IF YA MAKE IT.
I WILL ACCOMPANY THE SKULL.
A TOKEN OF MY AFFECTION.
KEEP THIS SAFE FOR ME-- UNTIL WE MEET AGAIN.
THAT'S WHAT GETS YOU GOING? THE 'ROID NOID OVER THERE?
HE'S NOT WITHOUT HIS CHARMS...
...BUT I JUST PUT A TRACKER ON HIM.
JUST LIKE THE ONE I SLIPPED INTO VOODOO'S POCKET.
AND SO BEGAN CONAN'S WALKABOUT FROM THE HYBORIAN AGE--

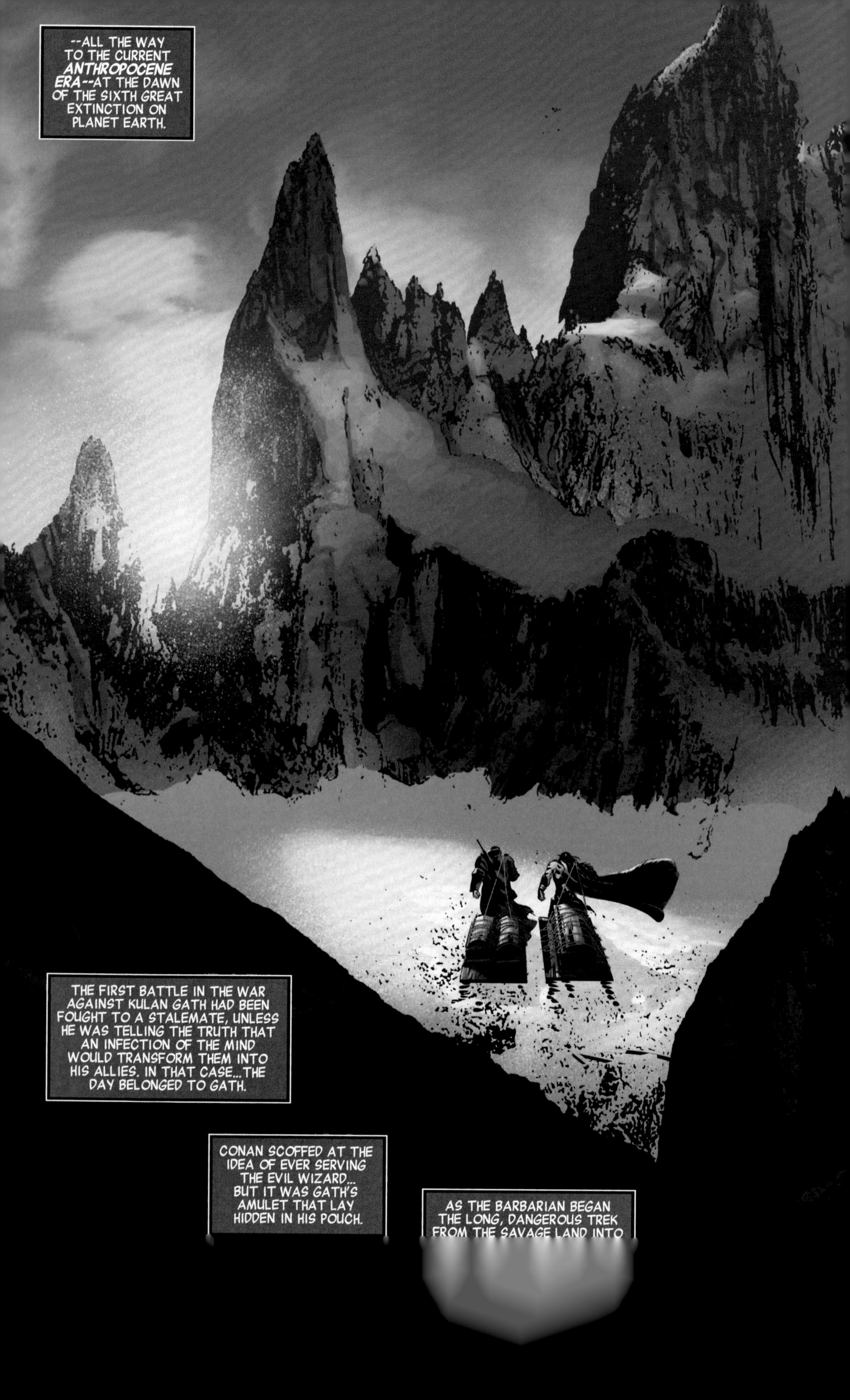
--ALL THE WAY TO THE CURRENT *ANTHROPOCENE ERA*--AT THE DAWN OF THE SIXTH GREAT EXTINCTION ON PLANET EARTH.
THE FIRST BATTLE IN THE WAR AGAINST KULAN GATH HAD BEEN FOUGHT TO A STALEMATE, UNLESS HE WAS TELLING THE TRUTH THAT AN INFECTION OF THE MIND WOULD TRANSFORM THEM INTO HIS ALLIES. IN THAT CASE...THE DAY BELONGED TO GATH.
CONAN SCOFFED AT THE IDEA OF EVER SERVING THE EVIL WIZARD... BUT IT WAS GATH'S AMULET THAT LAY HIDDEN IN HIS POUCH.
AS THE BARBARIAN BEGAN THE LONG, DANGEROUS TREK FROM THE SAVAGE LAND INTO

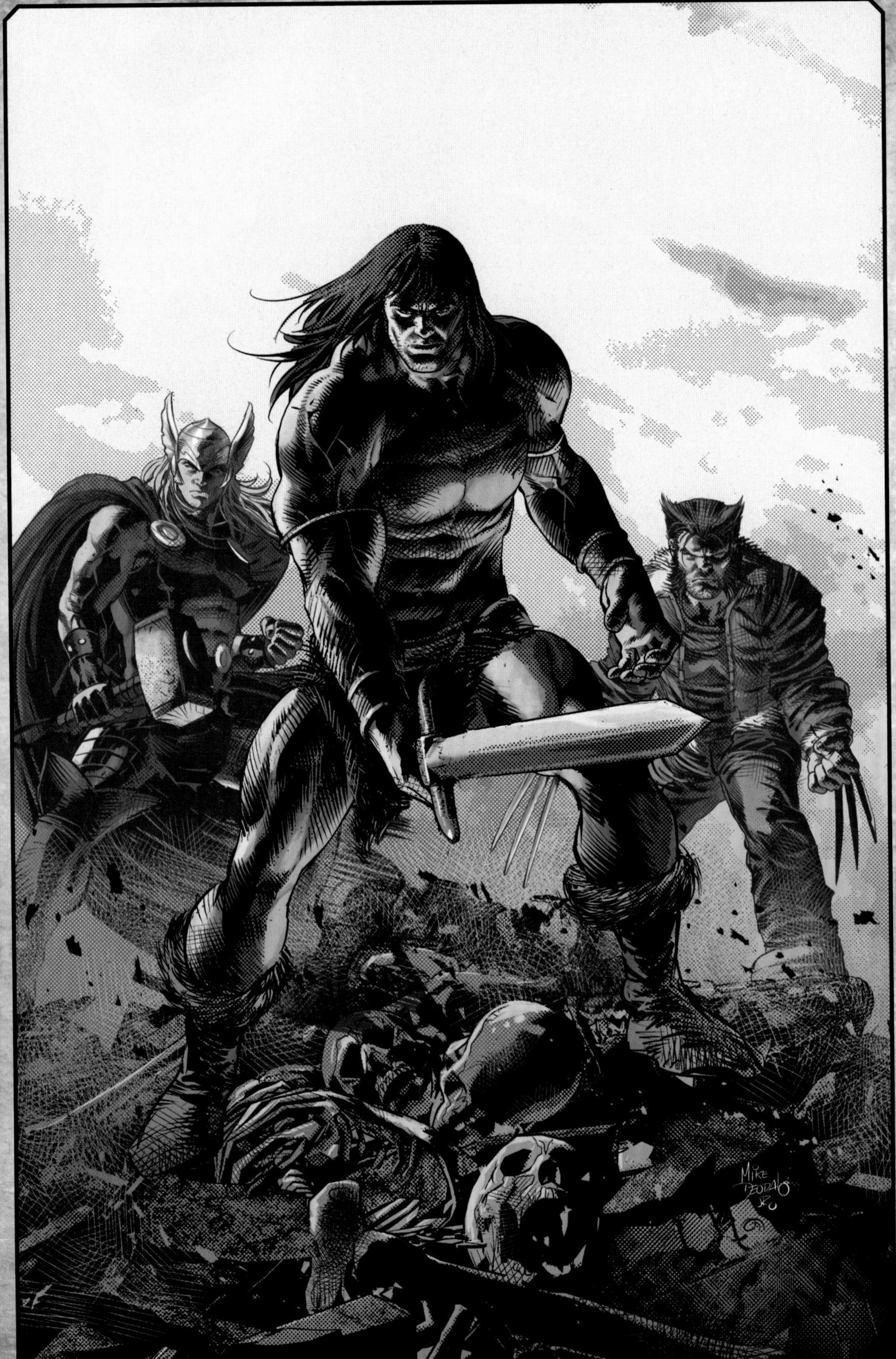

Mike Deodato Jr. & **Frank Martin**
1 VARIANT

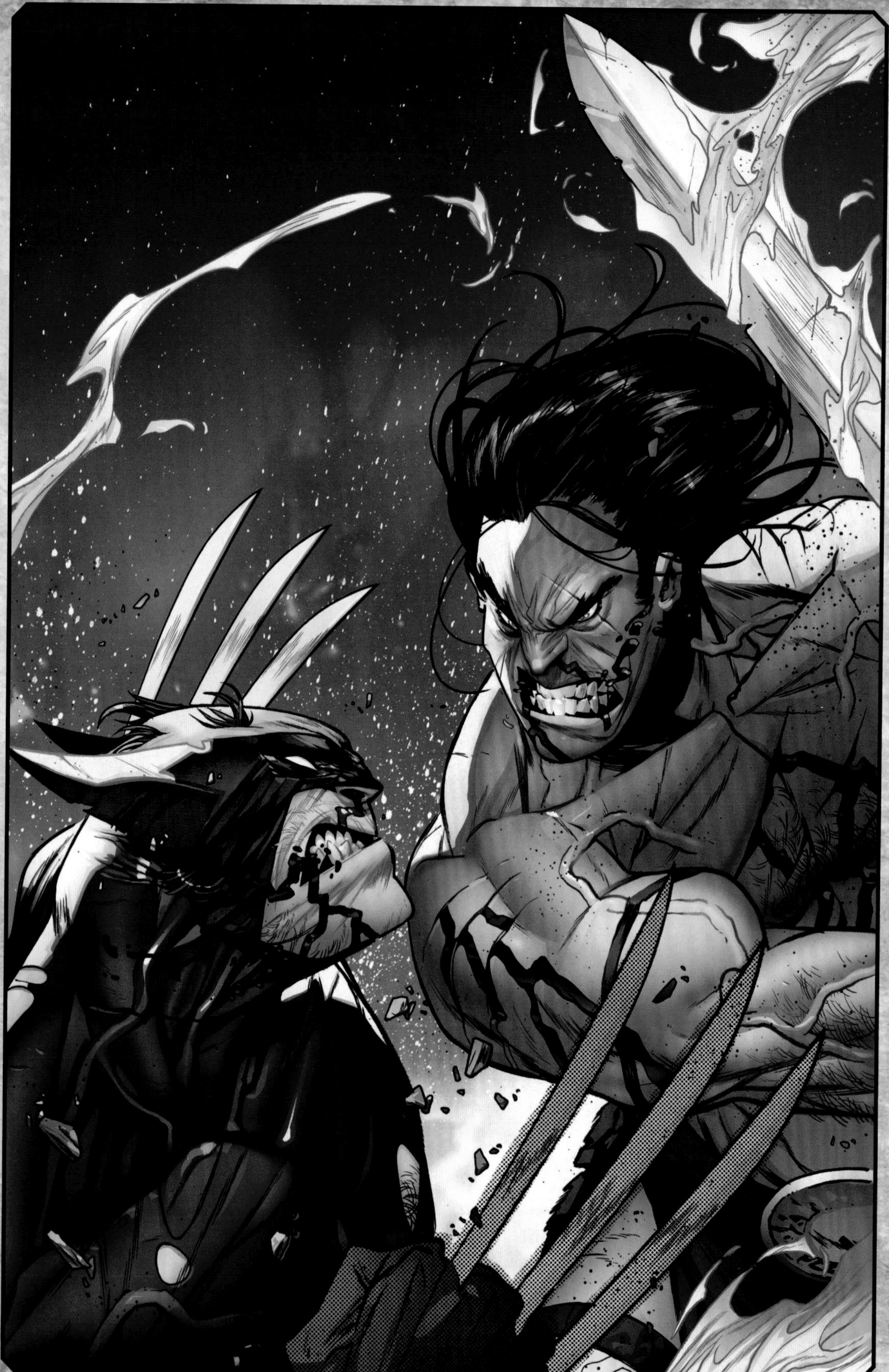

Kim Jacinto & **David Curiel**
1 VARIANT

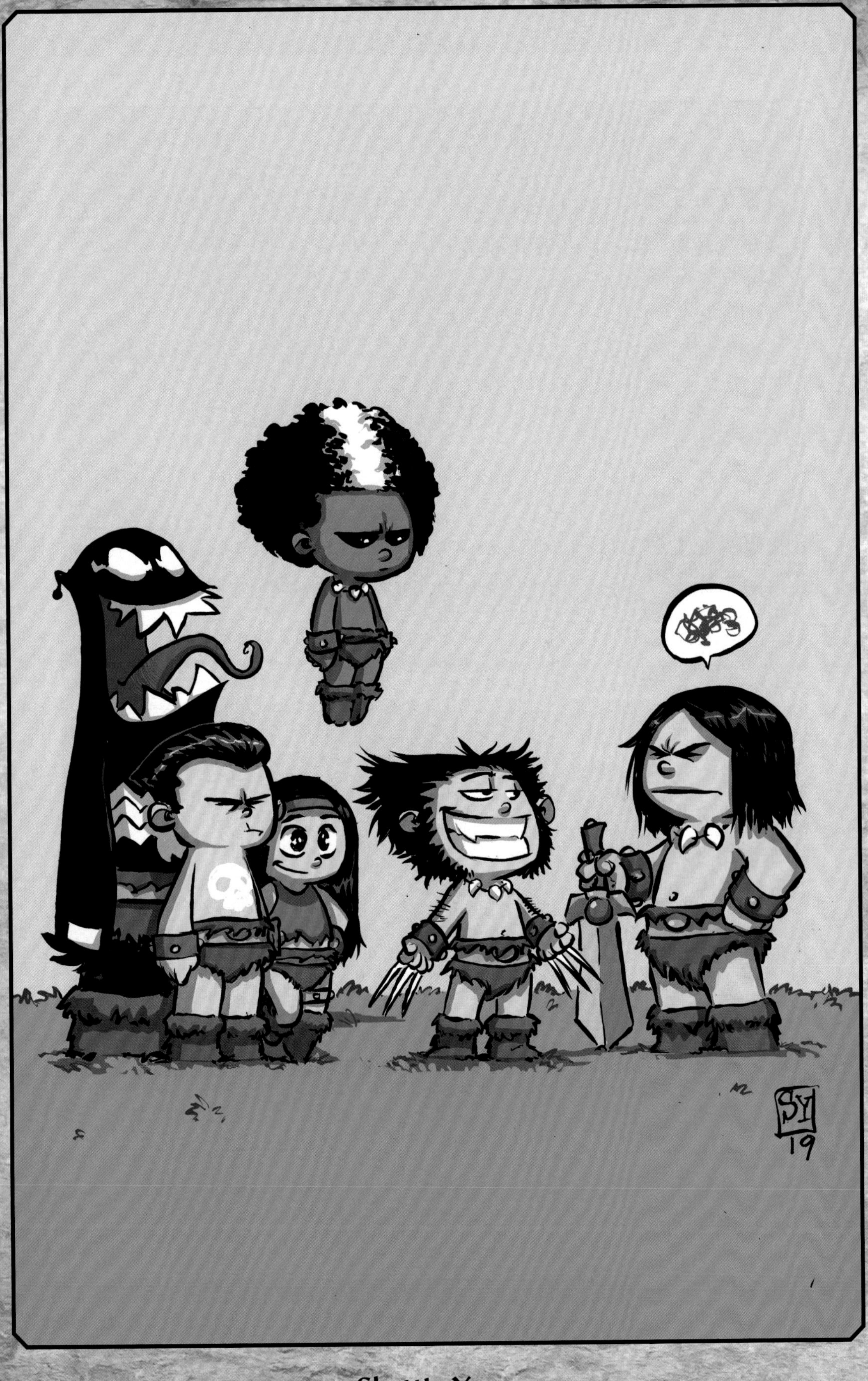
SY
19

Skottie Young
1 VARIANT

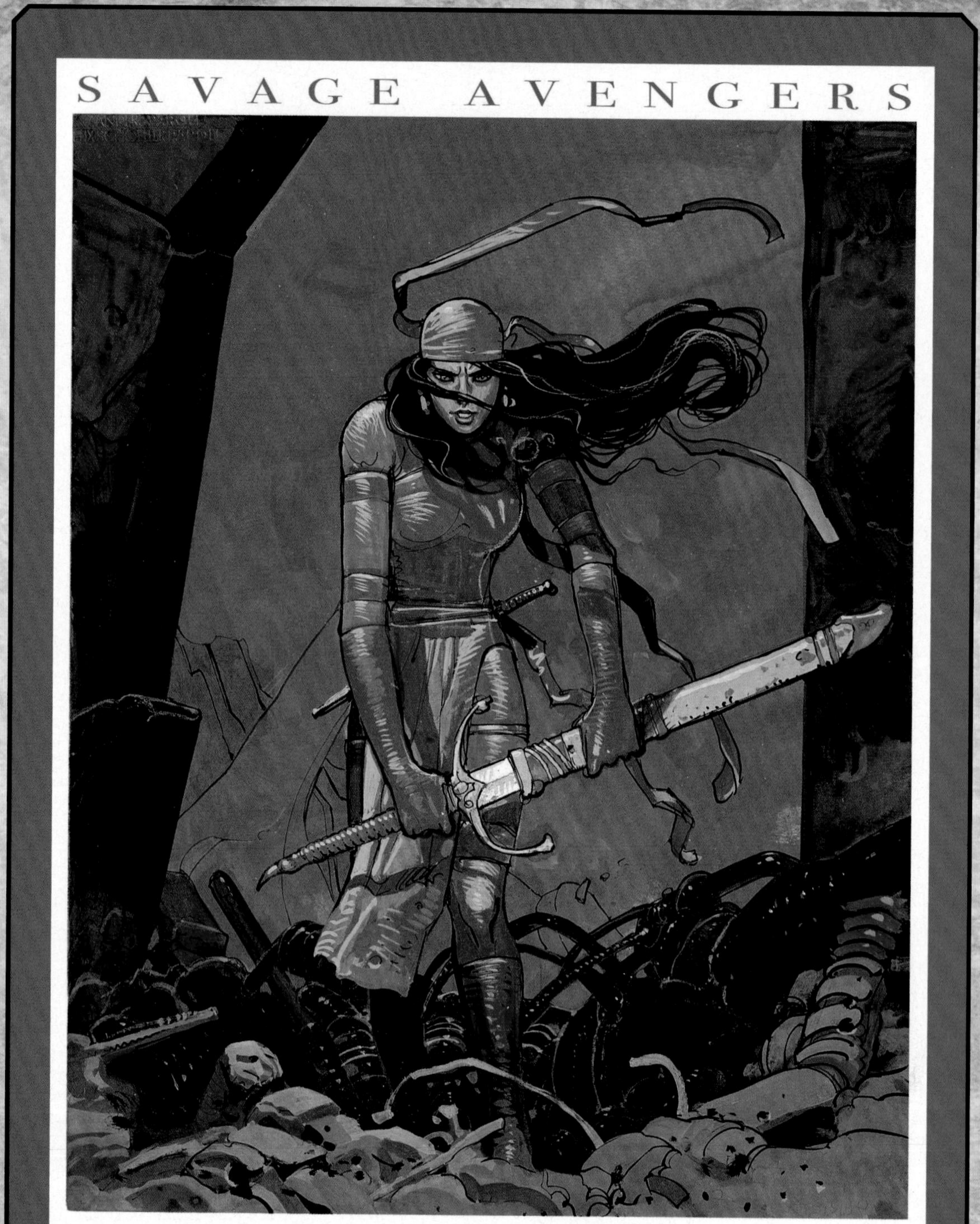
SAVAGE AVENGERS
ELEKTRA

Moebius
1 HIDDEN GEM VARIANT

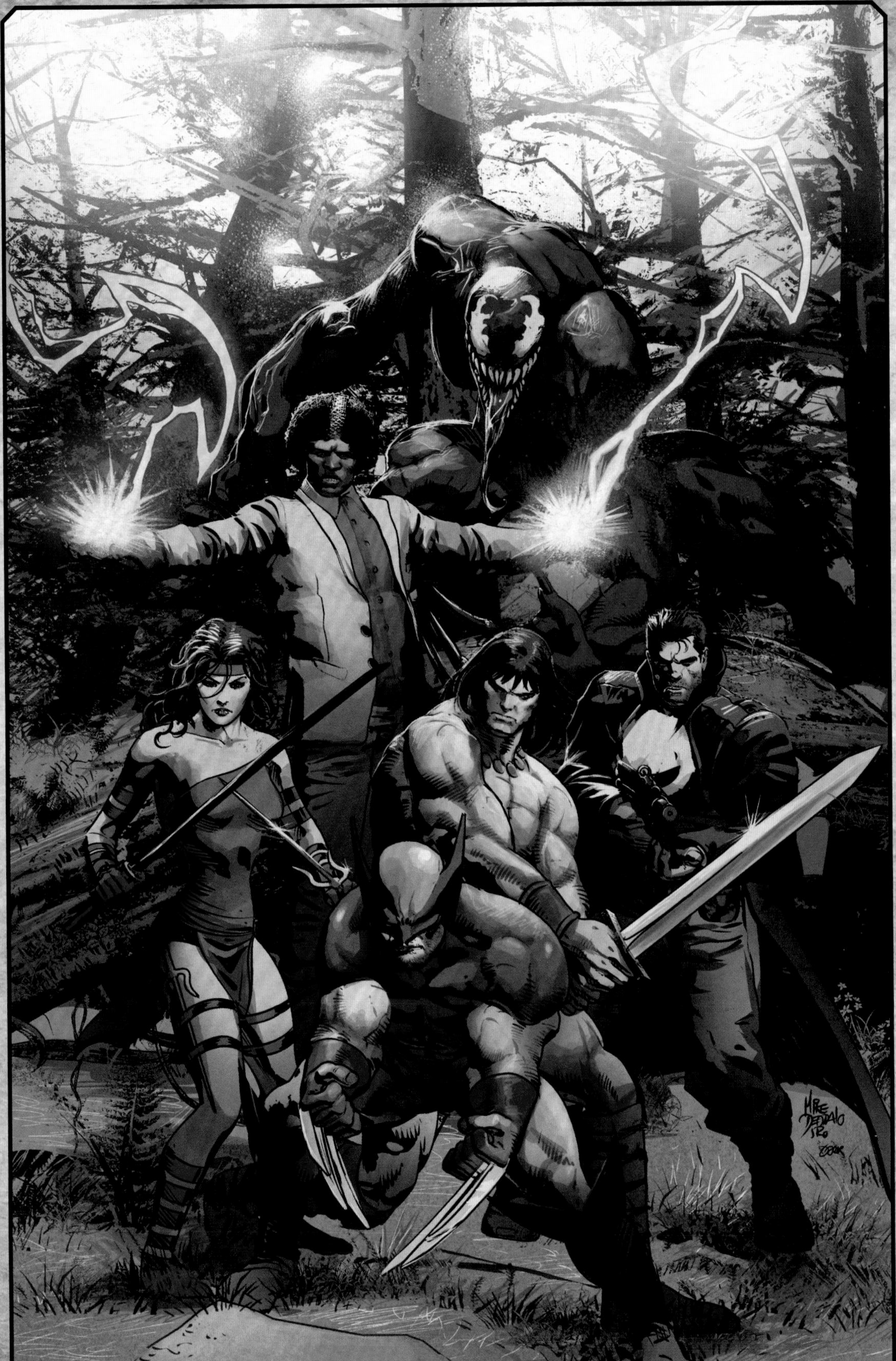

Mike Deodato Jr. & **Frank Martin**
2 VARIANT

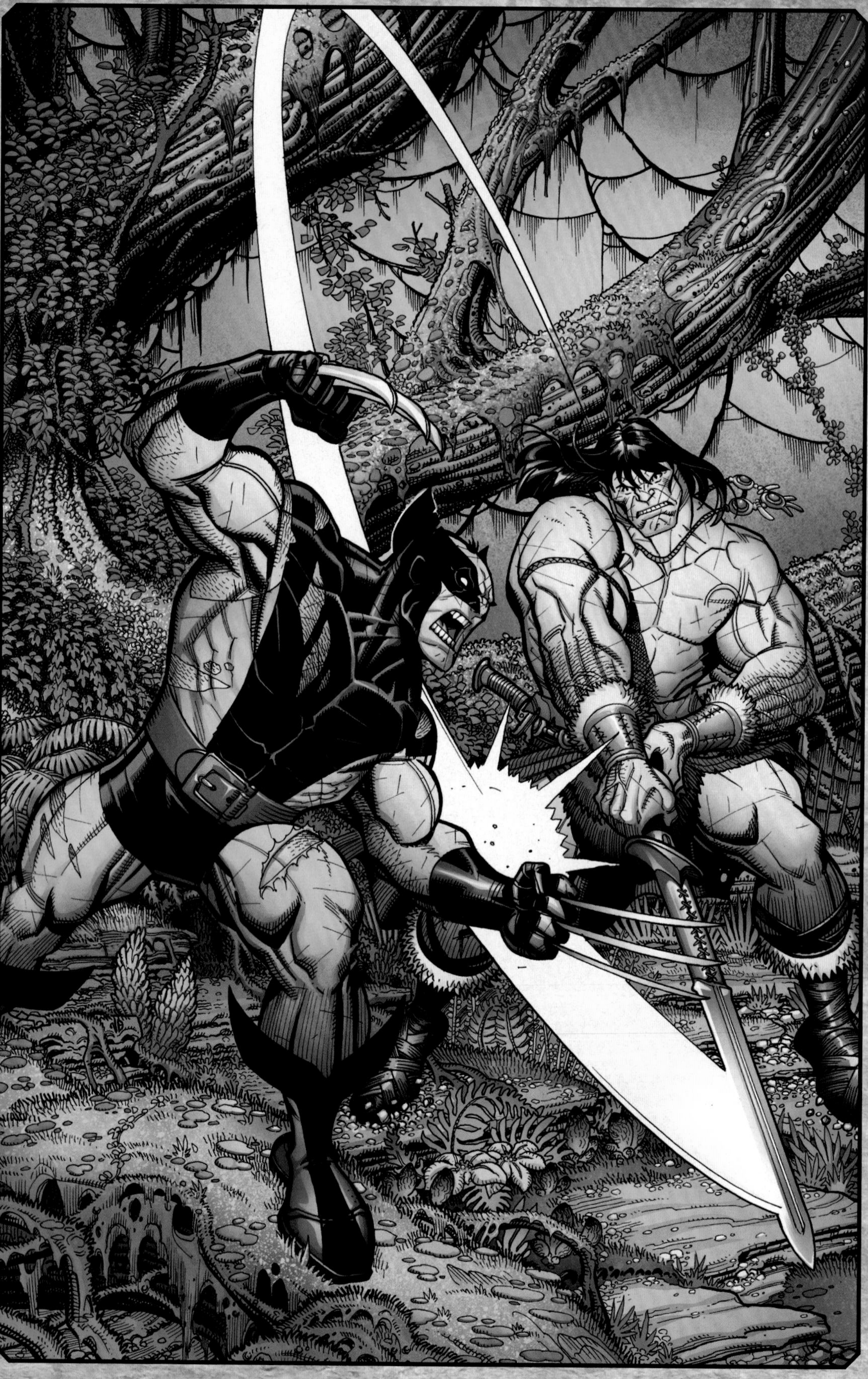

Nick Bradshaw & Richard Isanove
2 VARIANT

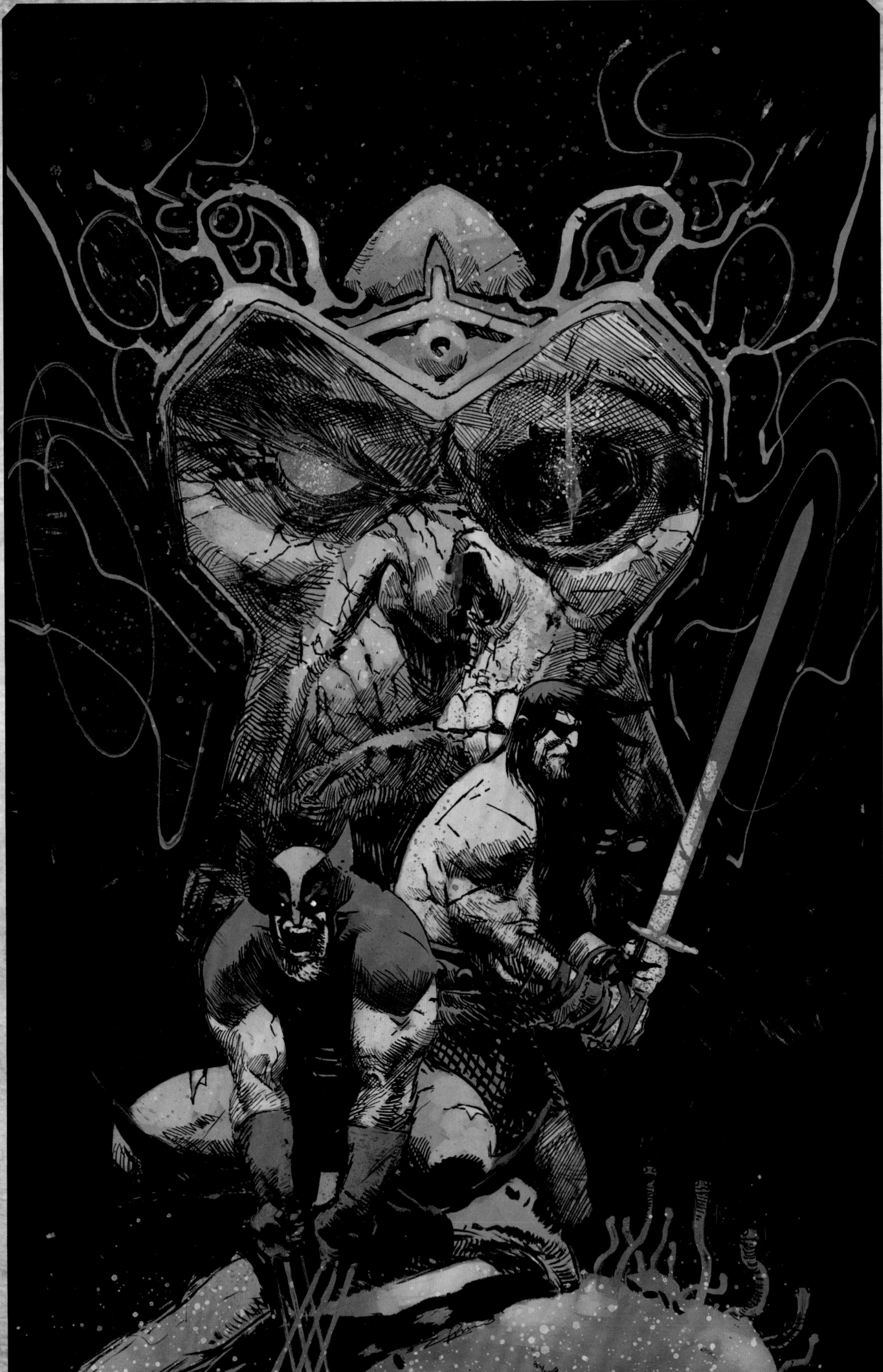

Gerardo Zaffino
4 VARIANT

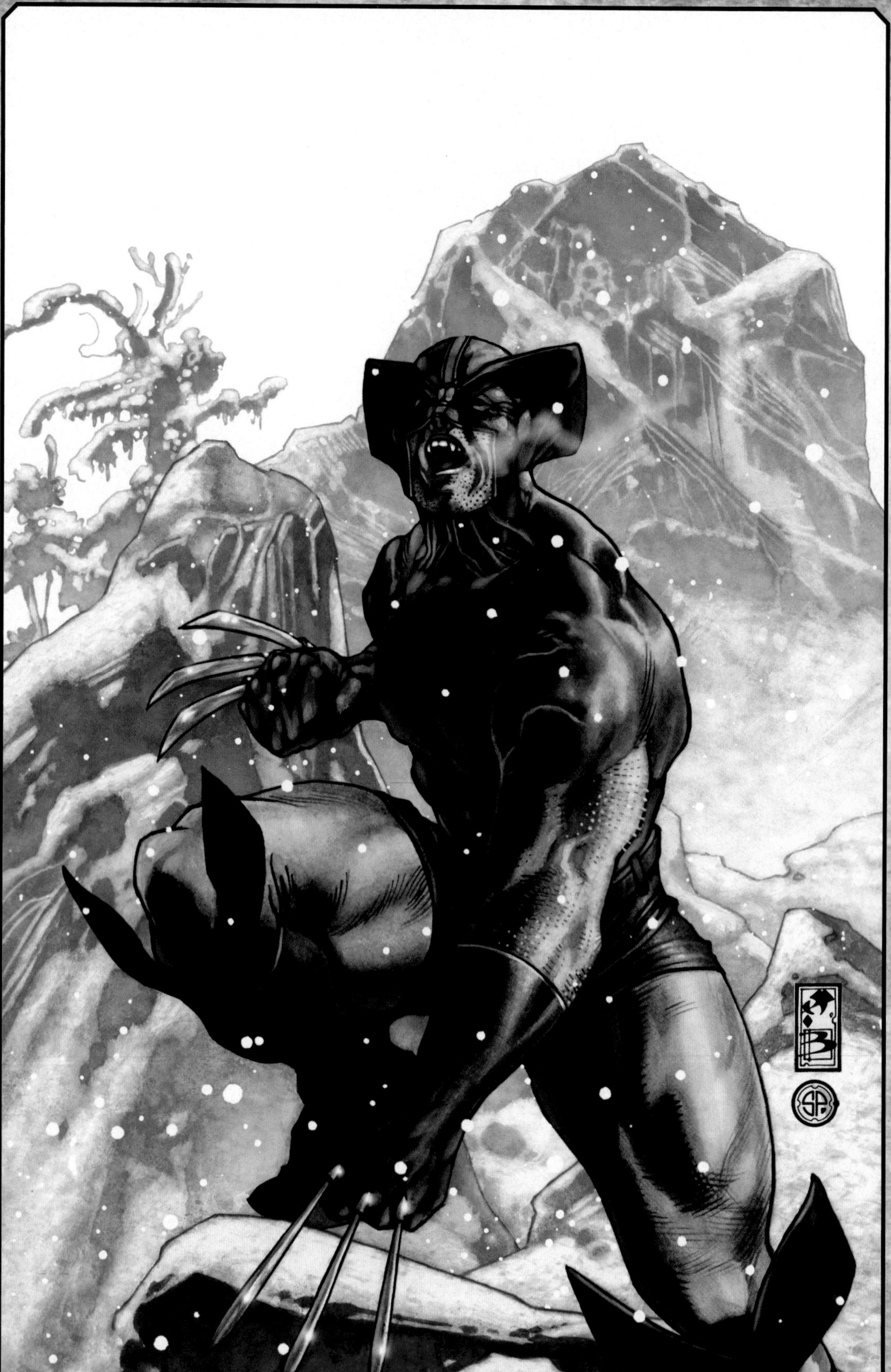

Simone Bianchi & **Simone Peruzzi**
1 VARIANT

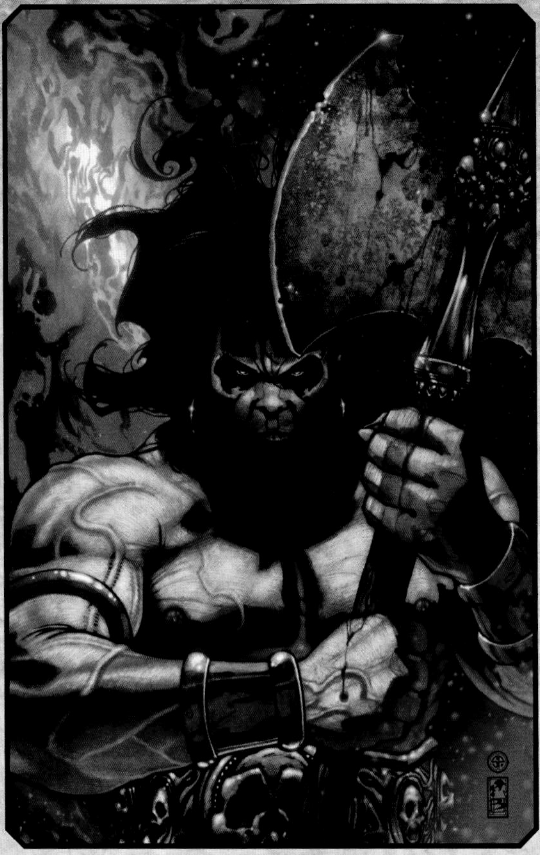

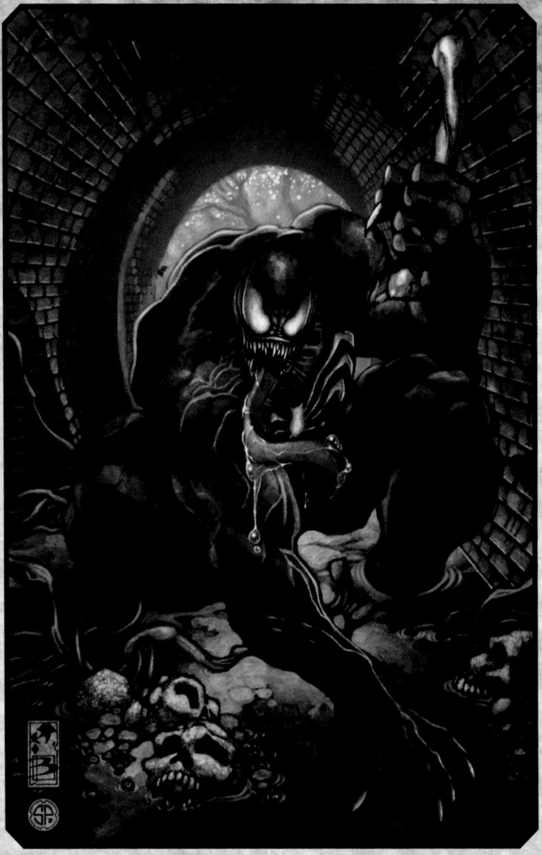

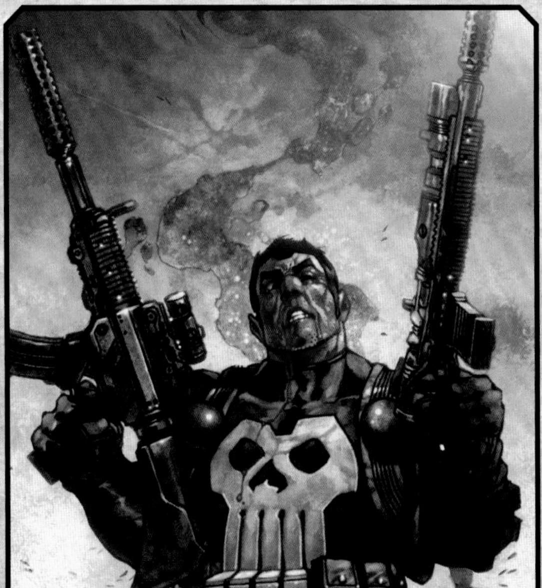

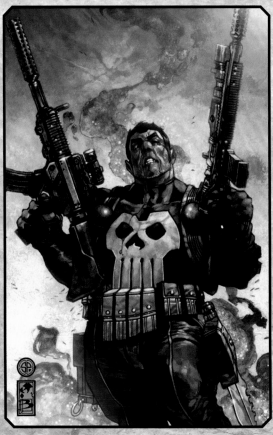

Simone Bianchi & Simone Peruzzi
2-4 VARIANTS

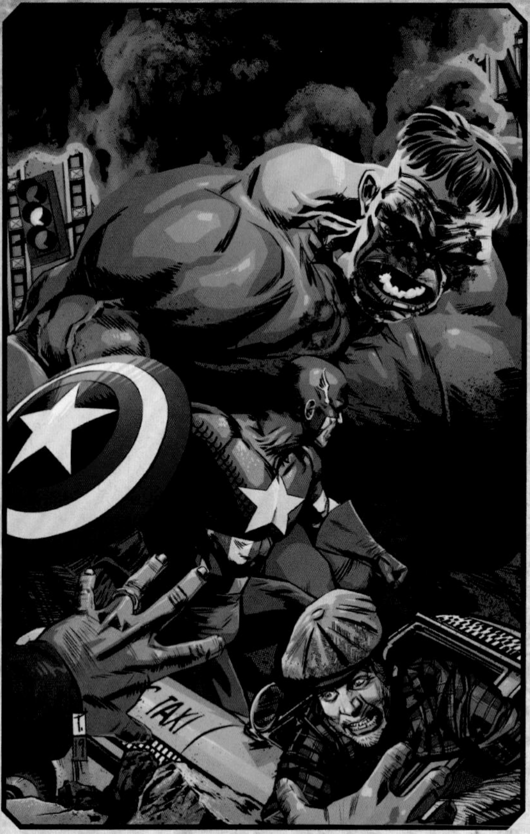

Tomm Coker & Michael Garland
2 MARVELS 25TH TRIBUTE VARIANT

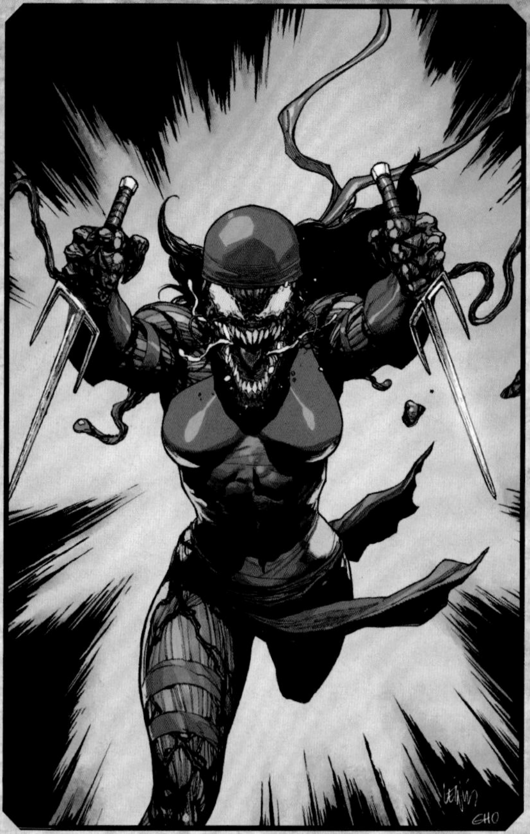

Leinil Francis Yu & Sunny Gho
3 CARNAGE-IZED VARIANT

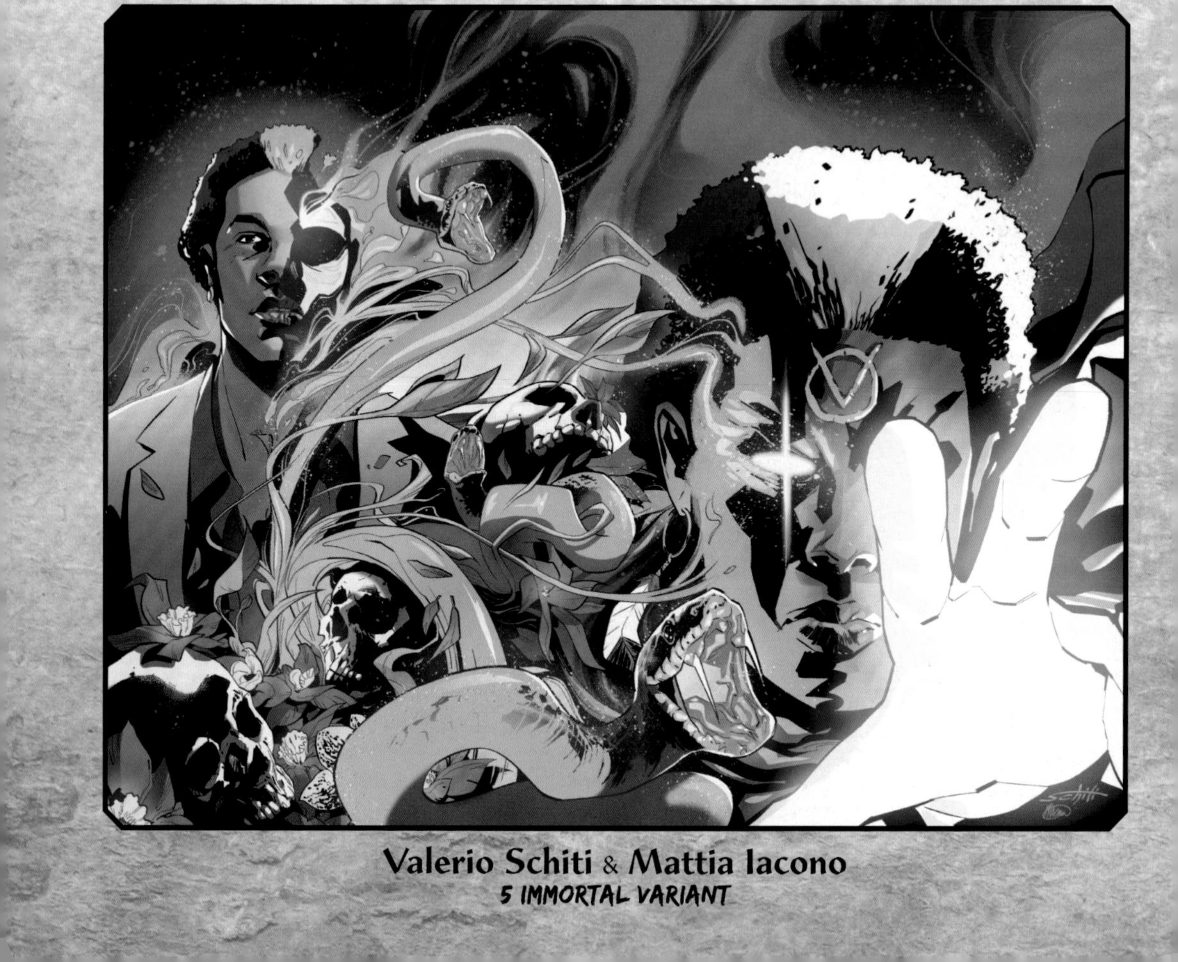

Valerio Schiti & Mattia Iacono
5 IMMORTAL VARIANT